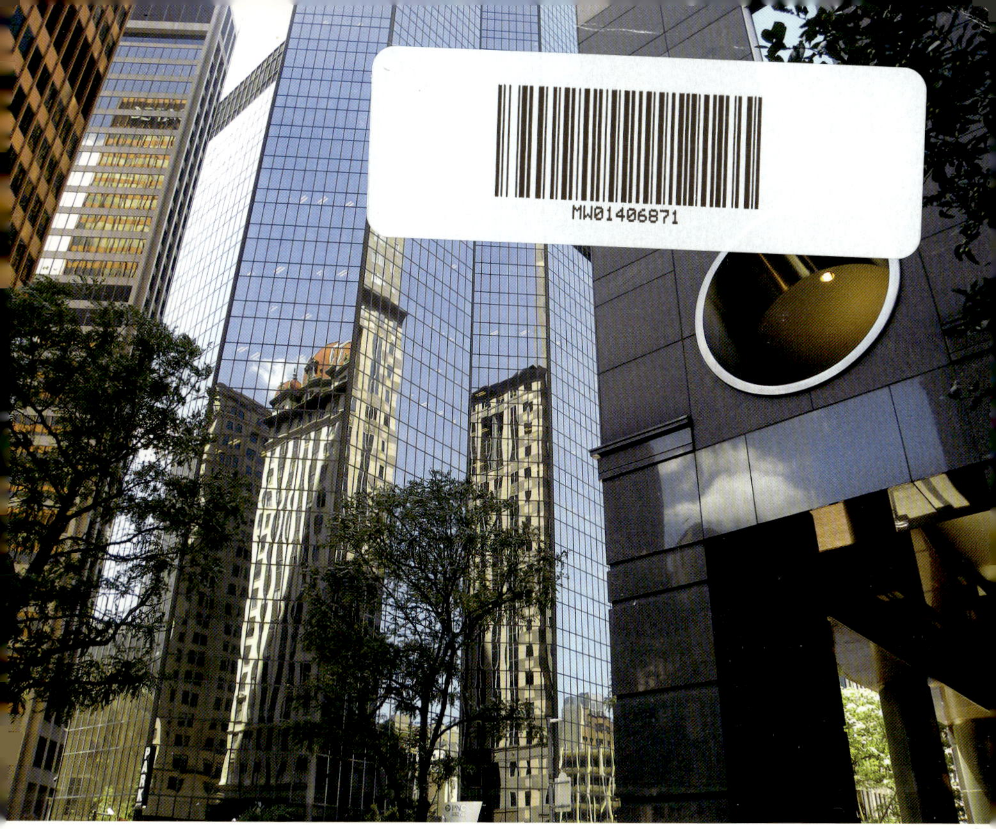

Pittsburgh Architecture in the Twentieth Century

Notable Modern Buildings and Their Architects

Albert M. Tannler

Pittsburgh History & Landmarks Foundation

PHLF

Pittsburgh History & Landmarks Foundation
100 West Station Square Drive, Suite 450
Pittsburgh, PA 15219-1134
412-471-5808
www.phlf.org

© 2013 by Pittsburgh History & Landmarks Foundation
All rights reserved. Published 2013
Printed in the United States of America

Author: Albert M. Tannler
Editors: Louise King Sturgess and David J. Vater, RA
Designer: Greg Pytlik of Pytlik Design Associates, Inc., with assistance from Beth Buckholtz

ISBN-978-0-9788284-9-3
Library of Congress Control Number: 2013950257

This book is typeset in Minion with Formata subheads. It is printed on 80# Opus Silk Text by Migliozzi Printing Services, Pittsburgh, PA, and Knepper Press Corporation, Clinton, PA.

Column capital, former Pitcairn National Bank

Contributors

Lead Donor
Sports & Exhibition Authority of Pittsburgh and Allegheny County

Benefactors
The Fine Foundation
Walter C. Kidney Library and Publications Fund of the Pittsburgh History
   & Landmarks Foundation

Patrons
Nadine E. Bognar
Alfred M. Oppenheimer Memorial Fund of The Pittsburgh Foundation

Partners

Alan L. Ackerman
Anonymous
Thomas W. Armstrong
Allen Baum and Liz Witzke-Baum
Dave Borland
David M. Brashear
David Burstin
Barry Chad
Phyllis K. Davidson
Arnold and Selene Davis
Mary and John Davis
Sally and Jim Dawson
James K. and Sara C. Donnell
Seymour and Ruth Drescher
Paul and Kitty Emery
Senator Jim Ferlo
Robert Z. Fierst
Brown Fulton
Gabriel and Karen Funaro
Bill and Ann Garrett
Anne and David Genter
Mary Louise Green
Phyllis Hamilton
Jeanne Hanchett and Phil Wedemeyer
Anne and John Harmon
Gary and Maristel Hunt
Cheryl Hurley
Rabbi Walter Jacob

David and Jeree Kiefer
David A. Kleer
Karl F. Krieger
Nancy and Edward Krokosky
Charlotte Lang
Brent K. Lazar
Claire and Larry Levine
John Lovelace
John A. Martine, AIA
Douglas and Angela Marvin
Jean H. McCullough
Jack Miller, in memory of
   Walter C. Kidney
Bill and Mary Anne Mistick
Suzan Mohney
Rona Moody and Fizz Stuart
Bob Moore and Scott Wise
Mary Beth Pastorius
Joyce Pearl
Ray and Trevi Pendro
Clinton Piper
The Pittsburgh Parks Conservancy
Preservation Pittsburgh
Sandra Preuhs
Marirose and John Radelet
Matthew Ragan and Laura Serzega
Dorothy and Nicholas Rescher
Jerome and Cynthia Richey

Partners (continued)

Anne Robb
Wilfred and Ruth Rouleau
Ann Fay Ruben
Steve Salvador
Paul and Cathy Schaughency
Strada Architecture, LLC
Louise and Martin Sturgess
Oscar E. and Emily W. Swan

Kathy and Lou Testoni
Frampton Tolbert
David J. Vater
Howard and Jane Voigt
Helen A. Wilson
Michelle Yanefski and Andrew Moss
Carol R. Yaster and William J. Levant
Arthur P. Ziegler, Jr.

Illustration Captions *(for photographs not captioned elsewhere)*

Cover photo/page i: Twentieth-century skyscrapers in downtown Pittsburgh (EQT Plaza near Liberty Avenue)
Inside front and back cover: Detail, Mifflin School, Lincoln Place
Page vi: U.S. Steel Tower, view from Sixth Avenue at Bigelow Boulevard, downtown Pittsburgh
Pages viii–ix: Parkstone Dwellings, Point Breeze
Page xiv: Prospect Street, Mt. Washington, with The Lofts of Mount Washington (formerly, Prospect School, Pittsburgh Public Schools)
Page 32: Hazelwood Coke Works, J&L Steel Corporation, early 1960s
Pages 44–45: 201 Stanwix Street Place (colonnade of the former Bell Telephone Building), looking toward St. Mary of Mercy Church and PPG Place, downtown Pittsburgh
Page 46: Lobby, Mt. Lebanon Municipal Building
Page 58: Highland Towers, Shadyside
Page 82: 1124 Cornell Road, Thornburg
Page 90: Urban Room, Omni William Penn Hotel, downtown Pittsburgh
Page 112: St. Agnes Center of Carlow University, Oakland (formerly, St. Agnes Roman Catholic Church)
Page 122: South Park Golf Club House
Page 126: Cecelia and Robert Frank House, Shadyside
Page 144: Richard King Mellon Hall of Science, Duquesne University, The Bluff
Page 154: Manchester Bidwell Corporation Headquarters, North Side
Page 160: Alcoa Corporate Center, North Shore
Page 174: Sarah Mellon Scaife Galleries, Carnegie Museum of Art, Oakland
Page 180: Betty and Irving Abrams House, Shadyside
Page 192: Civic Arena, Lower Hill (September 16, 1961)
Pages 204–205: Children's Museum of Pittsburgh, North Side
Page 206: David L. Lawrence Convention Center, downtown Pittsburgh
Pages 218–219: Phipps' Center for Sustainable Landscapes, Schenley Park
Page 220: Highland Towers, Shadyside

Opposite: Entrance detail, Holy Rosary Roman Catholic Church, Homewood

Contents

Introduction
Foreword xi
Preface xv
Definitions of Modern Architecture 1
The Eve of Modernism 10
How Modern Architecture Came to Pittsburgh 15

Guide
Notes on the Language of Architecture
and the Contents of the Guide 47
Maps
    Downtown Pittsburgh Area 50
    Beyond Downtown—North 52
    Beyond Downtown—East 54
    Beyond Downtown—South and West 56
Austro-Germanic Secessionism 59
California Craftsman—Thornburg 1900–1912 82
Art Moderne, Art Deco, and the "House of Tomorrow" 91
American Gothic 1905–1938 112
Expressionism 123
Gropius and Breuer in Pittsburgh 127
The Legacy of Frank Lloyd Wright 133
Miesian 145
Brutalism 155
Corporate Industrial Design 161
The Legacy of the International Style 175
Postmodernism 181
*Modern Landmarks—Relocated, Concealed,
Unfinished, or Demolished* 192

Epilogue
Twenty-first Century Architecture in Pittsburgh 207

Appendices
Illustration Sources 221
Acknowledgements 223
Notes 227
Bibliography 251
Index 265

Introduction

Foreword

Lu Donnelly

"Modernism" is a slippery term; each generation uses it to mean something fresh or new. Architectural writers have applied the term to every style from Greek Revival to Frank Lloyd Wright's organic architecture, from Mies van der Rohe's glass boxes to Philip Johnson's PPG Place. At last, we have Albert Tannler's lucid explanation of the evolution of the term and its relationship to Pittsburgh's architecture in the twentieth century. In this guidebook Tannler traces the roots of our architectural modernism to the German and Eastern European movements developed in the late nineteenth century, and he places Pittsburgh squarely in their mainstream. Our city may not have numerous examples of modernist architecture, but what is here is often among "the first" and is most admirable.

Tannler has chosen some of the best examples of these buildings from Austro-Germanic Secessionism to Postmodernism, rather than presenting an exhaustive inventory. This allows room for photographs and discussion of each example, giving the reader a better understanding of how and why the architects and their patrons chose to design the notable buildings that they did.

I was invited to write this foreword not as an expert on Modernism, but as someone uniquely aware of Pittsburgh's architectural heritage. That heritage has been documented in several major surveys, all conducted or begun in the twentieth century.

The first regional attempt to identify significant local architecture began in 1932, when architect Charles Morse Stotz oversaw the Western Pennsylvania Architectural Survey (1932–35) of pre-1860 buildings in twenty-seven western Pennsylvania counties. Sites in thirteen counties were described and illustrated in C. M. Stotz's book, *The Early Architecture of Western Pennsylvania*, published in 1936.

Opposite: Books based on twentieth-century surveys, displayed on a twentieth-century Art Deco desk in the James D. Van Trump Library, Pittsburgh History & Landmarks Foundation

Thirty years later, the Pittsburgh History & Landmarks Foundation (PHLF) conducted the first county-wide architectural survey in the United States (1966–67). In the resulting publication, *Landmark Architecture of Allegheny County Pennsylvania* (1967), by James D. Van Trump and Arthur P. Ziegler, Jr., Mr. Ziegler (then PHLF executive director and survey co-coordinator) wrote: "Our first problem was to determine what [architectural] landmarks exist and then to record them as a basis for further action."

A more comprehensive county-wide survey was undertaken by PHLF between 1979 and 1984. I worked as survey assistant, beginning in 1978, and directed the survey between 1982 and 1984. Approximately 6,000 significant historic resources were recorded and 400 were discussed and illustrated in Walter C. Kidney's book, *Landmark Architecture: Pittsburgh and Allegheny County* (PHLF, 1985). Landmarks Design Associates Architects and PHLF conducted a specialized survey of African-American Historic Sites in 1991–92, and in 1995 PHLF published *A Legacy in Bricks and Mortar: African-American Landmarks in Allegheny County*, by Frank E. Bolden, Laurence A. Glasco, and Eliza Smith Brown. Based on the growing knowledge of the region's architectural heritage, PHLF published its most impressive volume in 1997 (still in print): *Pittsburgh's Landmark Architecture: The Historic Buildings of Pittsburgh and Allegheny County*, by Walter C. Kidney.

Survey efforts have continued into the twenty-first century. I served as the volume editor and principal author of *The Buildings of Pennsylvania: Pittsburgh and Western Pennsylvania*, published in 2010 by the Society of Architectural Historians, in association with the University of Virginia Press. The book is based on a survey that began in 1996, documenting architecturally interesting structures in thirty-one western Pennsylvania counties.

Often the age of a building, structure, or landscape—collectively referred to as cultural resources—is a factor in determining its significance. According to Federal guidelines, cultural resources are not eligible for consideration as historic until fifty years *after* their construction (or design, in the case of landscapes). Therefore, PHLF's 1967 survey considered cultural resources erected/designed in or prior to 1917, and its 1984 survey considered cultural resources erected/designed in or prior to 1934. In 2013, cultural resources erected/designed in or prior to 1963 are eligible for consideration as historic if: they represent a significant work of a master designer; contain finishes of construction or exceptional artistic merit; are the last surviving example of a type; or were directly associated with a person or event that influenced our nation. Recording, evaluating, and seeking to preserve architectural

Foreword

landmarks is not a static activity. It is a recurring and ongoing responsibility, requiring the critical evaluation of each new generation.

Modernism has now come of age for our evaluation. This guidebook allows us to confidently place Pittsburgh's earliest modern buildings in their proper context and helps us to better understand their evolution and significance. It is an essential addition to the literature on local architecture, a model for other cities, and a resource for those who want to ensure that our most notable twentieth-century buildings continue to be cared for and used or reused in ways that inform, delight, and enrich the daily experiences of all those who live in or visit our city and county.

An art glass screen in an apartment in Highland Towers (1913–14)

Architecture, shielding you though you don't realize it from danger and inconvenience, can also be something that makes you glad, though you aren't always conscious of it, that you are where you are.

—WALTER C. KIDNEY
IN PITTSBURGH
(APRIL 27–MAY 3, 1988)

Preface

In 1900, British designer and architect Charles Robert Ashbee visited Pittsburgh and was profoundly shaken by what he saw and experienced. He later wrote that Pittsburgh, one of the "greatest and wealthiest" cities in the United States, was "everything that a city should not be." He noted the natural beauty of the landscape and the impressive bridges but found:

> *noble rivers ... covered with a black slime, the scum of her works and factories. ... Across these streams engineers had built bridges, fine, purposeful and dignified structures ... but the steel ties were disfigured by the placards of tradesmen. All around was a chain of hills of such natural beauty, that the lie of the land seemed to rival that of any city in the world. As little regard was paid to the trees as to the streams, the finest points of view were disfigured by advertisements and used as midden heaps. As the city burnt soft coal ... the city was always covered with a dense pall of smoke and soot. I looked into the history of the ... city and found her full of records of the heroism of past times, the early war of Independence and the struggle with France; one little landmark alone had been saved by some pious ladies from afar. I asked one of her leading citizens if nothing could be done to record or accentuate those things. "Nobody knew of them," he said, "and nobody cared."*[1]

Visitors today—many pleasantly surprised—discover that a city whose industrial squalor was unmatched in America for over a century has become not only an attractive, livable city, but one full of architectural landmarks, some well known, some not.

During the latter half of the twentieth century, environmental devastation and civic indifference were reversed. Despite substantial architectural losses, splendid historic buildings and neighborhoods survived and were restored, and twentieth-century clients and architects gave metropolitan Pittsburgh new and impressive buildings, structures, and landscapes, including: the sole surviving supper room designed by Viennese-American architect and designer Joseph Urban; the nation's first modern subdivision; the first Wrightian "Usonian" house in Pennsylvania (a house type Frank

Lloyd Wright named and first built in 1937); the largest and grandest of the nine houses Walter Gropius and Marcel Breuer designed during their five-year partnership; the world's first aluminum-clad skyscraper; the world's first modern garden plaza designed over a parking garage with retail space; the nation's first (partial) realization of Le Corbusier's concept of towers in a park; and the nation's first publicly sponsored, privately financed urban redevelopment project.

Major construction materials and technological innovations important to twentieth-century architects and contractors were pioneered, developed, and made in Pittsburgh, including iron, steel,[2] aluminum, glass—both functional and ornamental—and wire cables, Westinghouse elevators, light bulbs, alternating current, natural gas, petroleum, railroad airbrakes, switches and signals, and atomic energy for generating electric power.

This guidebook—the first devoted solely to twentieth-century buildings in metropolitan Pittsburgh—explores how Pittsburghers became aware of what was happening in architecture throughout the United States and Europe and commissioned distinguished architects to design notable churches, schools, apartment buildings, private residences, banks, clubs, commercial buildings, theaters and entertainment venues, municipal buildings, corporate skyscrapers, parks, bridges and highways, and more. Approximately eighty buildings, structures, and landscapes designed and erected between 1903 and 1999 are featured in the Guide section of this book. The sites are located on maps of downtown Pittsburgh and the region. Additional information on architects and their Pittsburgh buildings is cited in the bibliography. The endnotes have a broader reach: they document and also direct readers to additional sources of information and areas of inquiry; some will edify, others may entertain.

As we travel through the twentieth century, readers will meet clients, architects, and architectural historians and writers, and they will hear their opinions, concerns, and insights. Especially relevant is the scholarship of James D. Van Trump (1908–95) and Walter C. Kidney (1932–2005), architectural historians with the Pittsburgh History & Landmarks Foundation. Van Trump, who has been called "Pittsburgh's premier architectural writer and historian,"[3] became actively engaged with twentieth-century architecture in 1956 when he first wrote for *The Charette*, an architectural journal founded in 1920 by the Pittsburgh Architectural Club. In addition to his many articles, Van Trump served as the journal's assistant editor, editor, and co-publisher. After *The Charette* was sold in 1971, Van Trump wrote about contemporary and historic architecture for other publications for another decade.

Preface

On November 17, 1963, Van Trump received a letter about *The Charette* from Henry-Russell Hitchcock, arguably then America's most distinguished architectural historian:

> *I continue to be amazed at the range of material that you include— as many historical articles as in the SAH [Society of Architectural Historians] Journal and as a result a coverage of Pittsburgh, Philadelphia, and Pennsylvania architecture of the past, including the rather recent past, such as no other part of this country has, [and] at the same time [you include] a great deal of current work in the same areas and many special articles on all aspects of present-day architecture that rival those in national magazines.*[4]

Identifying and documenting notable twentieth-century landmarks builds a case for their preservation. In any region, the built environment contributes to the quality of life, reveals how we live, and is worth exploring. The historic preservation movement especially has encouraged public interest in discovering the story of a place by touring and learning about the significant structures that have survived. The architecture we save informs us about our history, connects generations, enriches lives, and inspires future designers. With this guidebook in hand, we encourage our readers to explore a selection of notable twentieth-century landmarks in the Pittsburgh region, and, in the process, to become familiar with the design vocabulary that distinguishes notable modern architecture throughout North America.

This 1998 photograph of a stair railing (now gone) in Richard Kiehnel's 1909 Brushton School in Pittsburgh's Homewood neighborhood illustrates the transformation from the sinuous, curvaceous floral patterns of first-generation Art Nouveau modernism into the abstract, symmetrical patterns of second-generation Secessionism.

Definitions of Modern Architecture

What does the word "modern" mean? In 1923, *Webster's New International Dictionary of the English Language* noted that "modern" comes from the Latin *modernis*, meaning "just now."[1] A dictionary published in 1995 defined modern as "belonging to the present or to recent times."[2] Twentieth-century museum curators, academic historians, architects, and clients periodically defined—and redefined—"modern" and "modern architecture."

Early use of the term "modern architecture" referred to contemporary reinterpretations of traditional, established styles. For example, architect and publisher William T. Comstock wrote in *Modern Architectural Designs and Details Containing Eighty Finely Lithographed Plates, Showing New and Original Designs in the Queen Anne, Eastlake, Elizabethan, and Other Modernized Styles* (New York, 1881): "The present styles, while bearing many characteristics of their prototypes, do not adhere strictly to any of them."[3] The author further noted that his illustrations "will be found to cover almost every question that can arise in detailing a modern dwelling."[4]

Sixteen years later, in 1897, a newspaper account of the first architectural exhibition held in Pittsburgh stated: "Ancient and modern styles of architecture will be represented in the collection,"[5] but the buildings illustrated in the catalogue were the prevailing classical and picturesque forms of the time.[6]

In May 1899, Louis Sullivan spoke to the Chicago Architectural Club on "The Modern Phase of Architecture." He did not use the word "modern" in the text but told his audience that "you are called upon … to express the life of your own day and generation" and denounced "a fraudulent and surreptitious use of historical documents, however suavely presented, however cleverly plagiarized, however neatly repacked."[7] Sullivan's talk was later read when a group of architectural clubs (including the Pittsburgh Architectural Club, established in 1896) met in Cleveland on June 2–3, 1899 and formed the Architectural League of America. Its motto was "Progress before Precedent," asserting that precedent should not be followed blindly and that "progress demands of us that we make our work express our civilization as correctly as the works of antiquity interpreted their times."[8]

Another discussion of the term appears in *A Dictionary of Architecture and Building: Biographical, Historical, and Descriptive*, edited by New York architect and critic Russell Sturgis and published in 1902. There is no separate entry for "modern," "modernism," or "modern architecture," but the entry in Volume I on "Design," in particular "Design II: Ancient Art and Modern Position," written by British Arts and Crafts architect and educator William R. Lethaby, noted:

> Others had hoped that a "modern style" would come of the use of new materials; but this is easily seen to be fallacious, as the real question is of the spirit which is to enlighten all our work, not of the matter of a small part of it. Is our architecture to be "modern art," when steel and aluminum are used, and not "art" when wood and stone are employed? … I claim for the sphere of modern architecture all buildings, all materials used in their construction, and all the workmanship involved in erecting them. The real purpose of our art is the expressive use of materials for the satisfaction of worthy needs.[9]

For Lethaby, "modern architecture" permits the "expressive use" of both traditional "wood and stone" and of modern "steel and aluminum."

The use of "modern," as applied to architecture, was not yet widespread in the United States. Frank Lloyd Wright would offer his own variation in 1908 when he referred to his work and the work of his colleagues in Chicago as "the New School of the Middle West."[10]

By 1916, "modern" and "modernist" had arrived in both the text and index of books such as C. Matlack Price's *The Practical Book of Architecture*. He devoted a chapter to "new styles applied to familiar uses, and old styles applied to the new uses."[11] The latter included tall office buildings, grand urban hotels, and railroad stations, among others, which still—in 1916 in America—followed historical models. The former, for Price, began with *Art Nouveau* (new art)—"no previous school of design had produced works in any way similar to the creations of the '*art nouveau*'" which, at its best, "awakened an appreciation of graceful form and of the inexhaustible possibilities of deriving decorative motifs from plant forms." Yet in Price's view, Art Nouveau had a short life and was "to all intents and purposes a 'dead style'."[12]

What interested Price was the Austro-Germanic architectural movement known as Secessionism: "the secessionists, as their name would imply, rebelled against what they regarded as the slavish copying of archaeological forms, and sought new means of expression." Secessionist architecture was "as nearly 'original' as it is possible to be" and influenced contemporary

Secessionist detailing in terra cotta on the façade of the 1913 Stengel House, Oakland

design (i.e., in 1916) in Germany and France; indeed Price proclaimed it "the forerunner of the 'Modernist' school of today" in Europe.[13] He noted that the movement had appeared in the United States "on a small scale": "The great American Secessionist in architecture is Frank Lloyd Wright, of Chicago, whose work … has extensively influenced many contemporary architects of the Middle West. The exact place of this school of architectural design has yet to be determined."[14] (*For Secessionist architecture in Pittsburgh see pages 59–81 of the Guide*)

The terms "modern" and "modern architecture" would come into their own in the United States in the mid-1920s. Modern design arrived in 1925 as *Art Moderne*. The *Exposition Internationale des Arts Décoratifs et Industriels Modernes* (International Exposition of Modern Decorative and Industrial Art), a World's Fair originally planned for 1915 but delayed by World War I, was held in Paris from April through October 1925. Germany was not invited and the United States government declined to participate: "Herbert Hoover, at the time secretary of commerce, had consulted V.I.P.'s in the art, educational and business worlds, who advised that there was no modern design in America."[15] Americans did visit the Paris fair and many more learned of it from illustrated design magazines.

> *The exposition contained many different examples of art—from the highly sophisticated, hand-crafted furniture of Emile-Jacques Ruhlmann, to low-relief, neoclassical sculpture and the geometrical purism of Le Corbusier and Amédée Ozenfant's* Pavillon de l'Esprit Nouveau—*but the American observers tended to overlook the differences, choosing instead to view the entire ensemble as an example of the moderne movement or Art Moderne. The overall impression was of an ornamental effect: lush, rich, and exotic materials, colors, and forms competing on the interiors and exteriors.*[16]

American architects, artists, and clients responded enthusiastically to Art Moderne. Simply put, it was "a decorative style at once traditional and innovative" absorbing "influences from a variety of sources and movements."[17] Art Moderne could adapt virtually anything—traditional architectural styles such as Classical or Gothic, natural floral or water forms, and technological innovations like the automobile and the airplane—into characteristic exaggerated, elongated, geometrized, or streamlined patterns.

While the enthusiasm for *moderne* would continue into the 1930s, change was imminent. In 1929, a new definition of modern architecture entered the American design vocabulary when *Modern Architecture: Romanticism and Reintegration* was published by a 26-year-old American architectural historian, Henry-Russell Hitchcock. *Modern Architecture* has been acclaimed for its "vast richness and lively ambiguity."[18] It was ambitious—it was a history of Western Architecture from 1750 to 1929— and its young author was as opinionated and sometimes verbose as he was erudite. According to Hitchcock, modern architecture had its roots in "painting, Cubist and Néo-Plasticist or otherwise abstract, which influenced architecture during [World War I] and immediately after" and its "central idea" is that "style of architecture depends on a method of construction."[19]

Hitchcock declared:

> *the newer manner ... is based on principles of design not inherited from the art of the past. Instead of composing in three dimensions in values of mass, the [leading modernist architects] compose in values of volume; instead of complexity as a means of interest they seek a strenuous unification; instead of diversity and richness of surface texture, they strive for monotony and even poverty, in order that the idea of the surface as the geometrical boundary of the volume may most clearly*

be expressed. ... [Ornament] makes the fullest unification impossible by breaking the surfaces.[20]

The leading practitioners of modern architecture, according to Hitchcock, were Le Corbusier (Charles-Édouard Jeanneret) of France, Walter Gropius and Ludwig Mies van der Rohe of Germany, and J. J. P. Oud of Holland. Together their work constituted an "international style."[21]

In 1932, an exhibition, *Modern Architecture—International Exhibition*, was mounted at the Museum of Modern Art (MoMA) in New York City, which had opened on November 7, 1929. Alfred H. Barr, Jr., who had been teaching contemporary painting and sculpture at Wellesley College, became the first director. The co-curators of the exhibition were Hitchcock and Philip Johnson, a 1930 graduate of Harvard College and a volunteer at MoMA (who later headed MoMA's Department of Architecture and Design). Barr had just turned 30, Hitchcock was 28, and Johnson was 25.

The exhibition "was conceived as a full-scale documentation of the first collective architectural effort in centuries to extract a consistent artistic style from a disciplined study of the technological possibilities and cultural needs of its time."[22] An exhibit catalogue[23] and a book, *The International Style: Architecture Since 1922*, written primarily by Hitchcock, were published to coincide with the exhibit.[24]

In the Preface to the book, Barr wrote:

The distinguishing aesthetic principles of the International Style as laid down by the authors are three: emphasis upon volume—space enclosed by thin planes or surfaces as opposed to the suggestion of mass and solidity; regularity as opposed to symmetry or other kinds of obvious balance; and, lastly, dependence upon the intrinsic elegance of materials, technical perfection, and fine proportions, as opposed to applied ornament.[25]

The book illustrated buildings designed by over seventy architects from fifteen countries, including six American firms. Two architects practicing in the United States, William Lescaze and Richard Neutra, had been educated in Europe and had come to America in the 1920s. The key figures in the exhibit and the book were Gropius, Oud, Mies, and Le Corbusier. The exhibition catalogue did not mention Frank Lloyd Wright, although five photographs and a model of one of his houses were exhibited.[26]

According to the MoMA curators, contemporary architecture was derived from abstract painting and sculpture, was to express innovative materials and technologies, and was no longer permitted to use ornament, or any architectural forms inherited from the past. Earlier architectural styles had been new and unprecedented—Art Nouveau, Secessionism, Expressionism, Wrightian—but they were now widely viewed as incomplete or tentative or stubbornly committed to traditional materials such as brick or wood; not really modern but "proto-modern," meaning "primitive, early, first, or precursor."[27]

With the arrival of Walter Gropius at Harvard University's Graduate School of Design in 1937 and Mies van der Rohe at the Armour Institute of Technology in Chicago in 1938 (renamed Illinois Institute of Technology), the newly defined modern architecture entered the curricula of the country's architecture schools.

Over the next two decades, the definition of modern architecture articulated in 1929 remained preeminent in American architectural education and practice. The term International Style opened the door to other "styles" of modern architecture that might differ in appearance yet remain faithful to the principles of abstract, non-ornamented form and the use of new materials and technologies. Those "styles" applicable to buildings in Pittsburgh during the twentieth century are discussed in the Guide.

By the 1960s, the rigidity and insularity of the prevailing concept of modern architecture came under fire. The widespread demolition of historic, inner-city neighborhoods, and of major architectural landmarks such as Frank Lloyd Wright's Larkin Building in Buffalo (1950), Louis Sullivan's Schiller Building in Chicago (1961), and McKim, Mead & White's Pennsylvania Station in New York (1963), resulted in the founding of regional nonprofit preservation organizations such as the Pittsburgh History & Landmarks Foundation in 1964. The National Historic Preservation Act was passed in 1966, signaling the beginning of a change in attitude and direction by many architects, city planners, and architectural historians.

Architectural historians writing near the end of the twentieth century questioned the assumptions of the MoMA curators in light of later events. According to Vincent Scully, Hitchcock in *Modern Architecture*:

> *will* not *deal with city planning, or with the building of cities, or with architecture as the construction of the human environment or, most of all, of the human community. ... He ... treats every building as if it were a painting in a gallery, isolated for him to see. And this is basically the way the late modernists saw their own buildings, as individual inventions, as wholly free from urbanistic conventions, responsibilities, and restraints as any abstract painting. ... This attitude combined

Twentieth-century buildings are reflected in the curtain wall of Four Gateway Center, as seen from Liberty Avenue in downtown Pittsburgh.

with other phenomena to destroy most of our cities, and it has not passed away yet among the perpetual avant-garde.[28]

The later influence of the schools of architecture came under fire as well. Carter Wiseman observed:

Many of the individual buildings designed by Mies, Gropius, and their American disciples had unquestionably architectural merit, but many lesser works by their imitators had contributed to an all-too-frequent sameness, particularly in the nation's cities. ... This sameness helped concentrate the attention of both the public and the professional architectural community on the physical variety that had been lost in the name of progress. Americans were coming to see that the "Victorian atrocities" and "Romanesque piles" so despised by many Modernists had much to recommend them after all, especially in the way they interacted with their architectural neighbors. Even some of the nation's slums that had been cleared with such zeal in pursuit of urban renewal were now recognized in hindsight to have been preferable in their scale and detail (not to mention their role in fostering a sense of community) to the faceless structures that often replaced them.[29]

Changes in the attitudes and approaches of the practicing architect and the architectural historian were decisive. In 1966, the same year as the National Historic Preservation Act, Robert Venturi, who was both a practicing architect and an architectural historian at Yale University, published *Complexity and Contradiction in Architecture*. Venturi wrote:

Architects can no longer afford to be intimidated by the puritanically moral language of orthodox Modern architecture. I like elements which are hybrid rather than "pure," compromising rather than "clean," distorted rather than "straightforward," ambiguous rather than "articulated." ... I am for messy vitality over obvious unity.[30]

In the 1930s through the 1960s, modern architecture referred exclusively to an architectural style in which architecture was derived from abstract painting and sculpture, was to express innovative materials and technologies rather than traditional ones, and was no longer permitted to use ornament or any architectural forms inherited from the past. Did "orthodox Modern architecture," to use Venturi's phrase, born in the late-1920s, die in the 1960s when historical architectural forms and materials once again became sources of contemporary architectural inspiration? The term still used to characterize contemporary architecture near the end of the twentieth century is "Postmodernism" (*see Guide, page 181*) and presents a paradox—now that modernism has been superseded by postmodernism, how do we describe "new" architecture? One is tempted to seek an alternative term to "modern" architecture—"progressive" architecture, *avant-garde* (in front) architecture—but historically "modern" dominated the characterization of architecture in the twentieth century, despite acquiring diverse, sometimes contradictory meanings.

Near the end of the twentieth century, architectural dictionaries amplified their definitions of modern architecture in the United States to include the use of historical references, yet were unwilling to compromise the cutting edge of newness. The twentieth edition of *Sir Banister Fletcher's A History of Architecture* (1996) stated:

Modernism ... emphasizes newness and exploits fully the construction and design potential offered by new building materials and technology. References may be made to historical precedent by overt or oblique

Definitions of Modern Architecture

Early-twentieth-century buildings in the Fourth Avenue National Register Historic District are reflected in the Postmodern PPG Place.

means, but there is a clear distinction implied between previous eras and the present. Often, too, more concern is focused on anticipating the future than on associating with the past.[31]

In the Pittsburgh region, where people were experienced in producing and developing "new building materials and technology," modernism was all about "anticipating the future," since the industrial squalor of the past had created an unlivable city.

The Eve of Modernism

Walter C. Kidney, architectural historian of the Pittsburgh History & Landmarks Foundation, described Pittsburgh in 1882, just before the twentieth century:

> The city itself was rather casually thrown together, though it had over 156,000 people and though annexations of a decade before had brought Oakland, Lawrenceville, East Liberty, and the string of communities on the south shore of the Monongahela [River] within its limits. There were no zoning laws to control the use of land, and would not be until 1923. There were no pollution laws to control the notorious, outrageous smoke of industrial plants, locomotives, steam boats, and private hearths, or the runoff from sewers, factories, privies, and mines that went into the streams.
>
> The citizens of Pittsburgh had rejected the idea of a park twice, and would not get one until Mary Schenley's gift of 1889 .... There were no Carnegie libraries yet, and no museums. ...
>
> Architecturally, this Pittsburgh of 1882 was typically American, though perhaps a little behind the times. In Boston ... and in Philadelphia, a new approach to design was rapidly evolving in which color, texture, and form were experimented

Pittsburgh around 1880, with the spires of St. Paul's Cathedral (now gone), downtown, and industrial plants along the Monongahela River shore

with as they had never been before. In Chicago and New York, commercial architecture was developing as engineers and architects faced the demands for bigger and especially taller buildings. These aesthetic and technical developments drifted into Pittsburgh rather than originating here.[1]

According to Kidney, H. H. Richardson's Allegheny County Courthouse and Jail (1883–88) and Emmanuel Episcopal Church (1883–86) introduced "a sudden change" in architecture in Pittsburgh. In many ways, Richardson's Courthouse was what we think of today as a modern building. It had a highly functional plan, a clarity of public circulation, ample fenestration bringing daylight into every principle space, fire-proof construction, iron beams, concrete floors, elevators, heating, plumbing, and ventilating systems, coordinated furnishings, and a logical, literate finesse to the exterior façades which developed an expressive unity and harmony. Furthermore, Kidney noted:

> The example of the Courthouse was enforced by that of Emmanuel Episcopal Church in Allegheny. ... This [Richardson] treated as an essay in low walls beneath a towering roof, with a front of three low arches beneath a huge gable filled with patterned brickwork: a design crudely simple, powerful, and massive.[2]

When completed in 1888, H. H. Richardson's Courthouse was the tallest building in Pittsburgh.

Three early Pittsburgh architectural exhibitions of contemporary design—1898, 1900, and 1905—were held in the Carnegie Art Gallery in Oakland's Carnegie Library and Institute (Longfellow, Alden & Harlow, 1892–95). The building was enlarged by Alden & Harlow in 1903–07, and the 1907 architectural exhibition was held in the new Carnegie Art Museum. At the center of this photograph is the Music Hall at the corner of Forbes Avenue and Schenley Plaza; to the left are the art and natural history museums; and to the far right is the library. The music library of the Carnegie Library of Pittsburgh now occupies the original Carnegie Art Gallery space

How Modern Architecture Came to Pittsburgh

Modern architecture came to Pittsburgh through a variety of circumstances over time. The Carnegie Library of Pittsburgh assembled an exceptional collection of current architectural books and journals—both national and international. The Pittsburgh Architectural Club, joined by the Pittsburgh Chapter of the American Institute of Architects (AIA), sponsored a series of architectural exhibitions that introduced architects and the general public to contemporary design in the United States and abroad. These Pittsburgh professional organizations, later joined by the Pennsylvania Society of Architects, published *The Charette*, an acclaimed regional architectural journal between 1920 and 1975. Visiting architectural exhibitions showed contemporary design that originated in Austria, Germany, Paris, and New York—and designs on paper or shown in photographs came to life through the patronage of Pittsburgh citizens, who commissioned new buildings. Finally, in an effort to reverse the region's legacy of industrial blight, the Allegheny Conference on Community Development was formed in 1943 to oversee the Pittsburgh Renaissance after World War II. Between 1946 and 1974, smoke-control and water purification laws were enforced, and massive clearances eventually resulted in the creation in downtown Pittsburgh of major new skyscrapers and green spaces, and in the redevelopment (unsuccessfully) of portions of the Lower Hill, North Side, and East Liberty.

Architectural Books and Journals

Knowledge of current architectural design and practice came to Pittsburgh initially through a library, not through an art museum or an educational institution. Architectural literacy began in Pittsburgh in 1895 at the Carnegie Library of Pittsburgh, two years before the first major exhibition of architectural design was held in 1897 at the Carnegie Library in Allegheny City (now Pittsburgh's North Side), and ten years before a school of architecture was established in 1905 at Carnegie Technical Schools, renamed Carnegie Institute of Technology (Carnegie Tech) in 1912 and Carnegie Mellon University in 1967.

The Bernd Collection of architectural books is one of the earliest and most important collections in the Carnegie Library of Pittsburgh. It was established through the generosity of businessman Julius Bernd and the foresight of head librarian Edwin H. Anderson: "Bernd's one stipulation was that [the gift] be used solely for the acquisition of books in a single category or department. ... architecture and decoration became the focus of the Bernd fund."[3] The first catalog of the Bernd Collection was published in 1898 and included 300 titles.

From 1896 through the 1940s, the Carnegie Library worked with the Pittsburgh Architectural Club to identify architectural books and journals for purchase. The Bernd Collection served as the core architecture library for students at Carnegie Tech and the University of Pittsburgh.[4]

The architectural and applied arts journals were of critical importance. Through photographs, plans, renderings, and building descriptions, they introduced local architects to current international architecture and design: *Der Architekt* (Austria); *The Builder, The Studio* (Britain); *Die Architekture des XX jahrhunderts [Architecture of the 20th Century]* (Germany, with text in German, French, and English); and *American Architect & Building News, Architectural League of New York Yearbook, The Craftsman,* and *The Western Architect* (United States), to cite a few examples. The journals published designs by architects who exhibited at the architectural exhibitions held in Pittsburgh between 1897 and 1916, and provided documentation of contemporary work in Vienna, Berlin, London, Boston, Chicago, New York, Philadelphia, and elsewhere. Architectural journals influenced the vocabulary of Pittsburgh architects and the appearance of Pittsburgh buildings prior to World War II.

In addition, *Construction Record* (extant issues 1910–16) and *Builders' Bulletin* (1916–present) provided concise information on construction contracts to be awarded and contracts awarded in Pittsburgh and western Pennsylvania.[5] Both were published weekly.

Architectural Exhibitions, Exhibition Catalogs, and *The Charette*

Architectural exhibitions were held in Pittsburgh (and Allegheny City) between 1897 and 1916. The illustrated exhibition catalogs are our primary, and, in some cases, only record of local architectural design during these years. Through these exhibitions, western Pennsylvanians saw not only examples of traditional design, but were introduced to the British Arts and Crafts movement, European Secessionism, and the midwestern Prairie School. A review of the first six exhibitions reveals their quality and significance.

The first documented local exhibition was the *Architectural Exhibition of Pittsburg, Pa.* held in the Carnegie Art Gallery of the Carnegie Library, Allegheny City, September 16 through September 25, 1897, sponsored by *The Builder*, a monthly Pittsburgh magazine. The catalog lists 146 entries accompanied by fifty illustrations of the work of twenty-one Pittsburgh architects representing sixteen firms.[6] The event received substantial newspaper coverage. According to the *Evening Record*:

> *Nothing of the kind has ever before been given in this city and the venture is exciting much interest among lovers of good architecture. About 200 invitations have been sent out for the opening night. … The exhibit will include plans, elevations and pictures of all kinds of buildings, churches, school buildings, business blocks, office buildings and residences. Ancient and modern styles of architecture will be represented in the collection, but the chief object of the exhibition is to show what Pittsburg has done and is doing in the world of artistic architecture.*[7]

The first official architectural exhibition sponsored by the Pittsburgh Chapter AIA was held in 1898. The "First Annual Architectural Exhibition" opened on May 2, 1898 and continued through the 31st. The catalog reveals a substantial exhibition: architects, architectural schools, and designers from twenty-two cities in twelve states (and the District of Columbia) submitted 766 entries. Architects from Altoona, Beaver Falls, Johnstown, and Pittsburgh represented western Pennsylvania. There were no exhibitors from abroad.[8]

The Pittsburgh Architectural Club (PAC), founded in 1896 by apprentices working in Pittsburgh architectural firms,[9] mounted its "First Annual Exhibition" at the Carnegie Art Gallery, June 9 through July 1, 1900. It was dedicated to the memory of H. H. Richardson. The PAC exhibitions were held regularly as a biannual until 1910 and thereafter as an annual exhibition until 1916. In 1900, there were 778 exhibits from the United States, England, and France. Many architects who had exhibited in 1898 entered designs in 1900.[10]

What made the 1900 exhibition significant was the large number of exhibitors—nineteen—from England. Charles Robert Ashbee was an architect, designer, educator, and preservationist. R. S. Balfour, Herbert Buckland, C. J. Harold Cooper, Lionel Francis Crane, Thomas Davison, F. C. Eden, Ernest George, Arnold Mitchell, Ernest Newton, Beresford Pite, F. Steward Taylor, Charles Harrison Townsend, Edward Warren, J. L. Williams, Edgar Wood, and Alfred Bowman Yeates were primarily architects. Walter Crane (Lionel's father) was a painter, illustrator and designer, and Francis Inigo Thomas was a landscape architect.

Most were active in the Arts and Crafts movement, an approach to art and design rooted in the theories of English critic John Ruskin (1819–1900), and the work of William Morris (1834–96)—painter; designer of furniture, glass, textiles, and books; poet and novelist; social activist; and preservationist (he founded the Society for the Protection of Ancient Buildings in 1877). They sought to revitalize the art and architecture of their time by using the materials and the techniques of medieval English craftsmanship. The Arts and Crafts Exhibition Society, established in London in 1888, gave the movement its name. Among the outstanding exhibits of British Arts and Crafts design in 1900 were Townsend's Whitechapel Art Gallery with its decorative mosaic by Crane; Wood's Lindley tower; and Ashbee's furniture, metalwork, and jewelry. Ashbee's Chelsea townhouses were among the over twenty contemporary English house designs on display.[11]

Ashbee was on a speaking tour of the United States in 1900 for the National Trust of Great Britain when he visited Pittsburgh from November 18 to 21 and attended the Fifth Annual Art Exhibition at the Carnegie Institute. Although impressed by the exhibition—he told a newspaper reporter it "is one of the finest he has ever seen"[12]—Ashbee was profoundly shaken by what he saw and experienced in the city. In his report to the National Trust, Ashbee wrote that Pittsburgh was "the only city I have visited in America that seems to be without any sort of public spirit or any sense of citizenship."[13]

In 1915, Ashbee returned to Pittsburgh to give the Convocation address at Carnegie Tech. By that time, Henry Hornbostel had established a School of Architecture at Carnegie Tech and had designed and built some half-dozen buildings on the campus. The "City Beautiful" movement had transformed the adjacent Oakland neighborhood into a civic center, with the enlarged Carnegie Institute and Library (1907), Soldiers' and Sailors' Memorial Hall (1910), the Pittsburgh Athletic Association (1911), and the Masonic Temple (1914). Ashbee noticed and told his audience that "I have a different opinion of the city now. The younger Pittsburgh is doing what the old Pittsburgh did not see and could not realize."[14]

Arts and Crafts societies had been founded in Boston and Chicago in 1897, and by 1901 Arts and Crafts associations, workshops, and publications were flourishing in the United States. Pittsburgh had no Arts and Crafts society, but local artists sympathetic to the movement displayed their work at PAC exhibitions until 1910 when the Associated Artists of Pittsburgh was founded.

At the 1903 exhibition, an additional dozen British designers, also affiliated with the Arts and Crafts Exhibition Society, displayed their work.

Although nothing is stated in the catalog, the 1903 exhibit stressed ecclesiastical design. Among the exhibitors best known to students of British architecture were John Douglas, Edward S. Prior, W. Bainbridge Reynolds, and Temple Moore.

If the 1897 and 1898 exhibitions provided a view of contemporary American practice, and the 1900 and 1903 exhibitions highlighted the British Arts and Crafts movement, the 1905 and 1907 exhibitions introduced Pittsburgh to the "Modern Movement" in Europe and to the "New School of the Middle West."

The Third Exhibition opened at the Carnegie Art Gallery on May 22, 1905. Titus de Bobula, born and trained in Budapest, but living and working in Pittsburgh since 1903, exhibited designs for twelve buildings, including seven in metropolitan Pittsburgh. (*For de Bobula see pages 60–65*) Also noteworthy were the first designs exhibited by Pittsburgh architect Frederick G. Scheibler, Jr. One of his four entries was "Apartment building, 'Old Heidelberg,' Braddock Avenue, Pittsburgh, Pa.," a design indebted to contemporary Austrian architecture. (*For Scheibler see pages 66–69*)

The 1907 architectural exhibition, sponsored by both the Pittsburgh Architectural Club and the Pittsburgh Chapter AIA, was held in November. It was the largest architectural exhibition hitherto organized in the United States and the broadest in scope. The printed catalog[15] for the month-long event listed about 1,420 exhibits; more than 1,500 were actually displayed. More than 88,000 visitors came to see American and European designs for buildings of every conceivable kind (such as a "small restaurant for automobilists" and a prize-winning French slaughterhouse), city plans, public monuments, bridges, landscapes, art glass, architectural ornament, ironwork, lighting fixtures, pottery and tile, pipe organs, furniture, sculpture, etc.

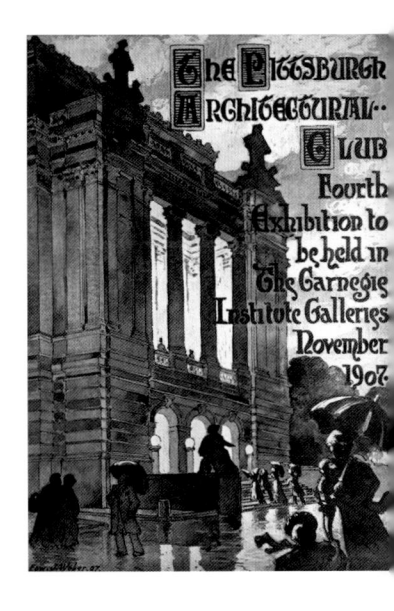

Christopher Monkhouse wrote: "What truly made the Pittsburgh Architectural Club's 1907 exhibition stand out from all previous exhibitions … was the final section, which filled two galleries. It bore the title 'Modern Movement' … ."[16] Great Britain was represented by the work of C. R. Ashbee, Charles Rennie Mackintosh, and Margaret Macdonald (Mackintosh's wife).

Pittsburgh Architecture in the Twentieth Century

One of the galleries in the 1907 Pittsburgh Architectural Club exhibition at the new Carnegie Art Gallery in the expanded Carnegie Institute in Oakland

Three of their countrymen appeared courtesy of their German publishers. Designs by more than two dozen Austro-Hungarian and German designers were presented by Ernst Wasmuth of Berlin, who published the journal *The Architecture of the 20th Century* (and who would publish the first book of Frank Lloyd Wright's work in 1910), and by Julius Hoffmann of Stuttgart, publisher of *Decorative Patterns*.[17] (H. P. Berlage of Holland, Eliel Saarinen of Finland, and Edgar Wood of Great Britain were among Hoffmann's exhibitors.) Prominent figures included Bruno Möhring,[18] who had organized the acclaimed German exhibit at the 1904 St. Louis Exposition;[19] Remigius Geyling, who created the chancel mosaic for Otto Wagner's Steinhof Church; Frantisek Kupka—"Naturalist, Symbolist, and one of the earliest [Czech] creators of abstract art;"[20] and Fritz Schumacher, who co-organized the 1906 Applied Arts Exhibition in Dresden. His works exhibited in Dresden were also exhibited in Pittsburgh.[21]

The 1907 exhibition was the first to exhibit Frank Lloyd Wright's work in Pittsburgh. His work would be shown again in 1913, but midwestern representation had been strong as early as 1898. Louis Sullivan, Walter Burley Griffin and his wife Marion Mahony, Hugh Garden and Richard Schmidt, Jens Jensen, Robert Spencer, George Maher, Dwight Perkins, and Vernon Watson were arguably the most important midwestern architects and designers whose works were displayed at PAC exhibitions or illustrated in the catalogs.[22]

The chairman of the planning committee for the 1907 exhibition was Richard Kiehnel. Years later, exhibition secretary Stanley Roush recalled: "We all worked like beavers for two months, Kiehnel giving practically all his time to the work."[23] (*For Kiehnel see pages 70–81*) When the exhibition closed, *The Western Architect* reported:

> *The International Exhibition of Architectural drawings of the Pittsburgh Architectural Club, held at Carnegie Institute, … was one of the most important ever held in the United States, rivaling the best of those held by the Architectural League of New York, and reflects the greatest credit upon the Pittsburgh Architectural Club.*[24]

Supplementing the construction journals discussed earlier, all architectural exhibition catalogs included advertisements by contractors, fabricators, artists, and artisans active in metropolitan Pittsburgh between September 1897 and December 1916.

In 1920, the PAC began publishing a journal, *The Charette*—a French word meaning "a final, intensive effort to finish a project, especially an architectural design project, before a deadline" and is sometimes spelled charrette.[25] The Pittsburgh Chapter AIA contributed for a time, and the Pennsylvania Society of Architects, headquartered in Philadelphia, participated in the 1950s and 1960s. The Carnegie Mellon University Architecture Archives has digitized the journal, which can be accessed and searched on its website. Martin Aurand, architectural archivist, characterizes the publication on the webpage:

> Charette *featured criticism and commentary on architecture as well as copious information about contemporary architectural projects, and the activities of sponsoring architectural organizations. During the Depression, it was a chatty vehicle for connecting architects and keeping the profession active. After World War II, it grew increasingly professional in content and appearance and expanded to cover the growing architectural scene.*[26]

James D. Van Trump was a key contributor. In 1963, the American Institute of Architects praised *The Charette* for "the best editing and design in a regional architectural journal."[27] In 1964, Van Trump became co-founder and architectural historian of the Pittsburgh History & Landmarks Foundation.

Visiting Exhibitions 1913–1932

In January and February 1913, the Carnegie Institute hosted an exhibition of *Kunstgewerbe* (Applied Art; also translated as Arts and Crafts) from the German Museum for Art in Trade and Commerce in Hagen, Germany, in association with the Austrian Museum of Art and Industry in Vienna. The catalogue (in English) defined the scope of the exhibition as "Work of modern German artists in Architecture, Drawing and Applied Design." The work of four decorative artists and twenty-seven architects was included in the Architecture section; one—Fritz Schumacher—had fourteen designs on display in Pittsburgh in 1907. A newcomer was Walter Gropius (*see pages 126–131*) of Berlin, who exhibited "A Gentleman's Sitting Room." The exhibition also traveled to museums in Newark, St. Louis, Chicago, Indianapolis, Cincinnati, and New York between April 1912 and April 1913.[28]

In 1926, "A Selected Collection of Objects from the International Exposition of Modern Decorative and Industrial Art, Paris, 1925," visited Boston, New York, Philadelphia, Cleveland, Detroit, St. Louis, Minneapolis, and Pittsburgh.[29] On November 23, 1926, members of the Pittsburgh Chapter AIA viewed the exhibition at the Carnegie Art Museum.[30]

The *Modern Architecture—International Exhibition,* held at the new Museum of Modern Art in New York City (February 9–March 19, 1932), traveled to various American art museums between March 1932 and December 1933. It was mounted at the Carnegie Art Museum June 3–25, 1932.[31] Robert Schmertz, then president of the Pittsburgh Architectural Club, reviewed the exhibit:

> *Let it be stated here that not all the buildings are good. Many are undoubtedly as false and tricky as some of our own fake half-timber houses, and can be classed as architectural scenery, pure and simple, but there are many which are direct and original solutions of the problems in hand, which make logical use of steel, concrete, and glass, and which achieve esthetic value through good proportion and carefully handled detail.*[32]

Architectural Patronage

The "Modern Movement" in Pittsburgh appeared first in the designs of Titus de Bobula (active 1903–06), Frederick G. Scheibler, Jr. (active 1904–30), and Richard Kiehnel (active 1908–16). If the visual language was Austro-Germanic, so initially were the clients: German or Hungarian social and athletic organizations, businessmen, academics, and clergy—both Roman Catholic and Protestant.

Richard Kiehnel's c. 1910 design for the Forbes School gateway (now gone) shows an exuberant use of geometric forms.

From left: Titus de Bobula, Frederick G. Scheibler, Jr., and Richard Kiehnel

The patrons of the Modern architecture of the next generation also had European, primarily German, roots, but they were Jewish. In 1925, Edgar J. Kaufmann, Sr., president of Kaufmann's Department Store in downtown Pittsburgh, "formulated plans … for the remodeling and redecoration of the first floor of [Kaufmann's]. Our purpose was to show all those who entered that utility is beauty."[33] The impetus for this remodeling may have been Kaufmann's response to the International Exposition of Modern Decorative and Industrial Art held in Paris, April through October 1925. Indeed, in November 1926, Kaufmann's held its own *International Exposition of Industrial Arts*: "The didactic purpose of the show was to demonstrate the evolution of design over time and demonstrate how the best modern forms are an outgrowth of what has gone before."[34]

Edgar J. Kaufmann, Sr.

Initially, Kaufmann asked celebrated New York designer Joseph Urban (*see pages 94–98*) to prepare plans for the department store remodeling. Urban's 1926 designs were not accepted but he remained a family friend.[35] The remodeling and redecorating commission went to Pittsburgh architect Benno Janssen, of Janssen & Cocken. Janssen had designed a Renaissance Revival addition to the Kaufmann store on Smithfield Street and Fifth Avenue in 1914; ten years later Janssen designed a Picturesque Norman house for the Kaufmann family in suburban Fox Chapel. Janssen—called "the most facile and talented of Pittsburgh's eclectic architects of the earlier twentieth century"[36] by Van Trump—produced an Art Deco masterpiece,

Opposite: The remodeled first floor of Kaufmann's (now Macy's) in 1930, with one of the Boardman Robinson murals illustrating "The History of Commerce"

24

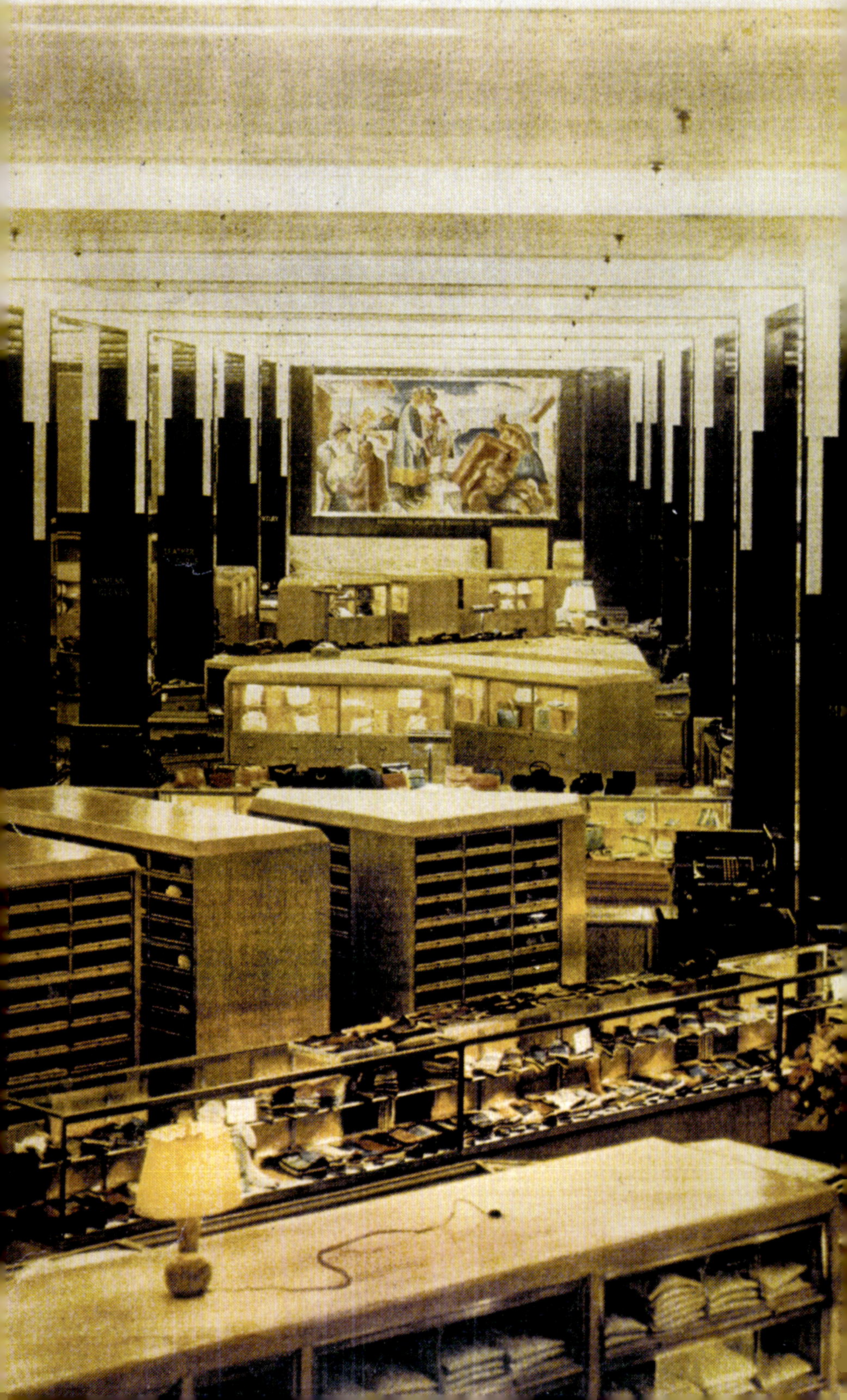

designed and installed between 1927 to 1930. The remodeled first floor opened to the public on May 1, 1930. On May 11, a twenty-four-page supplement to the *Pittsburgh Sun-Telegraph* published photographs and detailed descriptions of the project.

In his introduction to the supplement, "Art in Industry," Edgar Kaufmann wrote that "the development of art should be the cultural goal of America." He characterized Americans as a "fusion of many of the races of the earth … a complex and composite people," and stated his belief that American art should be "modern, [based on] principles of harmony rather than on personal distortions derived from older and devitalized nations."

The remodeling was an artistic and a technological triumph. The floor plan was radical and radial—customers moved from store entrances along diagonally placed aisles toward the central elevator bank, "like the spokes of a wheel." They paused at display cases of metal or imported wood, fabricated by nine different firms from around the country. "The world was searched for materials, new and proper for decoration. … The final choice fell upon stainless 'white bronze' for metal work, black carrara glass for columns, the beautiful avodire [light yellow hardwood] from Africa."

Details (above and opposite), including some survivors, now in Macy's

The structural columns were encased with 8,230 separate pieces of black Carrara glass—forty tons—developed by Pittsburgh Plate Glass (and named after the white, marble-like glass PPG had created as a substitute for the famed Italian marble). The tops of the columns were decorated (so to speak) with strips of light that illuminated and defined the edges of each column, rising to and spreading across the ceiling in a grid—a "linear lighting installation" composed of 10,000 Westinghouse Mazda lamps.

The floor was black and brown terrazzo—a mixture of marble chips and tinted mortar—laid in fourteen-inch by twenty-nine-inch diamonds edged with one-eighth-inch brass and then ground smooth and polished. General Bronze Co.'s Benedict metal—a recently invented metal alloy of copper, zinc, and nickel that was harder than bronze and exhibited a "peculiar gold like sheen"—was used on elevator doors, the railings around the mezzanine level arcade, and the frames of ten approximately

27

seven-foot-high by fourteen-foot-wide murals commissioned for the space illustrating "The History of Commerce," by New York muralist Boardman Robinson (1876–1952).[37] Cut and engraved glass in a leaf-and-berry pattern was designed by French artist Bernard Sauveur Akoun for the Arcade Grill and fabricated by artisans from his studio. The room was drastically remodeled in 1955, although some elements—display cases, elevator doors, ornamental grill screens, drinking fountains, and black Carrara glass panels in the entrance vestibules—remain. (*Also see page 194*)

Edgar Kaufmann, jr. (his lowercasing) labeled Janssen's design "bold art deco" and wrote that "Janssen influenced the Kaufmanns' tastes so that they became open to the trend of Wright's more profound art."[38] Edgar jr. studied art in Vienna and in Florence, Italy, from 1929 to 1934. When he returned, he discovered Wright's *An Autobiography* (1932), read it, and joined Wright's Taliesin Fellowship in Spring Green, Wisconsin, for five months.[39]

Edgar Kaufmann, Sr., met Frank Lloyd Wright in 1934 at Taliesin, while visiting Edgar jr., and subsequently commissioned Fallingwater (1935–37) and Kaufmann's private office (*see page 195*) in the department store in downtown Pittsburgh (1935–38); the office would be Wright's only realized work in the City of Pittsburgh (although Kaufmann commissioned some dozen projects from Wright, including several for Pittsburgh that never passed beyond the design phase).[40]

Richard Cleary noted:

> *A particular concern for Kaufmann jr. and his parents was the welfare of their friends in Austria, many of whom were becoming targets of discrimination both as Jews and as practitioners of modernist art and design, regarded as suspect by the political right. The family assisted a number of artists and designers in immigrating to the United States.*[41]

Hungarian-born artist László Gábor came from Vienna in 1935 and became art director of Kaufmann's Department Store. (Gábor later taught at Carnegie Tech; his course, "The Contemporary Home," was introduced in 1943 and "included discussion of the origins of the modern movement."[42]) Architect and author Bernard Rudolsky worked at the store in 1936; Walter Sobotka came to the United States in 1938. He obtained a position in 1941 teaching at the Research Bureau for Retail Training at the University of Pittsburgh,[43] founded by Edgar Kaufmann. Hans Vetter, who joined the faculty of Carnegie Tech in 1948, bringing "a new touch of Central European elegance and a new artistic spirit to the department,"[44] arrived in Pittsburgh through the intervention of Sobotka and Gábor.

"Gábor also helped Josef Frank and Oskar Wlach through the immigra-

How Modern Architecture Came to Pittsburgh

Frank Lloyd Wright prepared this perspective drawing (above) of Fallingwater (Fayette County, Pennsylvania) for Edgar Kaufmann, Sr., in 1935. In 1947, Kaufmann commissioned an ambitious cultural and sports civic center complex for the Pittsburgh Point from Wright. The first scheme was presented to the Allegheny Conference and met with disapproval; the second scheme was better received, in part because of the impressive colorful renderings prepared by Pittsburgh native Allen Lape Davison. The Scheme 2 west elevation (below) shows an aquarium at the tip of the Point backed by a 1,000-foot tower supporting cable bridges over the Allegheny River (left) and the Monongahela River (right). Kaufmann terminated the commission later that year and turned his attention to developing a cultural acropolis in the Lower Hill that did not involve Wright.

tion process."⁴⁵ Architect and designer Josef Frank had fled to Sweden in 1933, lived in the United States during World War II, and later returned to Sweden.⁴⁶ Oskar Wlach had partnered with Frank and Sobotka in the Viennese design firm Haus & Garten, which was seized by the Nazi government in 1938; Wlach came to the United States that year and established an architectural practice in New York in 1940.

Edgar Kaufmann, Sr., commissioned a house and office from Frank Lloyd Wright and a California house from Richard Neutra. He commissioned designs for Pittsburgh from Wright for a Civic Center at the Point (1947), a parking garage for the department store (1949), and an apartment building on Mount Washington (1952–53). In 1947, Kaufmann commissioned the local firm of Mitchell & Ritchey to prepare an exhibition and publication, *Pittsburgh in Progress*, that presented "a far more important vision for Pittsburgh than Frank Lloyd Wright's celebrated Point projects. ... Wright's plans would have spectacularly transformed Pittsburgh's Point, but did not find civic support. The Mitchell & Ritchey plan significantly reshaped the city."⁴⁷ It was an ambitious city-wide proposal that envisioned water and air pollution controls; new park and recreational areas adjacent to office and apartment towers; broad parkways and monorail mass transit; recreational use of the rivers; and a cultural center in the Lower Hill. (*For Mitchell & Ritchey see pages 155–157 and 197–200*)

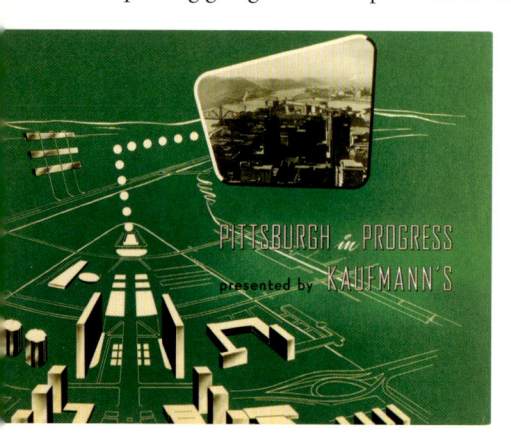

The Kaufmanns, Richard Cleary observed, "encountered boundaries that limited the scope of their ambitions in Pittsburgh society, but this liability was offset by the creativity of the people within the circles in which they moved." Other members of Pittsburgh's Jewish community became important creatively and/or as clients of contemporary architecture. Cecelia and Robert Frank commissioned a monumental house in 1938 from Walter Gropius and Marcel Breuer (*see pages 126–131*). Pittsburgh native A. James Speyer studied architecture in Chicago, but returned to Pittsburgh to design a house for Joan and Jerome Apt in 1951 and a home and studio for his mother, a sculptor, in 1963. (*For Speyer see pages 146–151*) In the 1950s, insurance adjustor Saul Lipkind and his wife Edith, and physician

Dr. Abraam Steinberg, commissioned Usonian houses from Taliesin Fellows Cornelia Brierly and Peter Berndtson. (*For Brierly and Berndtson see pages 132–143*) In the 1970s, Betty and Irving Abrams commissioned a house from Robert Venturi. Betty actively engaged with her architect to produce what is one of Venturi's best houses. (*For Venturi see pages 180–183*)

The Pittsburgh Renaissance

Roy Lubove, a social historian who wrote the first scholarly critique of the Pittsburgh Renaissance, observed that Pittsburgh had a "squalid image throughout most of its history."[48] The devastation came early and was noted by many nineteenth-century visitors—"Most of the flatland fronting on all three rivers was preempted by industrial and commercial enterprises. The desecration of a superb natural environment—one of America's most spectacular in its combination of water-breaks, topography, and verdure—was total."[49]

Pittsburgh did acquire "redeeming features" between 1888 and 1938, most notably H. H. Richardson's Allegheny County Buildings; Schenley, Highland, and Riverview parks; grand residences in the East End; and the Oakland Civic Center.[50] Yet, "political and topographical fragmentation … limited the community's ability to define and cope with its problems."[51]

Two early twentieth-century reports drew attention to the enormity of the problems and suggested possible remedies. The Pittsburgh Survey, undertaken in 1907–10 and published in 1909–14, "was a unique experiment in American social and community analysis. Never before had so many specialists been drawn together to explore so many facets of a community's life."[52] It was determined that "'progressiveness and invention' had gone into Pittsburgh the industrial center, and not Pittsburgh the community."[53] The published Survey was "a scathing indictment of the social and physical costs of untrammeled industrialism."[54]

In 1909, the Pittsburgh Planning Commission asked three well-known planners, including Frederick Law Olmsted, Jr., of Boston, to collaborate on a report, *City Planning for Pittsburgh*. The following year, Olmsted prepared *Pittsburgh: Main Thoroughfares and the Downtown District; Improvements Necessary to Meet the City's Present and Future Needs*, published in 1911. Olmsted's report did suggest much of the direction later taken:

> Clearly Olmsted's report had an impact on the shaping of twentieth-century Pittsburgh. As a key figure in the emerging American planning profession, he affirmed not only the legitimacy and priority status of many projects long part of the urban conversation but also the legitimacy and necessity of city planning itself for Pittsburgh. His report addressed

Pittsburgh was a symbol as well as a city. It was synonymous with the spectacular advance of American industry, and the byproducts: labor unrest, poverty, assimilation of a heterogeneous immigrant working force, and disruption of community cohesion. Pittsburgh was also the symbol of a broader metropolitan and regional complex whose one unifying force was business enterprise. Whether conceived as city, district, or region, Pittsburgh was an economic rather than a civic entity.

—Roy Lubove
Twentieth-Century Pittsburgh: Government, Business and Environmental Change (1969)

projects such as the widening of Fifth, Sixth, and Forbes avenues; the building of the South Hills [Liberty] Bridge and Tunnel; Schenley Plaza; the hump cut, all of which came to fruition before or shortly after World War I. ... Other proposals, such as the improvement of Grant [now Bigelow] Boulevard or the designing of the Point, took many more years before being implemented in some form.[55]

It would not be until 1943—185 years after the founding of Pittsburgh and 127 years after its incorporation as a city—that effective steps were begun to change its "squalid image." That year, the Allegheny Conference on Community Development (ACCD) was formed under the chairmanship of Richard King Mellon, a corporate leader and philanthropist, to bring together civic, business, and political leaders whose first task was to revitalize the downtown central business district and then address the needs of the regional economy. The priority projects were the creation of Point Park, smoke control, and flood control, but most activity on these three fronts had to be deferred until the end of World War II.

Key to any success was the cooperation of Mayor David L. Lawrence and Richard King Mellon and their ability to compel action in their respective areas of influence. "Point Park marked the beginning of the alliance of the Mellon-backed ACCD and the Democratic political machine headed by David Lawrence, elected to the first of four terms as Mayor in 1945."[56] Landscape architect Ralph Griswold observed:

Not a vestige of the natural beauty that [George] Washington had seen withstood the onslaught of industrial and commercial invasion. The Point became an indiscriminate hodgepodge of urban chaos ... when the air was cleared and the black, ugly confusion of the Point was revealed in full sunlight, a civic shudder shook the citizens. ... A complete new life, urban reincarnation, was the only hope. This was the challenge—a drastic challenge requiring equally drastic measures.[57]

Disagreements between highway planners and Point Park supporters, and between various schemes for the Park—should Fort Pitt be reconstructed, for example—were complications but did not derail action, as had often happened in earlier years. "By 1949, acquisition of the 36 acres was completed at a cost of $7 million, and the demolition began on 15 acres of freight yards, elevated freight-railway tracks and terminal, some 26 commercial buildings and the old Exposition Hall."[58]

The area had been designated as Point State Park by Pennsylvania Governor Edward Martin in 1945. Trees, flowers, and other vegetation native to the Point in the eighteenth century were planted. The 1764 Fort Pitt Block House, restored in 1895 as a museum, was integrated into the park landscape. Construction of the Portal Bridge began in 1961. It was designed and built to support an eight-lane highway that connected the Fort Duquesne Bridge (north over the Allegheny River) and the Fort Pitt Bridge (south over the Monongahela River), as well as to provide pedestrian and vehicular access to Point State Park. An impressive team of architects and engineers was involved: landscape architect Ralph Griswold; Pittsburgh architect Charles Morse Stotz; New York architect Gordon Bunshaft of Skidmore, Owings & Merrill; Pittsburgh highway and bridge designer and engineer George S. Richardson; and French structural highway engineer and pre-stressed concrete expert Eugene Freyssinet. Stotz recalled:

The Portal Bridge, with views of the Fort Pitt Museum and Fort Pitt Block House (above), and fountain at the Point (opposite)

> *I worked closely with Gordon. ... He recommended a very low, long, almost flat arch. That is a very difficult structure to build, because as an arch becomes flatter, the increased thrust at the spring line becomes critical. It could be done here because of new technology developed in prestressed reinforcing rods in the concrete structure.*[59]

The completed structure is not only functional—it is handsome. Visitors pass under its graceful, shallow arch and emerge to discover the surrounding hills and the three rivers of what was the gateway to the west in the eighteenth century. Point State Park was designated a National Historic Landmark ("Forks of the Ohio") in October 1960. The Fort Pitt Museum, designed by Charles Stotz, was dedicated on June 30, 1969. The park was officially dedicated on August 30, 1974 when the fountain was completed.

Improvements were being made in other areas as well. A smoke control ordinance was passed in 1941 but not enforced until 1946, when coal mining companies, industrial plants, railroads, and homeowners were required to abide by smoke control measures. Flood control was achieved after the U.S. Army Corps of Engineers erected ten dams on Pittsburgh's rivers and their tributaries between 1936 and 1956.

In 1946, a Pittsburgh Urban Redevelopment Authority (URA) was formed with Mayor Lawrence as chairman. That summer, the URA talked with The Equitable Life Assurance Society of the United States, headquartered in New York City, about funding the redevelopment of a twenty-three-acre site east of the thirty-six-acre Point State Park and bordered by Stanwix Street, to be known as Gateway Center. The project would become feasible because of new federal legislation:

> *The era of urban renewal officially began with the passage of a revolutionary bit of legislation known as Title I of the Federal Housing Act of 1949. Until then cities had been permitted to seize only those patches of private property needed to build public works like streets and schools. Title I extended the cities' authority by granting them the power to condemn entire slums, relocate the tenants and sell the bulldozed "renewal area" at a reduced price to a private developer who would rebuild according to city-approved plans.*[60]

The Gateway Center project was officially approved in 1950. "The extensive utilization of public powers and resources between 1945–1950 made Gateway Center, and thus reconstruction of the Golden Triangle, possible. It illustrated the tactics of the civic coalition in generating large-scale environmental change."[61] Equitable Life Assurance articulated its vision in an illustrated booklet, *Equitable Builds a Gateway*:

> *This is the story of a downtown business center. It is a place where office workers pause at the entrance to a gleaming skyscraper and view their surroundings ... graceful plazas, gardens, terrazzo walks. Once inside they enjoy comforts and conveniences well beyond the usual commercial office building. ... This well-ordered business district—open to the sun, and green with grass and foliage—is a foretaste of the future. It is Gateway Center in Pittsburgh, the nation's first comprehensive downtown business redevelopment accomplished without federal aid. The builder and owner ... is a private business enterprise, a life insurance company ... The Equitable Life Assurance Society of the United States.*[62]

Eight cruciform towers of similar design were proposed, although only three—One, Two, and Three Gateway Center—were constructed (1952–53). The twenty- to twenty-four-story high-rise buildings designed by New York

A rendering of downtown Pittsburgh with eight cruciform towers (proposed)

Nearing completion in 1952: Gateway Center One (left), Two (partially hidden), and Three (front right)

architects Eggers & Higgins and Irwin Clavan "have a decorative skin of polished chrome steel masking back-up masonry."[63] The curtain walls are patterned "with continuous verticals which read as modern abstractions of fluted pilasters and mullions with recessed windows and ribbed spandrels."[64] These modern adaptations of traditional flat columns, heavy vertical bars separating windows, and striped panels above and below windows provided exterior texture. The three buildings stand in a formal landscaped park, Gateway Plaza (1950–53), designed by Clarke & Rapuano (New York). This section of Gateway Center—the first realized—is located between Fort Duquesne Boulevard to the north, Liberty Avenue to the south, Commonwealth Place to the west, and Stanwix Street to the east.

Subsequently, a Hilton Hotel (now the Wyndham Grand Pittsburgh Downtown) was erected on Commonwealth Place (1957–59), and two apartment buildings—Gateway Towers (1962–64, now condominiums) and Allegheny Towers Penthouse Apartments (1964–67, now 625 Stanwix Tower Apartments)—were erected parallel to Fort Duquesne Boulevard. For the first time in the twentieth century, people were encouraged to live downtown, in upscale apartment buildings surrounded by landscaped plazas and close to a major park. The possibility of downtown living that is being realized on a much larger scale in twenty-first-century Pittsburgh was first envisioned in the Renaissance.

In 1955, new high-rise buildings of varying designs began to rise across Liberty Avenue and around the corner south on Stanwix Street, beginning with the Bell Telephone Company Building (1955–57, now 201 Stanwix Street Place); the State Office Building (1957, now River Vue Apartments); Four Gateway Center (1958–60); the IBM Building at Five Gateway Center (1962–63, now the United Steelworkers); and the Westinghouse Building at Six Gateway Center (1967–69, now Eleven Stanwix Street). These buildings border Equitable Plaza (1961–64), designed by Simonds & Simonds of Pittsburgh (*see pages 155–157*). Equitable Plaza and Four and Five Gateway Center are included in the Guide (*see pages 164–167*).

One, Two, and Three Gateway Center were praised in some circles, and criticized in others. Was the project indebted to the work of Le Corbusier?

> *"Le Corbusier made this prophetic sketch in 1922, now at last Office Towers in a Park"* exclaimed Architectural Forum *in a 1953 article [about Gateway Center]. And yet, according to an* Architectural Forum *article from 1949, the cruciform plan of the proposed office towers … was determined entirely by the real estate department of the City Investing Company [the New York City developer] without any initial architect's input and without any mention of Le Corbusier.*[65]

Another authority is of the opinion that "the concept of widely spaced towers in … open space seems very much rooted in ideas that were promulgated by Le Corbusier. He can stand as the prime example of the type of thinking that led to Gateway Center."[66]

There was some criticism from prominent architects and architectural writers. On April 13, 1960, Paul Rudolph, then chairman of the Yale University Department of Architecture, Paul Schweikher, head of the Department of Architecture at Carnegie Tech, and Joseph Hazen, editor of *Architectural Forum*, were interviewed by a newspaper reporter in Pittsburgh. Here are a few of their comments:

> *"The buildings at the Point* [sic] *don't have any relationship, one to the other,"* Mr. Hazen commented. *… they all look as if they just happened. Pittsburgh had a golden opportunity and missed it."*

> Mr. Schweikher described the rebuilding here *"as a kind of fragmented approach. The Urban Redevelopment Authority and the Allegheny Conference are full of men trained in fact-finding,"* he chided, *"but you don't find the artists and architects represented."*

Pittsburgh in the Spring of 1970, with the Renaissance nearing completion. Three Rivers Stadium is on the North Shore, between two pairs of bridges. The Manchester Bridge and Point Bridge (both close to the tip of the Point) would be demolished later that year. The Fort Pitt Bridge over the Monongahela River (right, barely visible) opened in 1959. The Fort Duquesne Bridge over the Allegheny River (left) opened in 1969. Gateway Towers, the Hilton Hotel (now the Wyndham Grand Pittsburgh Downtown), and State Office Building (now River Vue Apartments) border Point State Park. Gateway Center One, Two, Three, Four, Five, and Six rise behind. Beyond U.S. Steel Tower (the city's tallest building) are the Civic Arena (opened in 1961) and the Washington Plaza Apartments (opened in 1964), both in the Lower Hill

> *[Mr. Hazen]: What disappoints us is that in Pittsburgh you had big acreage to develop. Look at the first three Gateway buildings. They don't have any relationship to the Hilton. The Hilton is a screen for them.*[67]

The following year Jane Jacobs wrote about Gateway Center:

> *Every device—arterial highways, belts of park, parking lots—severs these projects from the working downtown, insures that their juncture will remain an abstraction on maps instead of a living economic reality of people appearing at different times on the same streets. American downtowns are not declining mysteriously, because they are anachronisms, nor because their users have been drained away by automobiles. They are being witlessly murdered, in good part by deliberate policies of sorting out leisure uses from work uses, under the misapprehension that this is orderly city planning.*[68]

Roy Lubove observed in his 1969 book that Pittsburgh's central business district "is being transformed into an enormous filing cabinet, which operates between the hours of 9–5. The expressionless ... façades of the Gateway offices tower over grass and walks; no shops, no entertainment, no restaurants of note, no nightlife."[69]

Gateway Center was a product of the 1950s and 1960s and reflected attitudes and policies regarding urban "renewal" that, while questioned at the time by some urbanists and designers, have since been widely discredited. Roy Lubove has written:

> *The Pittsburgh Renaissance was an extraordinary episode in American urban development. It had no precedent in terms of mobilization of civic resources at the elite level and wholesale environmental intervention. The achievement, however, was administrative and political in character; the civic coalition was dominated by corporate and political managers. ... Architecture and design were always secondary considerations in the Renaissance. Pittsburgh's natural endowments were not exploited fully, and imaginative improvement plans were ignored or made token progress.*[70]

In the 1980s, the Pittsburgh Cultural Trust began to restore and reuse historic buildings rather than demolish them, as a result of a commitment to preservation established between the Heinz interests active in the area and the Pittsburgh History & Landmarks Foundation, City of Pittsburgh, and Pennsylvania Historical and Museum Commission. The Pittsburgh Cultural District was established downtown, in a fourteen-square-block area, with a western boundary at Stanwix Street, across from Gateway Center.

Pittsburgh History & Landmarks Foundation scholarship recipient Nick Stamatakis wrote in the University of Pittsburgh student newspaper:

> *In fact, modern Pittsburgh is the success it is today not because of bipartisan long-term planning, but because after the dramatic projects of the 1960s, civic groups, budget constraints and Pittsburgh geography stopped more dramatic transformations from allowing the bulldozing of large swaths of the city.*[71]

Over time, more festivals and events are being held in Gateway Center and in Point State Park. The park was renovated between 2001 and 2013 by Pressley Associates (Cambridge, MA), through the leadership of the Pennsylvania Department of Conservation and Natural Resources, Riverlife, and Allegheny Conference. Most recently, downtown Pittsburgh is experiencing a housing boom. Two of the Gateway Center buildings—the former Bell Telephone Building and the former State Office Building—have been converted into apartment buildings offering a combined total of 376 units, which, when added to the 391 units in Gateway Towers and 625 Stanwix Tower, almost doubles the number of apartments and condominiums in Gateway Center. The increased residential population and the growing

A view from Liberty Avenue: Three Gateway Center, with its patterned façade of polished chrome steel and a reflection of Two Gateway Center

Gateway Towers (left), Wyndham Grand Pittsburgh Downtown (center), and River Vue Apartments (right) border Point State Park. Gateway Center One, Two, and Three rise behind.

number of downtown events have made Gateway Center a more active environment, from early morning to late evening.

The national importance of the city's Renaissance—an unprecedented "extraordinary episode in American urban development"—was recognized when the Pittsburgh Renaissance Historic District, nominated by the Pittsburgh History & Landmarks Foundation, was listed on the National Register of Historic Places in 2013.

In the twenty-first century, visitors take pleasure in the activities at Point State Park and on the three rivers, sit or stroll through the very different yet complementary gardens at Gateway Plaza and Equitable Plaza, and note the wonderfully distorted reflections of the neighboring Gateway buildings in the glass façade of Four Gateway Center. The unparalleled industrial squalor is gone.

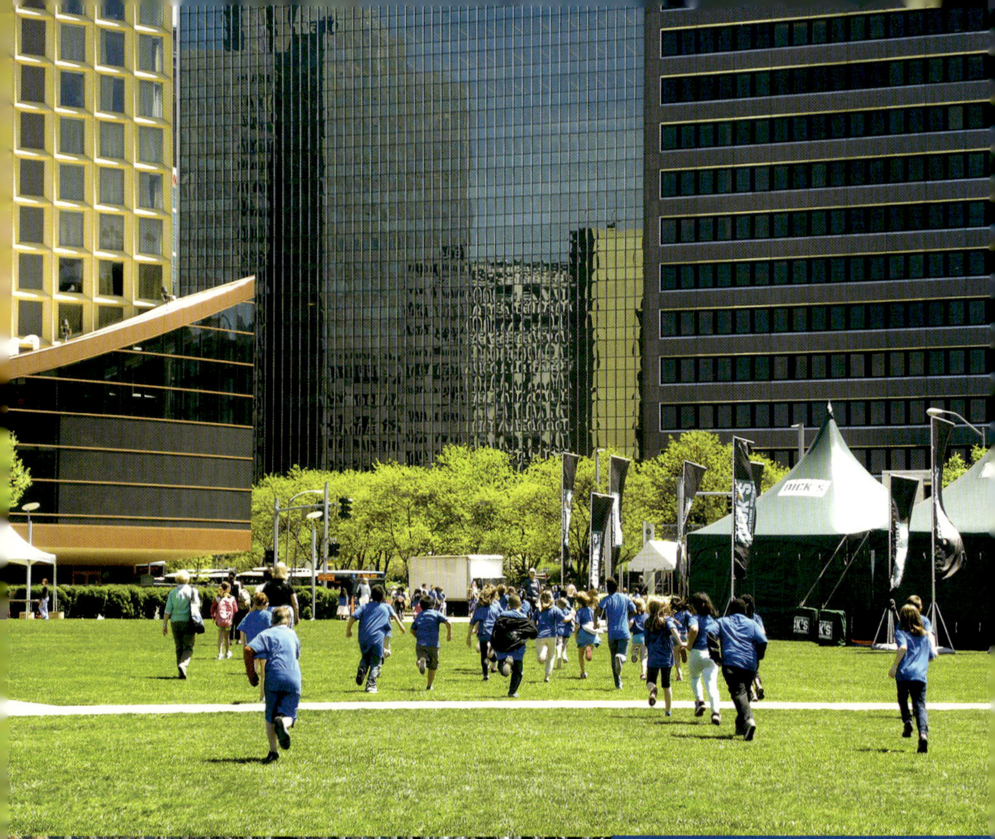
DICK'S

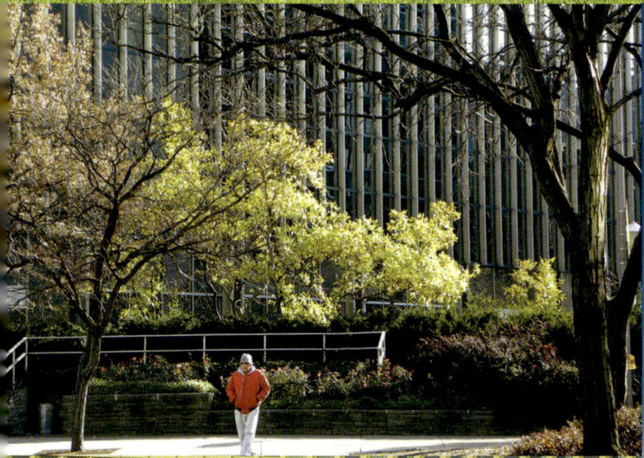

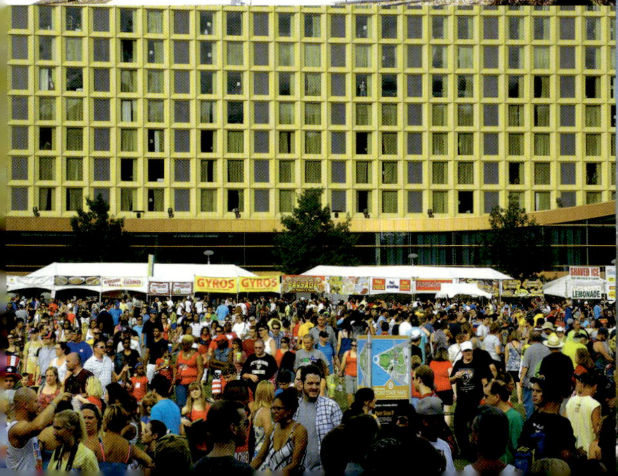
GYROS
GYROS
LEMONADE

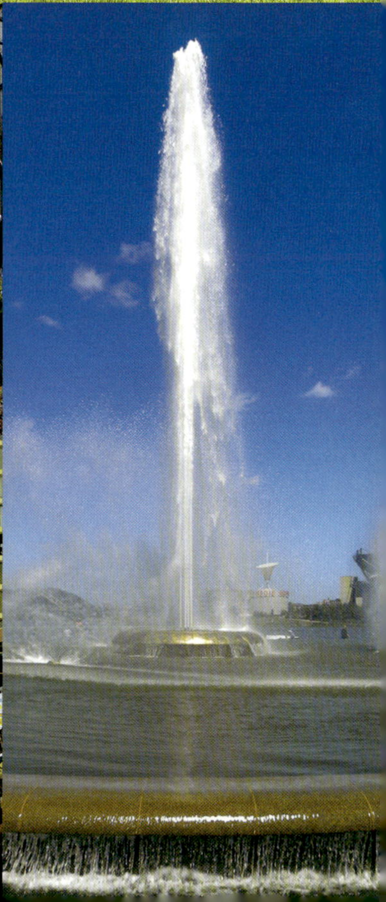

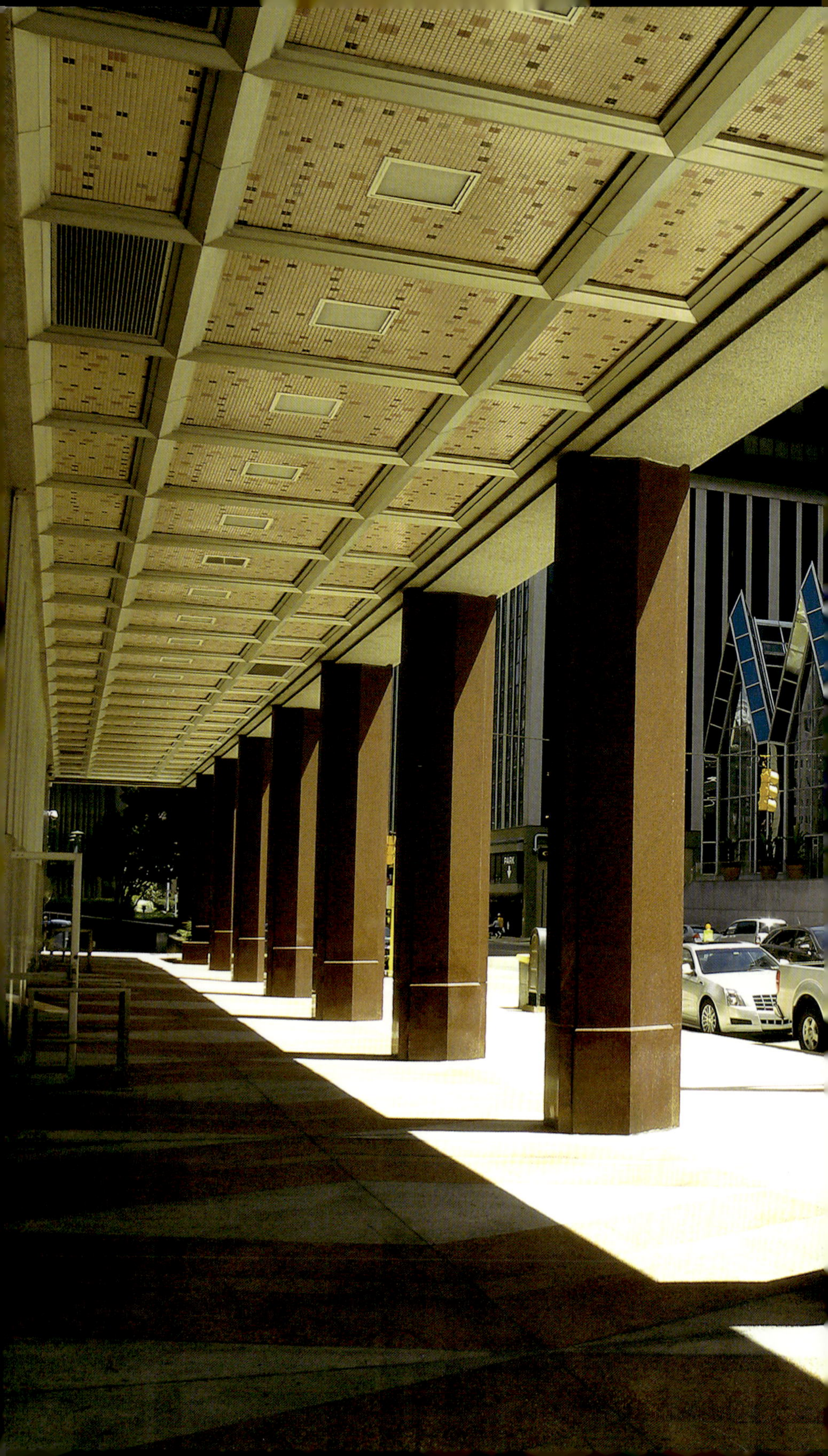

Guide

Notes on the Language of Architecture and the Contents of the Guide

In order to understand architecture, it is helpful to know two languages. One language is composed of specific vocabulary terms that define architectural forms, materials, decorative elements, etc. These are generally precise.

The second language is the language of "style," and that language is much more complicated and imprecise. Indeed, a "style of architecture may be defined differently from one text to another. Confusing the picture further, significantly different names may be used to describe the same style."[1]

Architectural styles are usually named by architects, curators, and academic historians. The problem is that they are usually broad *labels* applied to an era and are used to designate the appearance of a structure, but their terminology almost always fails to *define* anything structural, visual, spatial, in short, architectural: for example, art nouveau (new art); secessionist (to withdraw); Usonian (a term coined by Frank Lloyd Wright to mean "of the United States" and applied to a type of house design); and international style (too broad to be useful). The label rarely conveys meaning; someone must show you the visual elements, then provide the name.

The sites included in the Guide were chosen by virtue of their architectural interest and character, not because they illustrate any particular architectural "style." Nonetheless, for better or worse, stylistic labels are and will continue to be used. We have, therefore, chosen or adapted terms used in twentieth-century architectural guidebooks as a framework for our discussion of specific places within Allegheny County.

The following books provide more information about architectural styles:

- James Stevens Curl, *Oxford Dictionary of Architecture and Landscape Architecture*. 2nd. ed. (Oxford: Oxford University Press, 2006). Encyclopedic, but written from a British rather than an American viewpoint.

- Cyril M. Harris, *American Architecture: An Illustrated Encyclopedia* (New York: W. W. Norton, 1998).

- James F. O'Gorman, *ABC of Architecture* (Philadelphia: University of Pennsylvania Press, 1998).

- Steven J. Phillips, *Old House Dictionary: An Illustrated Guide to American Domestic Architecture 1600 to 1940* (New York: John Wiley & Sons, 1989).
- Marcus Whiffen, *American Architecture Since 1780: A Guide to the Styles*, rev. ed. (Cambridge, MA: MIT Press, 1992). Whiffen includes eight Pittsburgh buildings erected between 1888 and 1962 and three of these are illustrated.

The buildings in the Guide are grouped by architectural "style," from Austro-Germanic Secessionism to Postmodernism. The style is defined, biographical information on the architect or architects is provided, and a building or buildings by that architect or firm is described. If a city is not given with the architect's name, then the architect's office was (or is) located in Pittsburgh. More information is provided on architects who are not well known and are not already the subject of major biographies. The current name of the building is given in the headline, and the original name and other well-known names are given in parentheses. The houses included in the Guide are designated by the name of the original client. Building dates (design-construction) are also given when known. For comprehensive lists of buildings in Pittsburgh and Allegheny County by local and nationally known firms between 1950 and 2005, see *A List of Pittsburgh and Allegheny County Buildings and Architects 1950–2005*, by Albert M. Tannler (PHLF, third edition, 2005).

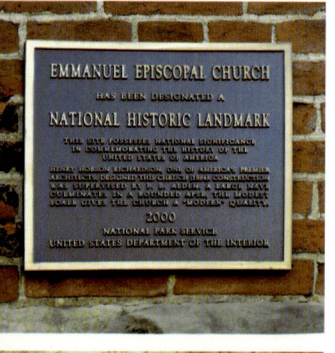

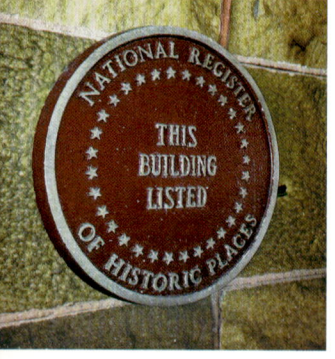

Historic designations are listed when they apply: National Historic Landmarks and individual buildings and districts listed on the National Register of Historic Places are designated by the federal government. The City of Pittsburgh designates City of Pittsburgh Historic Structures and City of Pittsburgh Historic Districts. The Pittsburgh History & Landmarks Foundation awards Historic Landmark plaques for individual properties and districts. Only the City designations, established through a legislative process, require a review process for property owners who are considering making exterior alterations to their historic buildings. PHLF's Historic Landmark plaques provide public recognition only and impose no restrictions on the property owner. Similarly, National Register and

Notes on the Language of Architecture

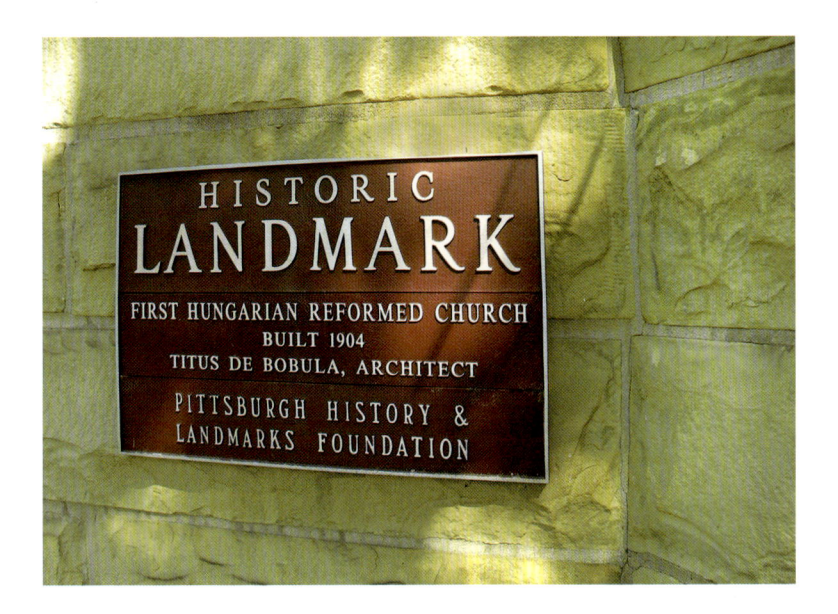

National Historic Landmark designations do not restrict how private property owners manage their property. These federal designations do bring benefits: if the property is threatened by a project using federal or state money, then a review process is required that could result in saving the designated property. Developers of National Register properties are eligible for federal and state income tax incentives if they choose to rehabilitate the property for income-producing purposes, and they can make a preservation easement donation to a qualified organization, thus realizing a federal charitable contribution deduction.

    This selection of approximately eighty sites is a sampling of notable twentieth-century architecture in Pittsburgh and Allegheny County. Seventy of them were selected because they retain their architectural character, and in most cases, they are visible from public sidewalks (weather and seasons permitting). Several private homes are not visible from the street. In those instances, please refer to the photographs in the Guide. The interiors of private residences are described since they are not open to the public; please respect owner privacy and property rights when visiting these places. Some of the houses have been, and presumably will be again, open for tours sponsored by the Pittsburgh History & Landmarks Foundation and neighborhood organizations. Several of the sites have been (or are being) restored or adapted for new uses. One site, Thaddeus Stevens School, is for sale. All the sites are worthy of preservation.

Pittsburgh Architecture in the Twentieth Century

Downtown Pittsburgh Area

The sites are listed in the order of a walking tour, from east to west, starting at Duquesne University and ending at Point State Park. The page number where the site is discussed or mentioned is given in parentheses.

1. Richard King Mellon Hall of Science (145)
2. U.S. Steel Tower (168)
3. Koppers Building (93)
4. Urban Room, Omni William Penn Hotel (96)
5. 525 William Penn Place (156)
6. Mellon Square (156)
7. 425 Sixth Avenue (former Alcoa Building) (162)
8. Alcoa Corporate Center (171)
9. O'Reilly Theater, Theater Square, Katz Plaza (189)
10. EQT Plaza (185)
11. Two PNC Plaza (152)
12. Market Square Place (100)
13. PPG Place (183)
14. 201 Stanwix Street Place (38)
15. United Steelworkers (166)
16. Eleven Stanwix Street (38)
17. Four Gateway Center and The Plaza at Gateway Center (164)
18. Gateway Center One, Two, Three (36)
19. 625 Stanwix Tower Apartments (37)
20. Gateway Towers (37)
21. Wyndham Grand Pittsburgh Downtown (37)
22. River Vue Apartments (38)
23. Portal Bridge, Point State Park (34)

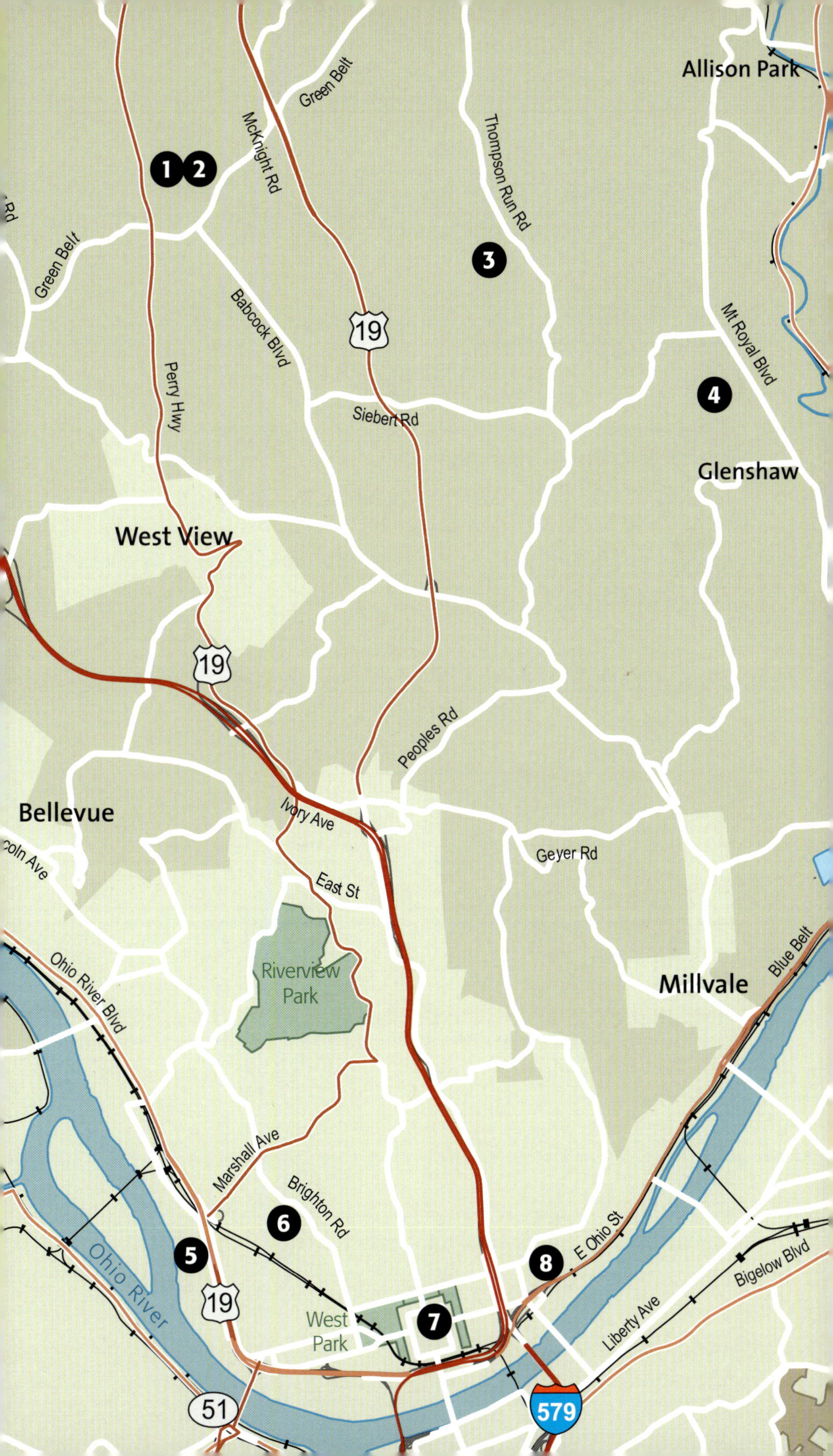
Allison Park
Green Belt
McKnight Rd
Thompson Run Rd
1
2
3
Green Belt
Babcock Blvd
19
Perry Hwy
Siebert Rd
Mt Royal Blvd
4
Glenshaw
West View
19
Peoples Rd
Bellevue
Ivory Ave
East St
Geyer Rd
Riverview Park
Millvale
Blue Belt
Ohio River Blvd
Marshall Ave
Brighton Rd
6
5
8
E Ohio St
Bigelow Blvd
19
West Park
7
Liberty Ave
Ohio River
51
579

Beyond Downtown—East

The general location of each of the following sites is shown. The page number where the site is discussed is given in parentheses.

1. 500 Second Street, Pitcairn (73)
2. Pittsburgh Mifflin School (103)
3. Hulda and Louise Notz House (135)
4. National Carpatho-Rusyn Cultural Center (63)
5. First Hungarian Reformed Church (64)
6. Apartment Building (200 East Elizabeth Street), Hazelwood (65)
7. Saul and Edith Lipkind House (140)
8. Mr. and Mrs. Jack Landis House (137)
9. St. James Roman Catholic Church (118)
10. Old Heidelberg (66)
11. Pittsburgh Student Achievement Center (72)
12. Destiny International Ministries (104)
13. Lemington Engine Company No. 15 (71)
14. Holy Rosary Roman Catholic Church (115)
15. Parkstone Dwellings (69)
16. East Liberty Presbyterian Church (115)
17. Highland Towers (68)
18. Sacred Heart Roman Catholic Church (117)
19. Calvary Episcopal Church (114)
20. Joan and Jerome Apt House (147)
21. Cecelia and Robert Frank House/Alan I W Frank House (127)
22. Frank Giovannitti House (178)
23. Betty and Irving Abrams House (181)
24. Tillie S. Speyer House (151)
25. Lydia A. Riesmeyer House (78)
26. The Episcopal Church of the Redeemer (120)
27. Pittsburgh Greenfield School (80)
28. Dr. and Mrs. Abraam Steinberg House (138)
29. Sarah Mellon Scaife Galleries, Carnegie Museum of Art (175)
30. University of Pittsburgh Cathedral of Learning Campus (120)
31. First Baptist Church (116)
32. George H. Stengel House (76)
33. Gardner Steel Conference Center, University of Pittsburgh (74)
34. St. Agnes Center of Carlow University (117)

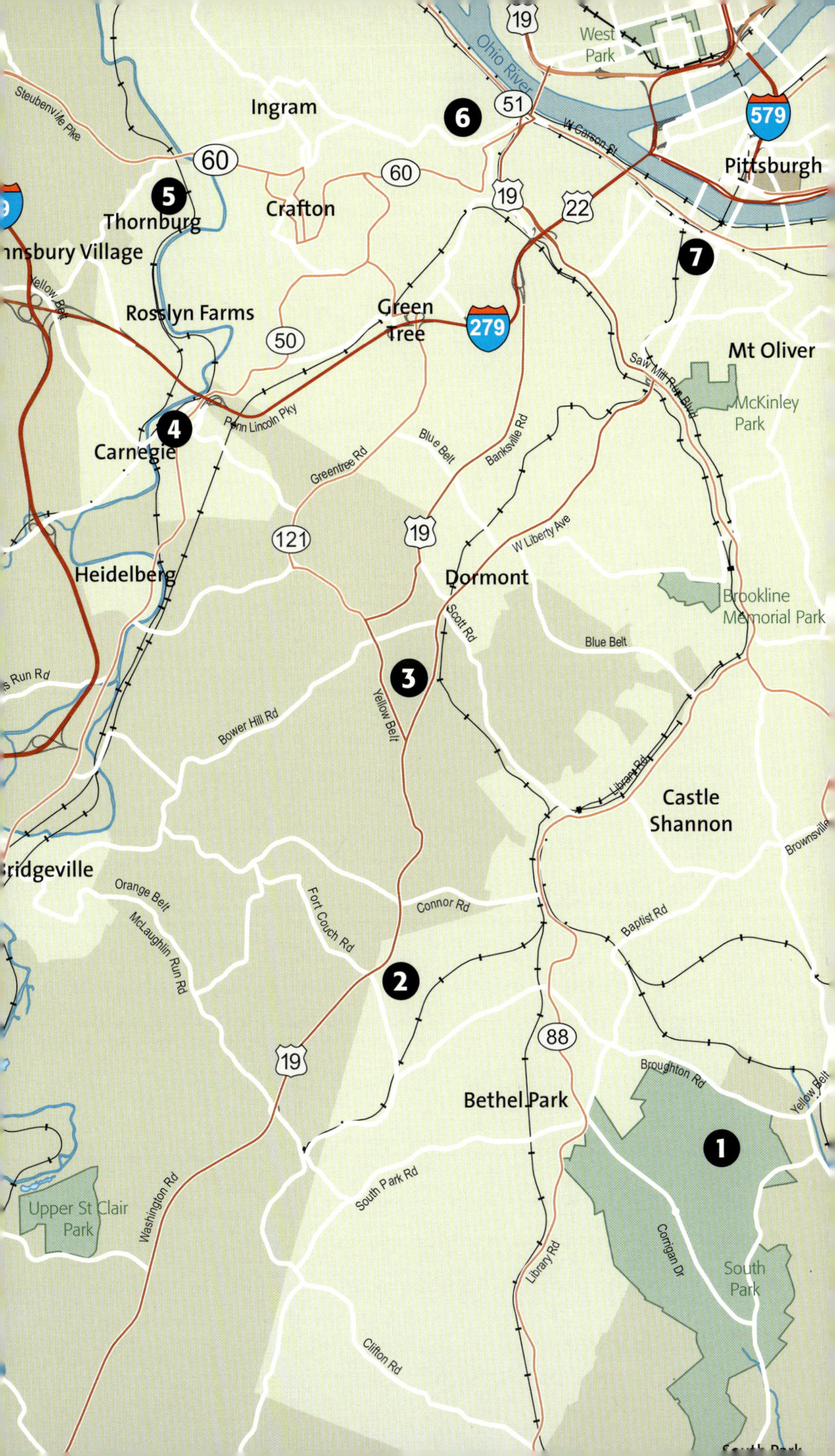
19
West Park
Ohio River
51
579
W Carson St
Pittsburgh
Ingram
6
Steubenville Pike
60
60
5
Crafton
Thornburg
19
22
7
Rosslyn Farms
Green Tree
279
Yellow Belt
50
Mt Oliver
Saw Mill Run Blvd
McKinley Park
4
Penn Lincoln Pky
Carnegie
Blue Belt
Banksville Rd
Greentree Rd
121
19
W Liberty Ave
Heidelberg
Dormont
Brookline Memorial Park
Scott Rd
Blue Belt
3
Yellow Belt
Bower Hill Rd
Library Rd
Castle Shannon
Brownsville
Orange Belt
Fort Couch Rd
Connor Rd
McLaughlin Run Rd
Baptist Rd
2
88
19
Broughton Rd
Bethel Park
Yellow Belt
1
South Park Rd
Washington Rd
Upper St Clair Park
Corrigan Dr
South Park
Library Rd
Clifton Rd

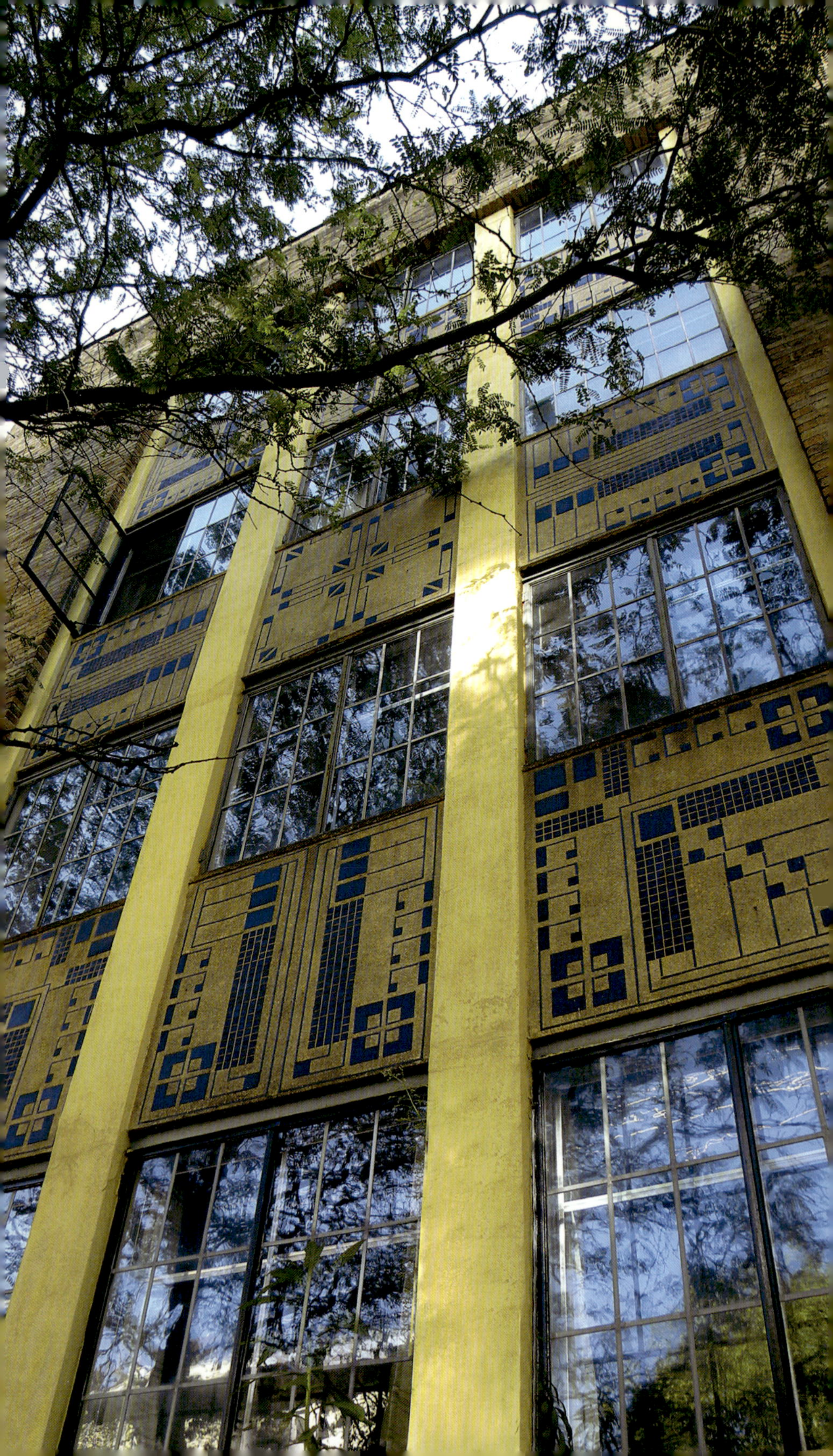

Austro-Germanic Secessionism

By 1900, Austrian and German architects and designers had turned the naturalistic and curvilinear forms of *Art Nouveau* (the German version is *Jugendstil* or "young style") into "simple geometrical elements arranged in complex patterns."[2] This school of geometric design became known as "Secessionist"—the term commemorates the withdrawal of prominent artists and architects from the official exhibition societies in Germany[3] and Austria in the 1890s. The Vienna Secession of 1897 commissioned a new exhibition building later that year. In January 1898, they published a magazine, *Ver Sacrum* (Sacred Spring), held their first exhibition from March through June (attended by Emperor Franz Joseph), and in November opened "Das Haus der Secession" (Secession Building), designed by architect Joseph Maria Olbrich, where they held their second exhibition. Due primarily to the activities of Otto Wagner (1841–1918), Vienna become the center of European Secessionism. Wagner was a professor of architecture at the Vienna Academy of Fine Arts from 1894 to 1914, author of *Moderne Architektur* (1896)—"the first modern writing to make a definitive break with the past, outlining an approach to design that has become synonymous with twentieth-century practice"—and a professional architect who employed many of his former students.[4] Secessionism spread throughout the Austro-Hungarian empire, including what is today Austria, Hungary, Slovakia, the Czech Republic, Slovenia, and parts of Poland.

Secessionist design first arrived in America via European architectural journals such as those available at the Carnegie Library of Pittsburgh. The Austrian and German exhibits at the 1904 St. Louis World's Fair impressed many Americans—none more so than Frank Lloyd Wright.[5] These displays provided the first American exposure to three-dimensional, polychromatic Austro-Germanic design. Until this time, most Americans had to be content with black-and-white two-dimensional illustrations in European and British design magazines. Wright experienced Secessionist art and architecture *in situ* when he visited Berlin, Darmstadt, and Vienna in 1910 on his first trip to Europe. Two years later, in 1912, C. Matlack Price called Chicago architects Louis Sullivan, Frank Lloyd Wright, and Walter Burley Griffin "secessionists at heart, and in terms of their own convictions and ideals."[6] What has come to be known as the midwestern "Prairie School" may be considered an American manifestation of Secessionism. As Wright stated in a speech in 1930:

> *I came upon the Secession during the winter of 1910. At that time Herr Professor Otto Wagner of Vienna, a great architect, the architect Olbrich of Darmstadt, the remarkable painter Klimt of Austria and the sculptor Metzner of Berlin—great artists all—were the soul of that movement. And there was the work of Louis Sullivan and of myself in America.*[7]

Three architects—a Hungarian, a German-American, and a German—brought this modern movement to Pittsburgh.

Titus de Bobula (1878–1961) was the second son of János Bobula, Sr. (1844–1903), a prominent Budapest architect, editor, and politician. Both Titus and his brother, János, Jr. (1871–1922), who became a successful architect and editor, studied architecture at their father's alma mater, Budapest Technological University.[8] In contrast to his father's and brother's settled existence, Titus adopted a peripatetic life (and the honorific "de"). In 1896–97, de Bobula was living in New York City where he worked briefly for McKim, Mead & White.[9] In 1900, his place of residence is identified as Stuttgart, Germany. In 1901–02, he was in Marietta, Ohio.[10]

De Bobula's 1900 design for a commercial, office, and apartment building was published in a leading Viennese architecture magazine, *Der Architekt*.[11] The style of the building was transitional: stylized and exaggerated curvilinear plant forms adapted from Art Nouveau, which originated in the early 1890s in Belgium, were juxtaposed with geometric forms, characteristic of the style which came to be called Secessionist. This transition is also evident in de Bobula's designs for three impressive churches—among his first buildings in metropolitan Pittsburgh: Holy Ghost Greek Catholic Church (Allegheny), dedicated in August 1903; St. John the Baptist Greek Catholic Church and Rectory (Homestead/now Munhall), dedicated on December 27, 1903; and St. Nicholas Greek Catholic Church (Duquesne). The plans for St. Nicholas were completed in May 1904, just a few weeks after the Austrian and German pavilions opened at

St. Nicholas

the St. Louis Fair. Remarkably, the Secessionist design exhibited in St. Louis in 1904 had appeared in Pittsburgh in 1903.[12]

Titus de Bobula was 25 when he arrived in Pittsburgh in 1903. His last documented building here was designed in 1906 when he was 28, although he is listed in Pittsburgh city directories through 1910.[13] Although he lived primarily in the Oakland neighborhood of Pittsburgh and rented a downtown office, the buildings de Bobula designed for his Central and Eastern European clients were erected in Allegheny City (Pittsburgh's North Side after 1907), Braddock, Carnegie, Munhall (although the area was originally part of Homestead), and the Pittsburgh neighborhoods of Greenfield and Hazelwood.

Although he "was but a fleeting figure on the Pittsburgh architectural scene,"[14] five of the churches he designed were erected—four Greek Catholic[15] and one Hungarian Reformed—as well as a Roman Catholic Church in Connellsville, Pennsylvania, southeast of Pittsburgh.[16]

4129–4137 Frank Street

Also realized were a rectory; a parsonage; a parish house, convent, and parochial school[17]; an apartment building; and six concrete row houses on Frank Street in Greenfield.[18] Fourteen of these buildings remain in metropolitan Pittsburgh, although only three church buildings, the former rectory, and the apartment building retain their architectural character. De Bobula also prepared designs for the Tree of Life Synagogue in Oakland, but the commission went to another architect.

De Bobula's professional visibility increased when he was asked to address the Sixth Annual Convention of the Architectural League of America, held in Pittsburgh, April 17–18, 1905. De Bobula spoke on "American Style" and said in part:

[The] national styles of Europe all contain the common base of the antique. ... all have the most important buildings built in a style of which the classical is the base, yet characterized by specially nationalistic treatments. Only we poor North Americans ... must copy, copy, I repeat, our buildings either conscientiously after the antique or after art nouveau, beaux art, modern English, Knickerbocker, etc., etc., styles.[19]

He advised his listeners:

Go back to our own archeological excavations of Yucatan and Mexico. Take the architecture of the 18th and 19th centuries of Central America, and the New England States, use them as only conditional assistance; use our fauna and flora and textile art of the Indians ... for the creation of decorative elements; use the spirit of the Aztec buildings, the receding terraces, for instances, as a healthy and appropriate example of monumentality.... Never forgetting the requirements of today ... using all the materials according to their nature; applying symmetry, proportion and direction, creating a decorative style of our characteristic conditions, being all the time intensively chauvinistic; sooner or later we must become the rightful representatives of an international style which, although American in its lines, will nevertheless contain the fundamental principles of a cosmopolitan art....

The following month, on May 22, the Pittsburgh Architectural Club opened its Third Exhibition at the Carnegie Art Gallery. De Bobula exhibited designs for twelve buildings, and seven of those were in metropolitan Pittsburgh. St. Michael's Parochial School in Braddock, St. Nicholas Greek Catholic Church in Duquesne,[20] an auditorium, "Montefiore Hall," and the Alpha Apartment Hotel in Pittsburgh were illustrated in the catalog, but Montefiore Hall and Alpha Apartment Hotel—both extraordinary designs—were never built.[21] In addition, he exhibited plans for a Roman Catholic church and a department store/office building in Marietta, Ohio, a courthouse in Mississippi, and a church and office building in West Virginia. Pittsburgh architect John T. Comes reviewed the exhibition, noting:

Pittsburgh has among its architects one who is devoted to the propagation of the style of art nouveau, of the Secessionist style, as it is known in Vienna. Titus de Bobula has outgrown the traditions and styles of former periods and is industriously endeavoring to develop a new style which he thinks is more American and reasonable than the copying of historic styles.[22]

The architect's photograph appeared in *Palmer's Pictorial Pittsburgh and Prominent Pittsburghers, Past and Present*, published in 1905, when de Bobula was 27. The photo (*see page 24*) shows a very young face beneath a very large bowler hat.[23]

In 1910, de Bobula married Eurania Dinkey Mock of Bethlehem, Pennsylvania, a niece of the wife of Charles M. Schwab, president of Bethlehem Steel.[24] They moved to New York City.[25] De Bobula's post-Pittsburgh years were marked by controversy. In 1919, he unsuccessfully sued Charles Schwab for defamation of character.[26] He returned to Hungary in the early 1920s and became a political activist and propagandist. On November 10, 1923, the front page of the *New York Times* read:

"Titus De Bobula Jailed in Budapest: Husband of Mrs. C. M. Schwab's Niece Arrested for Plot to Overthrow [Hungarian] Government." In the 1930s, he renewed ties to the brilliant and eccentric Serbian-born inventor Nikola Tesla and, in the words of Tesla biographer Marc Seifer, "was hired to design the tower, power plant, and housing for the inventor's 'impenetrable shield between nations'"—a futuristic electronic weapons system. Seifer refers to de Bobula as "the notorious architect and arms merchant."[27] The FBI took notice of his activities and kept a dossier. De Bobula moved to Washington, D.C., about 1936 and died there in 1961 at the age of 83. His *Washington Post* obituary identified him as a retired consulting architect best known for designing churches in Ohio and Pennsylvania.[28]

1. National Carpatho-Rusyn Cultural Center (St. John the Baptist Greek Catholic Church and Rectory)
915 Dickson Street, Munhall
Titus de Bobula, architect, 1903
National Register District; Local Historic District; Historic Landmark plaque

St. John the Baptist Greek Catholic Church was dedicated December 27, 1903, in what was then Homestead, Pennsylvania.[29] The building is de Bobula's oldest surviving building in metropolitan Pittsburgh, and was dedicated four months before the Austrian and German exhibitions opened in St. Louis.

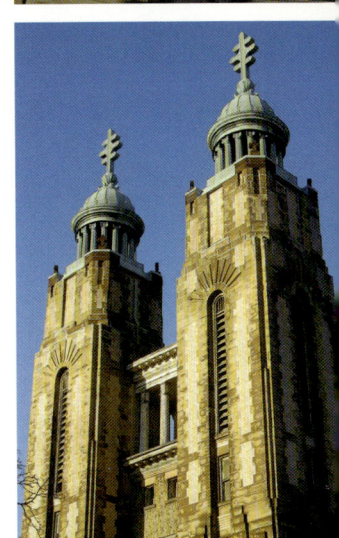

In his 1905 address, "American Style," de Bobula observed that "the classical is the base" of the "national styles of Europe." Here, the church and the rectory combine classical and Secessionist forms with a virtuosic exuberance. A dramatic conversation between the new and the old is manifested in the mingling of materials—buff brick, smooth and rough-cut sandstone, and stucco—angled buttresses, and geometric cruciform patterns that mount the two spectacular 125-foot towers. The towers are linked, however, by a classical colonnade. A similar colonnade frames the porch of the brick and sandstone rectory (now a private residence). The stained glass windows on the side of the former rectory incorporate cubic forms and abstract flower designs.

The church building has become a meeting and exhibition space celebrating Carpatho-Rusyn culture in America and the history of eastern Slavic peoples who originally lived in villages in the Carpathian mountains in what is today Slovakia, Ukraine, and Poland.

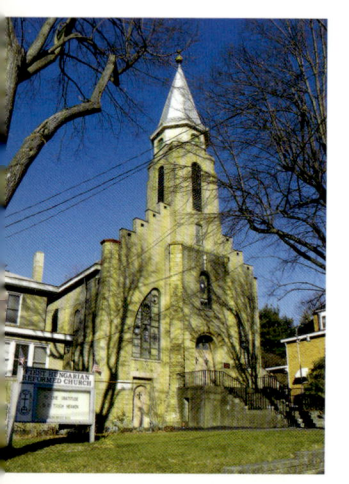

2. First Hungarian Reformed Church
221 Johnston Avenue, Hazelwood
Titus de Bobula, architect, 1903–04
Historic Landmark plaque

The architectural forms of the First Hungarian Reformed Church evoke medieval Romanesque and Gothic architecture, but in a highly original manner.[30] Nonetheless, St. John (discussed on the previous page) and First Hungarian Reformed, dedicated on April 6, 1904, have shared characteristics. The use of related but contrasting materials side by side—sandstone, cut both rough and smooth, and buff brick—is striking, as are the geometric shapes such as the sculptural buttresses, the stepped parapet gable, and the octagonal corner piers of the tower. The roughly carved stone arches here surround the entrance and the window above. The wonderfully preserved interior is notable for its opalescent glass windows that portray religious symbols and Reformed (Calvinist) luminaries such as John Calvin and Princess Zsuzsanna Lorántffy (*below*), a patron of Hungarian Calvinism.

As Walter C. Kidney noted: "most remarkably, the windows beside the tower are rampant arches, as if the sheer mass of the tower had exerted a gravitational pull on their crowns."[31]

3. Apartment Building
200 East Elizabeth Street, Hazelwood
Titus de Bobula, architect, 1903–04

This building, erected around the corner from the Hungarian Reformed Church, is an anomaly, and that is significant. If the ornate Alpha Apartment Hotel would be described several years later as "a structure that will compare favorably with the best apartment houses in the city,"[32] the Hazelwood building is an early-twentieth-century urban "dumbbell" model tenement, erected to provide affordable housing for members of Hazelwood's Hungarian community on land owned by the Hungarian Reformed Church. Designed in 1903 and completed in 1904,[33] it was the second model tenement built in Pittsburgh and is now the city's oldest surviving example of this building type.[34] The building is a three-story brick structure resting on a rough stone base composed of three rectangular sections. The center section has light courts on the south and north sides and is the "handle" of the dumbbell. Clearly, another section was to have been erected on the north side of the original building. A flat roof with a deep overhang extends above a band of soldier (upright) bricks; gently arched windows and concrete sloping door frames "decorate" the building, which retains a degree of simple elegance despite disfiguring alterations.

4. St. Peter & St. Paul Ukrainian Orthodox Church (St. Peter's & St. Paul's Russian Greek Catholic Church)
220 Mansfield Boulevard, Carnegie
Titus de Bobula, architect, 1906
Historic Landmark plaque

St. Peter's and St. Paul's Russian Greek Catholic Church was de Bobula's last recorded building in the Pittsburgh area.[35] The church's three great onion domes with wide overhanging skirts appear to float overtop the front façade with its three towers. The stepped roofline, vertical panels, and angled geometric buttresses are typical de Bobula forms.

Frederick G. Scheibler, Jr. (1872–1958) apprenticed in the Pittsburgh offices of German-trained Henry Möser; V. Wyse Thalman, who is said to have been trained in Europe; and Longfellow, Alden & Harlow, a firm with roots in H. H. Richardson's Boston office.[36] James D. Van Trump called Scheibler "a distinguished and unique pioneer of the Modern architectural movement in Pennsylvania."[37] Scheibler's most creative designs, produced from 1904 to around 1930, are variations of the design vocabulary developed by contemporary architects in Britain, Europe, and the United States. Scheibler's use of metal, wood, and tile in his interiors is masterly, and his designs for art glass demonstrate extraordinary virtuosity.

Scheibler never traveled far from Pittsburgh; we do not know if he attended the 1904 St. Louis World's Fair where he could have seen Austrian and German designs, but by 1905 his designs show the influence of Secessionism.

Scheibler's early work was influenced by J. M. Olbrich, whose designs Scheibler almost certainly encountered in architectural periodicals. Indeed, Martin Aurand noted: "Publications were *the* key for Scheibler."[38] He adapted designs by Scottish architect Charles Rennie Mackintosh (whose 1900 display at the Secession exhibit in Vienna had been very well received and whose work was exhibited at the 1907 Pittsburgh Architectural Club exhibition), by English architect M. H. Baillie Scott, and by German architect Peter Behrens. Secessionist elements in the work of Frank Lloyd Wright may also have influenced Scheibler.

The three buildings featured here are all apartment buildings; to encounter the full range of Scheibler's work—especially his residential architecture—see Martin Aurand, *The Progressive Architecture of Frederick G. Scheibler, Jr.* (1994).

5. Old Heidelberg

405–421 S. Braddock Avenue, Point Breeze
Frederick G. Scheibler, Jr., architect, 1905; additions, 1908
National Register of Historic Places; City Historic Structure;
Historic Landmark plaque

Old Heidelberg was commissioned by builders Robinson and Bruckman and was named by Fred Bruckman, whose family had emigrated from Heidelberg, Germany.[39]

> *There are four L-shaped apartments on each of three floors—*
> *each apartment occupying half of a T. The T-shaped forms afford*

a continuous street front, permit light and air to penetrate into courts at the rear, and allow for a more centralized arrangement of rooms. Each apartment has a living room, dining room, and two bedrooms that radiate from a reception room that is entered from the public stair hall.[40]

Martin Aurand has documented interior details inspired by Olbrich, Mackintosh, and Baillie Scott. Scheibler owned periodicals and books containing the designs he adapted. The façade displays fanciful details—panels depicting mushrooms—and decorative elements characteristic of Secessionist design: wave trim and panels of two-dimensional "cubes." There is also the exposed steel I-beam, which became a Scheibler trademark. A photograph of and brief commentary on Old Heidelberg was published in a 1908 article on American apartment buildings in *Der Architekt*.[41]

6. Highland Towers

340–342 S. Highland Avenue, Shadyside
Frederick G. Scheibler, Jr., architect, 1913–14
National Register of Historic Places; Historic Landmark plaque

Perhaps Scheibler's finest building, Highland Towers is a five-story U-shaped court building in warm earth-tone shades of tapestry brick. There were originally four apartments per floor, each with a solarium. The front façades of the side wings are broken by casement windows separated by cement plaster spandrels with glazed tile set in an abstract geometric pattern adapted from Peter Behrens (*see photo, page 58*). Concrete balconies decorated with a keyhole pattern and concrete columns frame the windows of the center section façade; art glass panels decorate the center of some windows. Scheibler has cleverly eliminated the need for any public corridors by having the apartment entrances open on the staircase towers at each corner of the inner court; the brickwork here is patterned. Exterior and interior glazed tile came from the Rookwood Pottery in Cincinnati. Martin Aurand suggests that Scheibler may have drawn upon Wright's Larkin Building (1904) and McArthur Apartments (1906) as well as Mackintosh's Glasgow School of Art (1897–1909)—and yet the building has its own character. Mackintosh-influenced art glass designs appear in the front doors. Kantero Kato, a Japanese designer and friend of Scheibler's, may have contributed to the design of the art glass screens, fabricated by the important Pittsburgh glass studio, Rudy Brothers, in the soleria in the center apartments[42] (*see photo, page xiii*).

7. Parkstone Dwellings
6937–6943 Penn Avenue, Point Breeze
Frederick G. Scheibler, Jr., architect, 1922
Historic Landmark plaque

Parkstone Dwellings accommodates four residences, two on each floor. Bright red doors announce the entrances to all four units and are grouped together in the center of the building. James D. Van Trump wrote that Scheibler's:

> *later manner, which to a degree reflects the lush, vespertine romanticism of the 1920s, is to be seen at its fullest flowering in the Parkstone Dwellings. … In this amazing building, which may be taken as his swan song, the long roof lines swoop low over walls of heavy schist stone and banks of heavily-leaded windows. Here the concrete toadstools at the entrance doors, like the reliefs on the Old Heidelberg, attest to his continuing interest in and use of natural forms. … The note of whimsey, not unapparent in his earlier work, has crystallized at the Parkstone in the amusing tile "rugs" which depend so realistically from the balconies.*[43]

Richard Kiehnel (1870–1944) was born in Breslau, Germany, where he later studied architecture. He arrived in Chicago in the 1890s and is said to have worked for Egan & Prindeville, who specialized in churches (they designed St. Paul's Cathedral in Pittsburgh). By 1900, Kiehnel was sharing an office with architect William J. Brinkman, a German-American trained at Burnham & Root, who specialized in church architecture. Their office was located at 163 Randolph Street, which housed ten architects, eight of whom had Germanic names.[44] In 1903–04, Kiehnel was living in Cleveland where he is said to have worked for architect J. Milton Dyer.[45]

Kiehnel moved to Pittsburgh and entered the office of Frederick J. Osterling, working there in 1905. He practiced alone briefly, exhibiting designs at the 1905 Pittsburgh Architectural Club (PAC) Exhibition—fairly conventional designs for a Colonial Revival country house and barn and an American Renaissance art museum, as well as a library and (most interesting) a German Town Hall competition design (the latter two designs were not illustrated). In 1906, Kiehnel and Pittsburgh architect John B. Elliott established the firm of Kiehnel & Elliott, with Kiehnel as the designing partner.[46]

Kiehnel became active in the PAC. His own entries in the 1905 exhibition and the 1907 exhibition—the house and barn displayed in 1905 were repeated in 1907 together with a design for a high school in the Jacobean style—suggest a cautious architect feeling his way in the United States. In 1908, Kiehnel, now enabled by the international presence at the 1907 PAC exhibition, began designing buildings in the Pittsburgh area that drew upon the visual vocabulary of the Austro-Germanic "Modern Movement."[47] The City of Pittsburgh Hospital at Marshalsea (1909) and the quintessentially Secessionist gateway (c. 1910) at Forbes School have been demolished, and his German Club interior (1910)—the only section he designed—has been eradicated.[48] Nine of Kiehnel's thirteen Secessionist projects remain. Most of these buildings were exhibited at PAC exhibitions and photographs in the exhibition catalogs provide original documentation.

In 1917, Pittsburgh Steel Company president John Bindley asked Kiehnel to design a winter home in Coconut Grove, Florida, near Miami. The house, *El Jardin* (The Garden), has been called "the first real Mediterranean Revival building in South Florida, the first to use a picturesque montage of architectural elements drawn from a range of sources—Spanish, Moorish,

Tuscan, Venetian."[49] The style achieved popularity as an appropriate one for a semi-tropical developing area with seemingly few strong architectural antecedents. In 1918, Kiehnel moved to Miami and opened a branch office of the firm. The Florida office became a leading practitioner of the Mediterranean Style and Art Deco in Miami, Coral Gables, Coconut Grove, and Winter Park. Kiehnel's Scottish Rite Masonic Temple, Miami (1922), has been called "the earliest Art Deco building in Miami"[50]; it predates the Paris exposition and is one of the first Art Moderne/Art Deco buildings designed and erected in the United States.

The partnership between Kiehnel and Elliott was dissolved in 1926. Richard Kiehnel practiced under the name Kiehnel & Elliott for the remainder of his career and the Pittsburgh firm became Kiehnel, Elliott & Chalfant. Between 1935 and 1942, Kiehnel edited a journal, *Florida Architecture and Allied Arts*, and in 1938 published *A Monograph of the Florida Work of Kiehnel and Elliott*. He died in 1944 at the age of 74.

8. Lemington Engine Company No. 15 (Lemington Engine Company No. 38)
7024 Lemington Avenue, Lincoln/Lemington/Belmar
Richard Kiehnel of Kiehnel & Elliott, architect, 1908–09

Engine Company 15 is, although small, paradigmatic. Cubic massing of the brick building was broken by round-arched engine doors on the first floor (the doors have been altered and are now rectilinear). Second-story windows are separated by pilasters (flat columns) decorated with an "Imperial Banner" motif, often used by Austro-Hungarian architects for state occasions, consisting here of four ringed ribbons, surmounted by seven spheres and edged with luxuriant foliage. Most striking is the tall narrow tower, topped by a gable roof set within two stepped gable ends. A cornice of symmetrical floral patterns circles the building. They are typically late Jugendstil, which deviated from Art Nouveau's "whiplash" curves in favor of more geometric, symmetrical patterns.

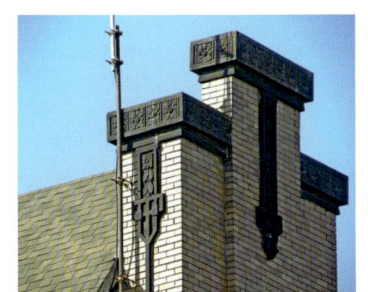

9. Pittsburgh Student Achievement Center (Brushton School)
Brushton and Baxter Avenues, Homewood
Richard Kiehnel of Kiehnel & Elliott, architect, 1909
National Register of Historic Places; Historic Landmark plaque

The entrance to the two-story rectilinear school facing Baxter Avenue is marked by an elegant terra-cotta arch ornamented with geometric flowers. (Terra cotta is clay molded into patterns and fired.) Warm, dignified, red-brick walls contrast with rich terra-cotta ornament surrounding the second-floor windows—laurel leaf bouquets (symbolizing wisdom) grow out of frames of one- and two-dimensional geometric squares and rectangles. A ledge, encircling the building, is decorated with jaunty fretwork. Each block-and-floral design is a modern variation on the ancient classical column capital or decorated top. The brick walls of the school form pilasters between the windows; the design and variations—capitals are sometimes divided in half—are repeated, creating a classically derived colonnade around the entire building.[51]

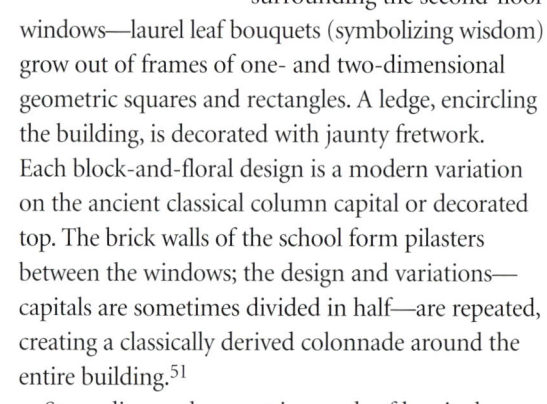

Stone diamonds are set in panels of herringbone brick framed in stonework between first- and second-floor windows. Bands of light-colored stone or terra cotta above and below the windows encircle the building and literally tie it together.

Inside, the original metal stair railing with a Jugendstil pattern similar to the one on the façade of the Lemington Engine Company was removed sometime after 1999 (*see photo, page xvii*).

In 1911, Kiehnel & Elliott substantially enlarged the school south along Brushton Avenue. In 1929, Kiehnel, Elliott & Chalfant added a handsome gymnasium, auditorium, and cafeteria building west on Baxter Street that replicated the Secessionist detailing on the 1909/1911 building.

Austro-Germanic Secessionism

10. 500 Second Street
(First National Bank of Pitcairn)
Second Street and Center Avenue, Pitcairn
Richard Kiehnel of Kiehnel & Elliott, architect, 1910
Historic Landmark plaque

This building, fifteen miles southeast of Pittsburgh, originally housed a bank, shops to the rear, and apartments above. The bank is gone, but shops and apartments remain. The rectilinear, buff-brick, three-story building has a smooth surface, broken only on the first and second floors by the protruding sills of the recessed windows. The third-floor windows are separated by herringbone panels and a cornice of inverted triangles. The apartment balconies, resting on heavy wood and iron supports, display ironwork in a wave pattern set within angular grillwork.[52]

The bank was differentiated from other parts of the building by large arched windows. The arches were originally filled with art glass; now only the main window over the doorway on Second Street retains its glass. Three glass boxes with cantilevered tops in green- and rose-colored glass—the outer two bearing a stylized geometric rose—recall a pattern by Scottish architect Charles Rennie Mackintosh. Mackintosh used this geometric rose often; it appeared in the music room of a "house for an art lover" exhibited in Pittsburgh in 1907.

The central doorway is framed by two five-sided columns adorned with elaborate ornament. Pendants composed of layered rectangles and cubes (like those decorating the third-floor windows) descend from a square capital decorated with a floral band; the center rectangle is adorned with a geometric rose.

Geometry defines the art glass transom windows. The window over the 500 Second

73

Street entrance to the upstairs apartments is composed of ribbons of clear and colored glass. The transom window over the apartment entrance at 215 Center Avenue is composed of glass circles, half circles, and triangular patterns of clear, crackled, and colored glass.

The Center Avenue apartment entrance has a distinctive semi-circular hood supported by brackets that are a larger variation of the rectangle/cube pendant used on the third-floor pilasters and on the entrance columns. The pattern, Martin Aurand has noted, is very like the entrance to the Home for Self-Supporting Women in Chicago, designed by architects Pond & Pond, a Chicago firm much influenced by contemporary Germanic design. Photographs of the Pond & Pond building were displayed at the March 1910 Pittsburgh Architectural Club Exhibition.[53] The use of this geometric pendant pattern on the Pitcairn bank is apparently its first appearance in Kiehnel's work, but the pattern occurs frequently thereafter.

The interior of the bank was wonderful and its loss is regrettable.[54] The interior pilasters that remain—decorated with naturalistic foliage, in particular a giant rose, and geometric forms that echo those on the exterior of the building—give us a sense of the bank's original grandeur.

11. Gardner Steel Conference Center, University of Pittsburgh (Central Turnverein)
O'Hara and Thackeray Streets, Oakland
Richard Kiehnel of Kiehnel & Elliott, architect, 1911–12
National Register District; City Historic District; Historic Landmark plaque

The Central Turnverein purchased property to erect a new gymnastics clubhouse[55] and began construction of the building in November 1911.[56] It was completed eleven months later at a cost of $100,000 and was dedicated on Sunday, October 20, 1912.[57] The *Chronicle Telegraph* reported: "The new building, which is of the modern progressive school of architecture, is one of the best equipped halls in the state."[58] A "turner," in German, is a gymnast (the English word has some of that meaning) and a turnverein is a gymnastics club. This program of physical education based on group gymnastics developed in Germany and Switzerland in the nineteenth century, and immigrants from those countries brought it to America. Physical education was the centerpiece of an organization that included a choral society and various social activities.

From the outside, the clubhouse is a compact, buff-brick building covered by a low, hipped roof with wide, overhanging eaves. The building at first appears to be a rectangle, but the plan is in fact L-shaped. On three sides of the long arm of the L, large two-story arched windows (six overlook O'Hara Street) provided maximum light to the gymnasium.

The first floor, set on a raised basement on the sloping corner site, is the taller of the two stories; its spare horizontal brickwork is given contrasting texture by five bands of soldier (upright) bricks—laid at approximately three-foot intervals—that wrap around the façade.

The entrances—two on Thackeray and one on O'Hara—exhibit straight lines and cubic forms. A chisel-shaped terra-cotta pattern, a "quotation" of a pattern that Viennese-trained Slovenian architect Jože Plečnik created for his Zacherl building in Vienna (1903–05), runs along the edge of the lintel across the top of the tall doorframe. Descriptions, plans, and excellent photographs of the Zacherl building appeared in *Der Architekt*,[59] and Wasmuth's *Architecture of the 20th Century* in 1906.[60] The lintel is supported with rectilinear brackets, another version of the layered geometric patterned brackets that first appeared on the Pitcairn bank. Wisps of the luxuriant foliage adhere to a centerpiece of interlocking blocks; below, laurel leaves border a long, narrow, geometric pendent. Double doors and a transom window filled with art glass face Thackeray Street.

The upper story is covered with an array of two-dimensional geometric patterning unique in Pittsburgh and rare indeed in the United States at this time. The basic pattern at its simplest consists of two sizes of two-dimensional blocks that alternate—one large block, two small blocks on a diagonal, etc. One variation consists of the pattern arranged in parallel rows. Another variation turns the pattern on its side and expands it.

A different design appears over the Thackeray Street doorways, marking them as the main entrances. This pattern is a narrow, flat column, marked at the base by incised lines and topped with an abstract "bouquet" that trails a pendent of ribbons.

A dramatic projecting band of molding encircles the building and separates the two floors. This richly conceived belt of diamonds, triangles, and three-sided cubes frames the bottom edge of the second story. Another bold geometric band originally decorated the face of the eaves above, but that, like an eyebrow window on the roof, is gone. The art glass transom windows remain; the original glass in the doors is gone. These designs are composed of geometric forms that spread outward in a symmetrical pattern. The pattern may depict, abstractly, a pair of candelabra.

The Turnverein is one of only a small number of American buildings before 1911 that exhibit such a forceful display of exterior geometric ornament.[61] It is a German-American architectural masterpiece—most appropriate given its client, its purpose, and its architect. It is one of Pittsburgh's five most important early twentieth-century architectural designs, together with Titus de Bobula's St. John's Church (1903), Frederick Scheibler's Old Heidelberg (1905) and Highland Towers (1913), and Kiehnel & Elliott's Greenfield School (1916).[62]

12. George H. Stengel House
4136 Bigelow Boulevard, Oakland
Richard Kiehnel of Kiehnel & Elliott, architect, 1913
National Register District; City Historic District; PHLF Historic District plaque

The Stengel House[63] in Schenley Farms is a three-story, "four-square" house (four rooms divided by a central hallway) of red brick with grayish-brown terra-cotta-and-stone trim. Below paired windows, separated by rectilinear panels filled with what looks like rough natural stone, the band of late Jugendstil ornament separates the third floor from the second. The columns between the windows— in the front they are terra cotta, on the sides and rear of the house they are wood—are severely geometrical. The brick porch piers flare outward at the top and are trimmed with stylized fern-like terra-cotta patterns. The central second-floor window is an arch decorated with wonderfully unconventional glass and terra cotta. Plečnik's chisel-shaped terra-cotta ornament reappears.

Windows on the first floor, in the front door, and on the stairway landing were made by Leopold Hanwell and were influenced by designs by Frank Lloyd Wright. Thick, rectilinear leading supports a tree-like pattern with chevron "leaves" extending upward from the "stem," topped by a diamond-shaped "flower." The glass is predominately clear with rough textured, translucent—but not transparent—inserts. This rough-textured glass is cathedral glass, available in a variety of textured surfaces, with names like granite, seedy, ripple, moss, fluted, etc. Richly colored opalescent glass panes are used sparingly. Wright emphasized the "cames," or strips, of lead or copper that bind and support the individual pieces of glass. American glass artists usually labored to conceal or minimize this structurally necessary "leading"; Wright made it part of the design. As he wrote in 1908, most of his windows "are treated as metal 'grilles' with glass inserted forming a simple rhythmic arrangement of straight lines and squares."[64]

Inside, the center hallway, the dining room, and the living room are paneled in golden oak. Glazed tile and copper decorate stone and brick fireplaces. The oak staircase railing is geometrically patterned openwork, and the newel post crown is composed of a series of geometric blocks. The stairway paneling and open woodwork is strongly reminiscent of the stairway in the Harry Rubins House in the Chicago suburb of Glencoe, designed by George W. Maher in 1903, and exhibited in Pittsburgh in 1907. Similar blocks—arranged in interlocking density—form the capitals of the oak columns on the main floor. These wonderful geometric column capitals bear an uncanny resemblance to those that decorate the exterior of Wright's Unity Temple (1905–09), Oak Park, Illinois, exhibited in Pittsburgh in 1907. The Stengel House resonates with rigorous geometric forms characteristic of both European and American Secessionist architecture and design.

13. Lydia A. Riesmeyer House
5818 Aylesboro Avenue, Squirrel Hill
Richard Kiehnel of Kiehnel & Elliott, architect, 1914

The Riesmeyer House is a two-and-a-half-story brick house with wood trim, symmetrical in shape, with a hipped roof and a front porch. One looks at it and recalls what America's leading architectural critic, Montgomery Schuyler, wrote about Pittsburgh houses in 1911: "unquestionably artistic but impossible to classify. ... Many Pittsburgh houses ... are of no style yet have style."[65]

There are exterior clues to the architect's identity—the Secessionist pendants decorating the second-story windows, the bold geometric brick pattern on the porch piers, and the geometric art glass window on the second floor. The client and her family were members of Pittsburgh's German-American community. Lydia A. Schaffer and Edward H. Riesmeyer were married in 1901. Edward was the manager of J. P. Schaffer, a heating company in downtown Pittsburgh, owned by Lydia's brother, John P. Schaffer. (In 1917, Schaffer commissioned a house at 5757 Wilkins Avenue from Kiehnel & Elliott.)

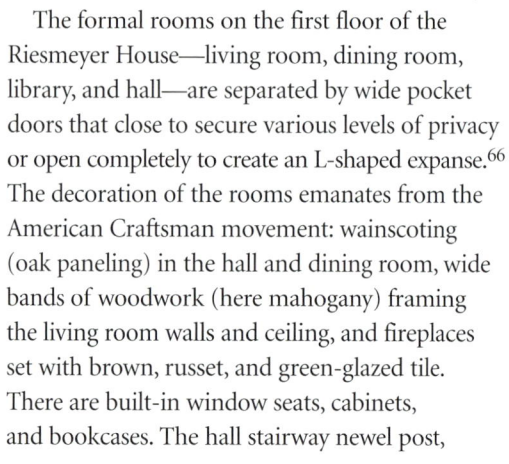

The formal rooms on the first floor of the Riesmeyer House—living room, dining room, library, and hall—are separated by wide pocket doors that close to secure various levels of privacy or open completely to create an L-shaped expanse.[66] The decoration of the rooms emanates from the American Craftsman movement: wainscoting (oak paneling) in the hall and dining room, wide bands of woodwork (here mahogany) framing the living room walls and ceiling, and fireplaces set with brown, russet, and green-glazed tile. There are built-in window seats, cabinets, and bookcases. The hall stairway newel post, capped by a lotus blossom held within a rectilinear grip, is rigorously geometrical at its base and sides; the base is identical to newel posts at the Central Turnverein.

    The Riesmeyer House doors and windows are even more extraordinary than those in the Stengel House, but the abstract floral patterns are gone. Here, geometric grids connect every part of the design through a web of leading. Within the grid, panes of variously textured cathedral glass are set with opalescent squares, diamonds, and triangles. Prominent elements of the pattern appear to float, although always tethered to and by the intricate leading. The rigor of the geometry notwithstanding, natural and artificial light continuously alters the colors of the glass, which appears vital and alive.

14. Pittsburgh Greenfield (Greenfield School)
1 Alger Street, Greenfield
Richard Kiehnel of Kiehnel & Elliott, architect, 1916 (constructed 1921)
National Register of Historic Places; City Historic Structure;
Historic Landmark plaque

Since the building faces a large playing field, visitors are oriented immediately to the main entrance and indeed to the whole main façade. Greenfield School is a large, buff-brick, three-story building with a T-shaped plan, built on a slope so that only two-and-a-half stories are visible from the front. The rear of the building rests on the edge of a bluff, revealing three brick stories supported by two stone-faced basement and sub-basement levels, rather like a hillside castle.[67]

Bands of light stone surround the base. Here too, are classically derived brick piers/pilasters, but the laurel leaves at Brushton School have been replaced by rigorously geometric blossoms. The pattern of cubic blossoms aligned on either side of a vertical stem is sometimes repeated, sometimes broken apart to form pendants. As at Brushton School, double bands of ornamentation form a garland that encircles the building.

The Greenfield doorway rises halfway up the center of the building. Two stone piers support a lintel bearing the school's name; the piers "ripple" or undulate in a manner quintessentially Secessionist. Kiehnel's model here is the Door to the Great Hall in Hermann Billing's Mannheim Museum (1905–07), illustrated in *Moderne Bauformen* in 1907.[68] The top half of the Greenfield entranceway is filled with glass; the doors below were crowned by a triangular pediment ornamented by Plečnik's chisel-shaped molding; this molding has been removed.

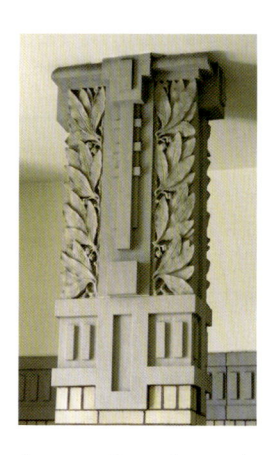

Inside, the Greenfield foyer was richly decorated with wall panels (still surviving) and free-standing columns (now gone) whose geometric and laurel leaf decoration recall Brushton School, but with more elegance and sophistication.

81

California Craftsman — Thornburg 1900–1912

National Register of Historic Places District

F our miles southwest of downtown Pittsburgh, the borough of Thornburg,[69] founded in 1909, rises on a terraced bluff in the Chartiers Valley. In 1806, Thomas Thornburg acquired over 400 acres of land, including the parcel on which the borough of Thornburg now sits. This parcel—some 250 acres—was acquired in 1899 by Thomas's heirs: Frank Thornburg (1856–1927); his cousin David; and members of their family. They established the Thornburg Land Company and began developing their share of the family estate into a planned suburban residential community.[70]

1899 to 1912 saw the development of the unique character of Thornburg. Construction of the first houses in 1900 engendered acclaim, followed by rapid growth: twenty-eight buildings were in place by 1905. During the intervening years, residents were attracted by the beauty of the region, the convenient rail links with the city, the novelty of the first golf course in the area, and the special character of the community emerging under the direction of its founder—a businessman, showman, and architectural aficionado.[71]

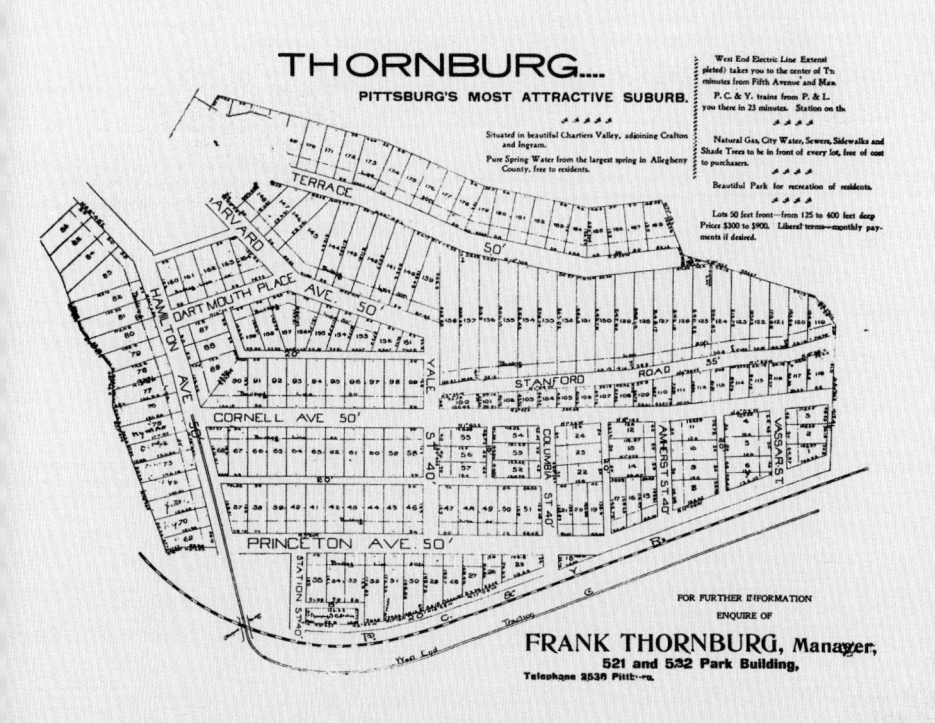

1132 Lehigh Road

Only two restrictions were placed on prospective residents: (1) houses must cost a minimum of $2,500, and (2) the first stories must be built of brick or stone to prevent fires. In 1900, the first five houses were erected along Princeton Road. These can be described as "simplified Queen Anne," a style found in abundance at the turn of the century in urban as well as suburban communities. Very soon, however, distinctive housing came into being: comfortable, informal, rustic yet sophisticated. Some houses wear the attire of the earlier "Shingle Style," others the emerging "Craftsman" style, and both traditional and contemporary ornamentation were used. However diverse such decorative elements may be, however varied the roofs or the fenestration, Thornburg houses appear to be family members who share primary building materials of fieldstone, brick, stucco, and wood shingling, and whose differing details are charming expressions of individuality.

A key factor in the development of the communal character was Frank Thornburg's interest in contemporary California architecture and his consequent influence on the design of the residences erected for his clients and neighbors. The April 1, 1905 issue of *Construction* magazine noted:

> *Frank Thornburg arrived home from Los Angeles, Cal., last Friday, after two months' absence. While away Mr. Thornburg, who laid out and is developing Thornburg, adjoining Crafton, secured 60 photographs of Los Angeles residences, and intends reproducing most of the dwellings at Thornburg. ... The 60 new photographs are mostly of houses of the mission type and some are very artistic.*[72]

If the homes of Thornburg were inspired by Frank Thornburg's photographs, they were realized, and adapted both structurally and aesthetically, by his cousin, architect Samuel Thornburg McClarren (1862–1940), who had apprenticed with Pittsburgh architects.[73] Houses erected in 1903 tilted the stylistic envelope toward California. Frank's second house at **501 Hamilton Road** (Frank's daughter Florence called it "a copy of a California house"[74]) recalls Los Angeles and Pasadena Shingle Style houses by Hunt & Egar, Locke & Preston,

1060 Stanford Road

F. L. Roehrig, Train & Williams, and 1898–1902 houses by Greene & Greene, soon to become the leading California Arts and Crafts firm. A two-story turret topped with medieval battlements protrudes from an otherwise symmetrical, wide-eaved stucco, shingle, and stone building. Originally, the unenclosed side veranda and a rear enclosed porch opened into the living room.

Albert Daschbach's house at **1060 Stanford Road** has a low-hipped roof with wide eaves, hipped dormers, and horizontal massing. Inside, rooms flow into one another and French doors lead to terraces and porches. An article in *House Beautiful* described the Daschbach interior (now altered).[75]

A 1903 house for Conrad Pfohl at **1124 Cornell Road** is Thornburg's first California-derived Spanish Mission building.[76] Other houses of special interest erected prior to 1905

1124 Cornell Road

include **1137 Cornell**, known as the "Cobblestone" house and, according to Florence Thornburg, is modeled on a California house. It shares common elements with 325 South Grand Avenue in Pasadena (c. 1895) by Locke & Preston (whose house nearby at 395 Grand Avenue was named "Cobbleoak") and an even more striking resemblance to the first Craftsman house design of Gustav Stickley and E. G. W. Dietrich (a former Pittsburgher), published in *The Craftsman*, May 1903. **1109 Cornell** resembles houses designed by Myron Hunt, an associate of Frank Lloyd Wright, who moved his practice from Chicago to Los Angeles in 1903.[77]

Two façades of 1137 Cornell Road

David Thornburg, co-founder of the community, was the Pittsburgh agent for Samuel Cabot, Inc. of Boston, makers of "shingle stain, brick and wood preservatives." Randell Makinson tells us: "The use of Cabot's transparent penetrating-oil stain was a critical factor in the Greene & Greene exterior color specification."[78]

In 1906, McClarren built a new home at **529 Hamilton Road**.[79] The first story is clad in brick. Long, thin, multi-tinted bricks are laid in an asymmetrical pattern called one-third running bond. The brick is "tapestry" brick, suggesting "a very old oriental rug" in which "differing color values of the individual bricks … are taken up and harmonized in the prevailing tone."[80] The description is Louis Sullivan's, who used similar brick frequently after 1905. The second story and attic are contained within a great triangular gable of stucco and wood framing that not only covers the entire house but extends beyond it toward the street. The grid of the wood trim is more of a geometric pattern than medieval half-timbering. Side, front, and rear dormers project from the great gable and reinforce the triangular pattern.

1132 Lehigh Road (above and below)

In 1907, McClarren created his Craftsman masterpiece for Frank Thornburg. The Thornburg "mansion" (as it was called by the neighbors) crowns the hillside at **1132 Lehigh Road** and was Frank Thornburg's third and final residence in the community. The house [*Historic Landmark plaque*] is an immense two-story shingle and stone V-shaped structure. At each end, open porches (one has since been enclosed) protected by deep eaves that encircle the house permit sweeping views of the Chartiers Valley. Inside, the wood-paneled living room with its stone fireplace and the formal dining room are impressive, but it is the two-story entrance hall at the core of the house that is its central feature: facing the front door, the two-story, free-standing brick fireplace dominates the room. The stairway behind the fireplace bench rises a half-story, winds behind the fireplace, and continues up to the

560 Hamilton Road

second floor. One ponders the source of the two-story entrance hall. In 1909, two years after the Thornburg House, the Heineman brothers designed a variant in the Hindry House in Pasadena.[81]

Californians, in the early twentieth century, "were haunted by romantic conceptions of a simpler, better day. ... They pictured the California of the eighteenth and early nineteenth centuries as a pastoral society in which Franciscan missionaries had converted Indians into contented workers."[82] Efforts began to preserve and restore the Spanish Missions, and elements of ecclesiastical and domestic Spanish Colonial architecture appeared in new buildings. The Spanish Colonial house at **560 Hamilton Road** called "Almo Terrace," designed by McClarren c. 1908, is a one-and-a-half-story, red-tile-roofed, U-shaped stucco house with rooms grouped around a central patio—a plan derived from ranchos of the 1830s and revived by Greene & Greene in their 1903 Bandini House in Pasadena. In 1912, McClarren designed an addition to the Thornburg School (now **545 Hamilton**) that doubled the size of the building and created an entrance hallway whose main exterior feature is a Baroque parapeted gable derived from Spanish Mission buildings.

In 1909, the Thornburg Land Company declared bankruptcy and the borough of Thornburg was established. Frank moved to Los Angeles in 1911. In 1913, McClarren and his family moved to St. Petersburg, Florida.

In Thornburg, McClarren created a residential architecture inspired by southern California yet attuned to southwestern Pennsylvania's landscape and climate. Nowhere is that regional character more apparent than in Frank Thornburg's house. This massive shingle and stone mansion—southwestern Pennsylvania's finest American Craftsman house—would not be quite as at home in southern California as it is here. The Thornburg Historic District was listed on the National Register of Historic Places in 1982.

California Craftsman—Thornburg 1900–1912

In 1912, Samuel T. McClarren doubled the size of the Thornburg School (originally designed by Pressley C. Dowler in 1909–10) and added a California Spanish Mission entryway. The building now houses a community room, library and Borough council meeting room, records room, and day care center.

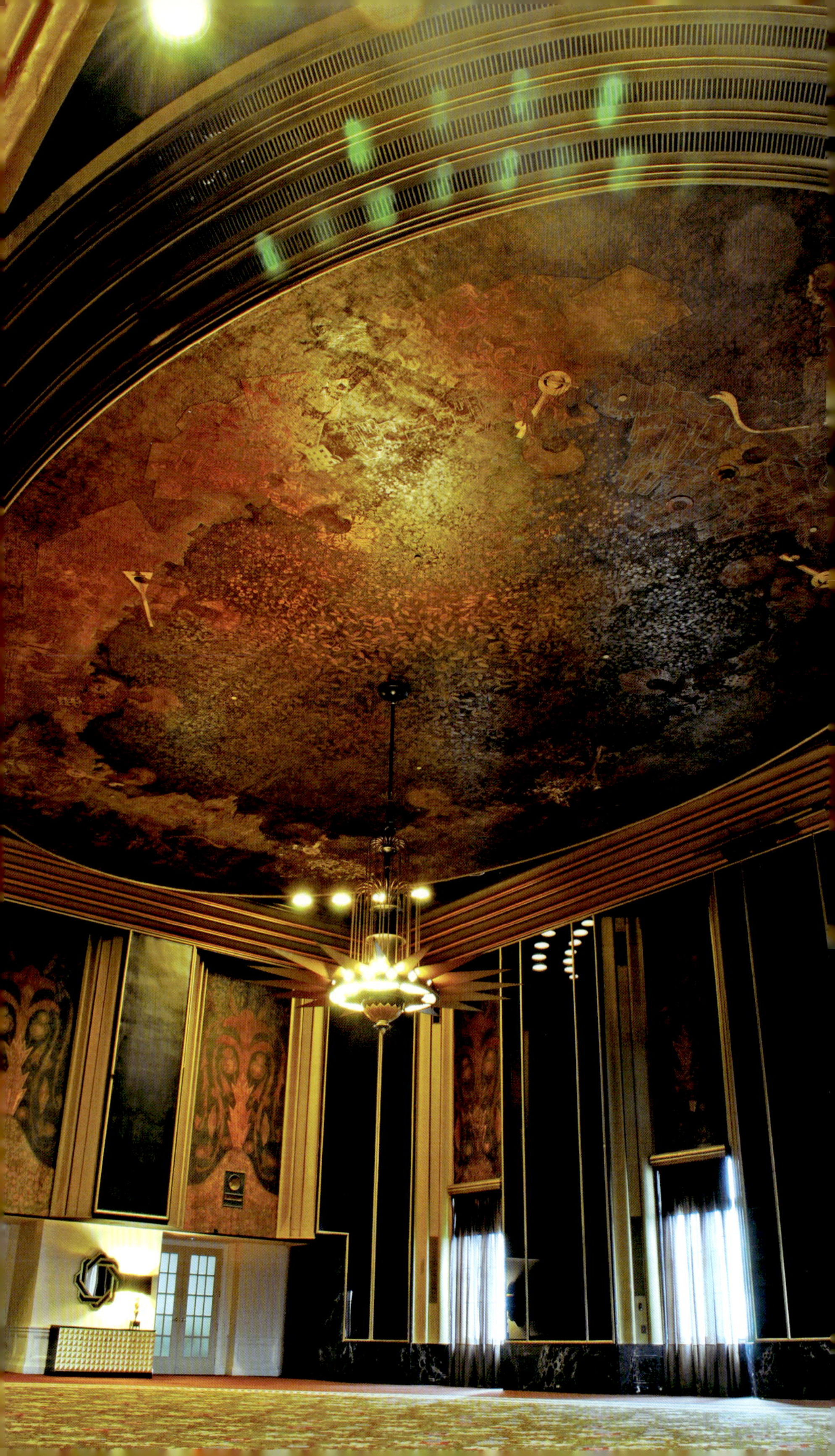

Art Moderne, Art Deco, and the "House of Tomorrow"

James D. Van Trump wrote:

> *Art Deco was a youthful style, at once traditional as well as innovative and dynamic. It created the last ornamental style known to Western art by marrying the machine with the old handicraft tradition. It was new as tomorrow, and yet old as history; it could be quite simple and austere or very intricate and complex. It summed up the past but it announced in no uncertain terms the present and the future. …*
>
> *The earlier Art Deco of the 1920s was often decorative, curvilinear, and graceful … but by 1930 the influence of Cubism and the machine became paramount, and the ever more abstracted, conventionalized, and geometric quality of its ornamental system displayed a new dynamism and a new vocabulary. Gazelles and maidens were replaced by airplanes and lightening bolts. …*
>
> *Once the beholder's eye has been opened to the all-pervasive presence of Deco in our streets, he will find it everywhere.*[83]

We have chosen to highlight a former theater, a commercial building, a hotel banquet room (*shown opposite*), a municipal building, a Five & Dime store, four public schools, and residential architecture inspired by the 1933–34 *Century of Progress Exposition* in Chicago.

Rubin & VeShancey was established in 1919 and continued until 1947. Both partners were active in the Pittsburgh Architectural Club and the Pittsburgh Chapter AIA. Hyman Louis Rubin (1893–1947) was born in Philadelphia. His family moved to Pittsburgh and Rubin graduated from Carnegie Tech in the class of 1915. He was the first Carnegie Tech student to win the John L. Stewardson Memorial Scholarship in Architecture. In 1921,

Rubin returned to Pittsburgh after an eighteen-month trip through England, France, and Italy where he studied at the American Academy in Rome. Meyer VeShancey (1892–1971) was born in Pittsburgh and attended Carnegie Tech, 1911–14. He worked as a draftsman with E. M. Butz, 1909–11, and for the Allegheny County Engineering Department, 1916–18. VeShancey continued his own practice after Rubin's death in 1947.[84]

15. Letter Carriers' Local 84 Union Hall (New Brighton Theatre)
841 California Avenue, North Side
Rubin & VeShancey, architects, 1927–28
National Register District

No "gazelles and maidens" frolic on the former New Brighton Theatre of 1927 (originally a theatre, bowling alley, and commercial complex), but it is one of the best Pittsburgh examples of Art Deco that is both "intricate and complex" as well as "decorative, curvilinear, and graceful": comic-tragic masks, surrounded by exuberant interlacing and exaggerated stylized flowers, crown the Brighton Place façade; below are panels of abstract cubic and curvilinear ornament. Elephant trunks cascade down the corners while extravagant floral ornament frames the California Avenue entrance.

Photographs of the building were included in *Zigzags and Stripes: Art Deco Style*, held at the Heinz Architectural Center, Carnegie Museum of Art in 1999.

The three-story, flat-roofed, cream-colored, terra-cotta-and-brick building has a one-story, Postmodern side-entrance addition designed by Brenenborg Brown Group Architects in 1997. Although the reuse of the building has closed off the original front doors facing Brighton Place, the architects have playfully recreated them in four colors of ceramic mosaic tile.

Art Moderne, Art Deco, and the "House of Tomorrow"

The Chicago firm of **Graham, Anderson, Probst & White** (GAPW) was the official successor to the distinguished and well-known architect and city planner Daniel H. Burnham, senior partner of Burnham & Root (1873–91) and D. H. Burnham & Company (1892–1912). Following Burnham's death in 1912, GAPW was established by Burnham's chief designers; senior partner Ernest Graham (1866–1936) had worked with Burnham since 1888 and senior designer Peirce Anderson (1870–1924) had worked with him since 1900. Edward Probst (1870–1942) joined Burnham's firm in 1898 and Howard White (1870–1936) joined the firm in c. 1888. Between 1898 and 1912, D. H. Burnham & Company designed eleven buildings in Pittsburgh; seven remain. Some—perhaps all—of the GAPW partners worked on these buildings.

16. Koppers Building
436 Seventh Avenue, Downtown Pittsburgh
Graham, Anderson, Probst & White (Chicago, IL), architects, 1927–29
National Register District;
Historic Landmark plaque

The Koppers Building, begun in 1927 and completed in 1929, exhibits a dignified exterior of gray, green, and bronze. The building has thirty-four "levels" above street level and three below; the first three floors are clad in polished granite; those above are clad in Indiana limestone topped by a copper-over-quarry-tile chateau roof; the building "set-backs" are at the twenty-first and twenty-ninth floors. At night, the flood-lit copper roof of this handsome building serves as a local landmark—the warm crown of light 475 feet above street level more than holds its own in comparison with the harder, brighter lights of more recent buildings.

The Koppers Building is the city's finest Art Deco commercial building. The copper-crowned façade and the subtly polychromatic lobby (housing shops on three levels overlooking the lobby corridors) are the most notable features of a building that combines elegance, dignity, and warmth. The three-story lobby is a restrained, yet rich, polychromatic delight, eschewing the silver (often chrome or aluminum) and black "streamlined" color scheme of many contemporary Art Deco buildings. The walls and columns are cream-colored marble infused with veins of pink, gray, red, brown, and green. Ceiling moldings and trim are gold, red, and green. Railings, light fixtures, elevator doors, lobby clocks, and mailboxes are cast bronze. The decoration is not particularly geometric (but the elevator doors are one of the few exceptions); rather, stylized floral—ferns and leaves—predominate. Four French tapestries created between 1922 and 1924 hang in the basement corridor, designed by Edouvard Benedictus (1878–1930) in 1922, Elizabeth Eyre de Lanux (1894–1996) in 1923, and Max Vibert and Y. Parigot in 1924.

Walter C. Kidney finds a touch of architectural mischief in the design when he writes: "Yet a little quiet humor crept into the design, with or without management's approval. The crowning chateau roof, being made of copper, can be taken as a pun, while the downstairs mailbox is a doll's-house version of the whole building, roof included."[85]

The owners of the Koppers Building have restored and refurbished the building; the marble and bronze now gleam as they did in 1929.

Joseph Urban (1872–1933) received his architectural training at the Vienna Academy of Fine Arts from 1890 to 1893. He co-founded a society of young artists, the Hagenbund, designed its gallery and many of its exhibitions, and served as its president. In 1904, Urban visited America where he was awarded a special gold medal for his interiors in the Austrian Pavilion at the St. Louis Exposition. In 1905, he began to design sets for the theater. His busy career as an architect and designer—culminating in his appointment in 1908 as chief designer for the Golden Jubilee of Emperor Franz Joseph I—took a decisive turn in 1910 when Henry Russell, impresario of the Boston Opera Company, saw Urban's Paris production of Debussy's *Pelléas et Mélisande* and offered him a job in America.

Urban served as general stage director for the Boston Opera, uniting for perhaps the first time the roles of set designer, lighting designer, costume designer, and stage director. When the opera company disbanded in 1914, Urban was asked to design his first Broadway play. This led to a meeting with Florenz Ziegfeld, creator of the Ziegfeld *Follies*; Urban would continue his theatrical design activities for *Follies* shows until 1931. Urban's longtime association with the Metropolitan Opera Company began in 1918. The next year publisher William Randolph Hearst hired Urban to design sets and lighting for a film company formed to showcase the talents of actress Marion Davies. He left Hearst's film company in 1925.

Urban had been approached by several Palm Beach, Florida, residents regarding architectural projects. While he continued to design for the theater and opera, he resolved to focus on architecture, as he had during the first seventeen years of his career. In Palm Beach, he turned to the Mediterranean style already in place. Among his best known Palm Beach projects are the Bath and Tennis Club (1925), the Sunrise Building (1925–26) and Paramount Theatre (1927), and his 1926 remodeling and enlargement of Marjorie Merriweather Post's grandly exotic home, Mar-a-Lago, designed by Marion Syms Wyeth.[86]

From 1927 to 1929, Urban designed buildings, façades, and interiors—often decorated with colorful lush murals—in an elegant Art Moderne/Art Deco manner. Among these designs were the Ziegfeld Theatre, the Bedell Store, and the Central Park Casino (all demolished) in Manhattan, and banquet rooms and restaurants across the country, including the Urban Room in the William Penn Hotel in Pittsburgh.

With the 1929–30 Atlantic Beach Club on Long Island (demolished), a new "cubist" austerity entered Urban's design vocabulary; this was also used in his 1930 New School for Social Research in Manhattan and in the 1932 Urban Room in Chicago's Congress Hotel (gone). As geometric as these buildings and spaces were, they stood apart from their European cousins through Urban's use of bright interior colors and subtle lighting. Indeed, Urban's final commission was a gigantic exercise in lighting and color when he became lighting director for the *Century of Progress Exposition* set to open in Chicago in 1933.

The most recent literature on Urban—*Joseph Urban: Architecture, Theatre, Opera, Film*, by Randolph Carter and Robert Reed Cole (New York: Abbeville Press, 1992), and John Loring, *Joseph Urban* (New York: Abrams, 2010)—ignore Pittsburgh's Urban Room, and misattribute designs Urban created for it.[87] Yet the Urban Room in the William Penn Hotel is the sole survivor of the "many supper rooms and restaurants" Joseph Urban created between 1928 and 1932 in Chicago, Cincinnati, Detroit, New York, and Pittsburgh.

17. Urban Room, Omni William Penn Hotel (William Penn Hotel)
530 William Penn Place, Downtown Pittsburgh
Joseph Urban (New York, NY), designer, 1929
The hotel is in a National Register District and is individually listed on the National Register of Historic Places. Both the hotel and the Urban Room have been awarded Historic Landmark plaques.

In 1927, the Pittsburgh Hotels Company commissioned Janssen & Cocken to design a Grant Street addition to Pittsburgh's grand hotel, the William Penn—a logical commission since Benno Janssen and his former partner Franklin Abbott had designed the original hotel building on William Penn Place in 1914 for Pittsburgh industrialist Henry Clay Frick. Construction began in 1928. Then, later that year, the William Penn was sold to hotel developer Eugene C. Eppley. The original 1927 plans called for extending the seventeenth-floor ballroom into the new addition, but this would have meant removing, at great expense, structural supports in the original exterior east wall of the hotel. Instead, Eppley commissioned Urban to design a new room connected to the ballroom but entered by lower doors that would leave the support system intact. The room Urban designed could be used as an extension of the ballroom or as a separate reception or banquet room.

Urban's banquet room has walls of black Carrara glass, outlined in gilt trim, rising from a black-and-green marble base to a four-tiered concave gilt molding. The elliptical ceiling painting, which is surrounded by four gold concentric rings, has a border of twelve colorfully dressed women playing musical instruments in a field of golden flowers. Behind the players, across a blue waterway, exotic buildings are set against a blue sky. The sky serves as the background for a filigree of golden branches in the center of the painting. Fourteen wall paintings, or murals, depict an exotic tree set within a flower bed. Blossoms and branches are purple, pink, green, brown, and the colors most characteristic of Urban: "Gold, blue—particularly a blue green which some now refer to as an Urban blue—and white and black." Otto Teegen, Urban's associate, wrote: "but there was never a sameness in the character of these projects, and he always established a new palette for each job and the mood desired."⁸⁸

Pittsburgh electrical contractor R. G. Frame, who worked with Urban, recalled: "It was not Mr. Urban's intention to illuminate the room highly but rather to achieve 'mood' lighting effects. This was achieved by … a group of twelve recessed high wattage lighting units [in each corner of the ceiling] and a large inverted shallow cone unit in the center below the ceiling mural [*sic*]." The central lighting fixture was:

> about 9 ft. in diameter and possibly 2 1/2 ft. deep with the large diameter at the top and open. It was constructed of bronze and the visible exterior was composed of concentric ribs with minimal decoration. Lights placed within this fixture were directed upward to illuminate the mural. … The fixture was supported by a set of four cables … [anchored at the corners of the ceiling painting] intended to resemble the strings of a musical instrument.⁸⁹

The enlarged William Penn Hotel opened on May 9, 1929. One news account reported:

Eugene C. Eppley, president of the group of twenty-one hotels extending from Pittsburgh to Los Angeles ... was host at the buffet luncheon to more than one thousand guests. The luncheon was served in the Joseph Urban Room, one of the many new additions to the hotel. It is on the seventeenth floor, and is regarded as one of the most beautiful public rooms in the country. It is named after its designer and decorator.[90]

The architect and his wife were present and Urban spoke at the luncheon (his remarks, unfortunately, were not recorded).

Urban's three-tiered bronze chandelier was removed in the 1950s; it is said that it had become the repository for countless hard dinner rolls lobbed during countless parties. It was replaced by a sunburst fixture set into the ceiling painting. In 1979, the hotel cleaned the murals—the colors had so darkened over time as to be indistinguishable—and replaced the carpeting and drapes. In 1996, the William Penn Hotel refurbished the room as part of a multi-million-dollar hotel renovation. The refurbishment repaired water damage and cleaned the ceiling painting; cleaned and relit all fourteen murals—for almost twenty years only five of these murals had been visible; cleaned and repaired the marble, black glass, and gilt trim; and installed new draperies and carpeting.[91] Draperies no longer hide the wall murals or cover sections of the black Cararra glass walls—these now regain their Moderne configuration. Someday, it is hoped, the original vibrant colors of the ceiling painting and the murals will be restored.

William Henry King, Jr. (1884–1953) was born in Baltimore, Maryland. His father, a lumber merchant, moved his family to Washington, D.C., and then to Pittsburgh at the turn of the twentieth century. In 1906, at the age of 21, King was working as a draughtsman in the office of MacClure & Spahr; during this period he produced a *Drawing for a Small House* for an AIA competition, later published in *The Builder*. In 1907, he joined the Pittsburgh Architectural Club.

He enrolled in Carnegie Technical Schools; while there he exhibited student work at the 1910 and 1911 Pittsburgh Architectural Club exhibitions. He graduated in 1910 with a Bachelor of Science degree in Architecture, then attended the Ecole des Beaux-Arts in Paris, from 1911 through 1913.

In 1914, King was working as a draughtsman at his home in Pittsburgh's East End. In 1915, he opened an architectural office at 801 House Building in downtown Pittsburgh and exhibited designs for two houses at that year's Pittsburgh Architectural Club exhibition. King worked as a civil engineer in 1918, perhaps in connection with the war.[92] He resumed private practice in 1919 and in 1923 moved to Mt. Lebanon. In 1928, he designed the Mt. Lebanon Municipal Building, one of the area's outstanding Art Deco buildings, completed in 1930.[93]

King moved to Washington, Pennsylvania, his wife's hometown, in the early 1930s. While living in Washington, he took a position in 1943 with the Pittsburgh firm of Janssen & Cocken. He returned to Mt. Lebanon in 1944 and subsequently worked for architects Pressley Dowler and Hoffman & Crumpton. He died in Mt. Lebanon in 1953 and is buried in Washington, Pennsylvania.

18. Mt. Lebanon Municipal Building
710 Washington Road, Mt. Lebanon
William H. King, Jr., architect, 1928–30;
Rothschild Doyno Collaborative, architects for renovation and restoration, 2004
Historic Landmark plaque

Four silent figures stand watch over their community—not threatening, not too familiar—but dignified, as befits their age. From their roof-top vantage point, this hooded quartet atop the Mt. Lebanon Municipal Building surveys the community, as it has since 1930. At the top of the building, the governmental eagle—wings spread—proclaims the seat of municipal authority, while a stylized bronze bas-relief panel, "Wisdom in Government," is set above the main entrance. Chevron panels (a repeated V-shaped pattern) on the Washington Road façade provide abstract decoration between the windows. Inside, the aluminum stair railings and lighting fixtures in the dramatic two-story lobby are richly geometric and sleekly streamlined (*see photo, page 222*).

In addition to the municipal offices, the building originally housed the Mt. Lebanon Police and Fire departments. The Police and

Fire departments moved to a new Public Safety Center that opened in 2003. The Municipal Building was renovated and restored in 2004 by Rothschild Doyno Collaborative; the firm was committed to "preserving and restoring the ... distinguished interior and exterior art deco features."[94] The four large fire-truck doorways were replaced with large windows and doors, and the former fire-truck garage now houses the Commission Chambers.

This building exemplifies a change of direction, as Walter C. Kidney observed: "Municipal buildings in the 1920s tended to be classical. ... but now and then a Moderne example appeared as well toward the end of the decade."[95]

G. C. Murphy Company, founded by George Clintock Murphy in McKeesport in 1906, was one of the region's must successful businesses. By 1930 there were 170 stores in Connecticut, Illinois, Indiana, Kentucky, Maryland, Michigan, New Jersey, New York, Ohio, Pennsylvania, and West Virginia. At the height of the Depression between 1930 and 1936, Murphy's built some forty new stores. "In addition to the stores Murphy's purchased, a few new locations were constructed or remodeled to the company's specifications. Beginning in 1925, they were designed by Murphy's in-house architect, **Harold E. Crosby**, who became the first and only employee of the newly created construction division on July 8."[96] Harold Crosby (1899–1958), a Missouri native, had graduated from Iowa State College in 1922. After serving as company architect from 1925 to 1946, he was vice president of Murphy's Construction Division from 1947 to 1955.

19. Market Square Place (including G. C. Murphy Company Store No. 12)
 Forbes Avenue at Market Square, Downtown Pittsburgh
 Harold E. Crosby, architect, 1930; Strada Architecture, LLC, architects for renovation and restoration, 2006–09
 City Historic District

Market Square Place, located at 222 Fifth Avenue, incorporates seven historic buildings in an award-winning, LEED Gold, mixed-use development by Millcraft Industries, Inc. of Washington, Pennsylvania. Forty-six loft apartments, underground parking, new street-level retail, and a new downtown YMCA

G. C. Murphy Company was at 219 Forbes Avenue (center).

have created an eco-friendly community and helped rejuvenate the Market Square area. The National Trust for Historic Preservation recognized Market Square Place with a Preservation Honor Award in 2012.

One of the historic buildings is the former G. C. Murphy Company's regional flagship store in Pittsburgh, erected in 1930 at a cost of $250,000. The Forbes Avenue façade at 219 Forbes displays fully developed Art Deco terra-cotta ornamentation on a buff-brick façade. Above the third-floor windows, half-circles (the rising sun?) peak out from behind triangles decorated with cubes and tiny triangles tinted salmon and green. Above, four "frozen" fountains jet upward past the roofline from a bed of lush vegetation. Panels of stylized ferns and flowers dot the façade. A band of geometric ornament and "219" in a jaunty script appear over the original service doorway (*see photo, page 226*).

The façade on Fifth Avenue had received "a new streamlined front of salmon-colored tile"[97] in 1940, but the original 1930 façade was restored in the 2006–09 renovation by Strada Architecture.

101

The distinguished character of Pittsburgh Public School buildings was recognized in 1986–87 when forty-nine schools, designed and built between 1850 and 1940, were listed on the National Register of Historic Places; the nomination was prepared by the Pittsburgh History & Landmarks Foundation. Some of these buildings have been sold and have been adapted for other uses; a few are extant but closed. Two buildings by **Edward J. Weber**—Mifflin (1932) and Lemington (1937)—and two buildings by **Marion M. Steen**—Prospect (1931/1936) and Stevens (1940)—are featured in this chapter. There are other school buildings erected in the 1930s of merit but none better. (*Schiller School, designed by Edward Weber in 1939, is featured on page 125.*) Mifflin, Lemington, and Schiller are listed on the National Register and are City of Pittsburgh Historic Structures. Prospect is on the National Register, but the Pittsburgh Board of Public Education declined to include Prospect among the schools nominated as City of Pittsburgh Historic Structures. Stevens is a City Historic Structure but was not fifty years old when the National Register nomination was submitted.

Edward J. Weber (1877–1968) had apprenticed with Peabody & Stearns in Boston and had attended the Ecole des Beaux-Arts in Paris before working for MacClure & Spahr in Pittsburgh. He achieved some success in the 1920s as a Roman Catholic ecclesiastical architect, writing two books on church architecture, and he designed churches, convents, and intricately patterned brick parochial schools, such as St. Colman's in Turtle Creek and Central Catholic in Oakland. After Link, Weber & Bowers dissolved in 1931,[98] Weber worked sporadically. His finest buildings during this period are the schools he designed for the Pittsburgh Board of Public Education.[99]

After graduating from Carnegie Technical Schools in 1908, Marion Markle Steen (1886–1966)[100] worked for Henry Hornbostel as a draftsman on campus buildings. In 1918, he left Pittsburgh and briefly worked in Chicago, returning later that year to head the architectural department of the Carnegie Land Company. In 1922, he joined the family firm, James T. Steen & Sons. While there, he also designed Oliver (1924/1928) and Herron Hill (1928) schools. Between 1935 and 1954, Steen served as supervising architect of Pittsburgh schools. In this capacity, he hired Edward Weber to design several buildings.

20. Pittsburgh Mifflin (Mifflin Elementary School)
1290 Mifflin Road, Lincoln Place
Edward J. Weber of Link, Weber & Bowers, architect, 1932
Strada Architecture, LLC, architects for renovation and addition, 2002–05
National Register of Historic Places; City Historic Structure;
Historic Landmark plaque

Mifflin School is dramatically sited on a hilltop in Lincoln Place in the Thirty-first Ward on the southeastern edge of the City of Pittsburgh. Mifflin follows the rectilinear, central-block-with-frontal-wings plan. The stepped-back, two-story gymnasium and auditorium wings on each end flow into the tall and narrow central block. At first glance, the building appears to be "streamline" Moderne, with smooth buff-brick walls terminating in elegantly rounded corners. The gymnasium and auditorium doorways are surrounded by wide Egyptian Art Deco borders.

The first-story wall curves inward to frame a grand, oversized entrance topped by an ornamental tablet framed by abstract flowers. Cloverleafs filled with floral tracings top wall piers (*opposite and bottom*). The walls are not smooth but reveal patterns of parallel waving lines incised in the exterior brickwork, and the decorative cornices circling the roofs are not flat, but rounded. The strange eclecticism of the façade, which grows increasingly wonderful the longer one views it, appears to be a marriage of the Moderne and sixteenth-century Mannerism which enlarged and exaggerated Classical Renaissance forms.

This mixture of contemporary and historical styles is found in the polychromatic auditorium. A ceiling of aluminum panels is the principal Art Deco element; Art Deco decoration also appears on the geometric metal air grilles which sport a maple leaf motif. Most of the auditorium decoration recalls Georgian neo-classicism. Wooden paneling and paneled columns are topped with light-blue capitals. Green-and-white medallions and a green scalloped border decorate the white plaster covering those areas not paneled in wood. White metal chandeliers are trimmed with gold. At the rear of the auditorium, white plaster panels framed in wood hold green-and-white medallions similar to those on the ceiling. The rear exit is surrounded by wooden classical pilasters and topped with a scrolled pediment.

21. Destiny International Ministries (Lemington School)
7061 Lemington Avenue, Lincoln-Lemington
Edward J. Weber, architect, 1937
National Register of Historic Places; City Historic Structure;
Historic Landmark plaque

Destiny International Ministries purchased the former Lemington School building in 2008. The community-based organization has opened a non-denominational church in the building and plans to add an all-boy's school (K–6), day care center, and social service agency.

The former school building exhibits the tripartite pattern of gymnasium, classroom block, and auditorium. The exterior is buff brick with gray stone trim; the brick walls are not smooth but are enlivened by extruding bricks that give the surface texture. It is easy to miss this interesting wall treatment, however, because of the extravagant terra-cotta ornament. Under the cornice is a frieze of polychromatic children's faces, and over the gymnasium and auditorium doorways a child's face stares out from what appears to be a Mayan-inspired head dress—wide ruff topped by a lamp of learning and great plumes— surrounded by decorative panels, all in vivid green, purple, red, blue, and gold (*see photo, page 224*). Gold Mayan terra-cotta panels decorate the chimney and sections of the façade; a polychromatic, somewhat sinister Comedy mask adorns the rear wall of the auditorium. Black geometric Art Deco ironwork and colorful Mayan patterns ornament the interior of the auditorium. The elegantly curved cornice moldings and the loving attention given to the brick wall surface link this building to Mifflin School.

Another Weber design that uses vivid colors in an Art Deco idiom is the Dunkle Gulf Service Station in Bedford, Pennsylvania, in orange, blue, green, and yellow glazed tile designed in 1933.[101]

22. The Lofts of Mount Washington (Prospect School)
161 Prospect Street, Mt. Washington
M. M. Steen of James T. Steen & Sons, architect, 1931/1936; Paul Rodriguez Architect, architects for renovation, 2013–14
National Register of Historic Places; Historic Landmark plaque

Prospect School, as erected in 1931, was a three-story, rectilinear, buff-brick block with stone facings around entrances and under the first-floor windows. The most distinctive feature of the original exterior (later enlarged) are "dog-tooth" piers. Primary ornament consists of metal ventilating panels of delicate intertwining circular lines under the second- and third-floor windows and an eagle (*see page 275*) standing guard above the main entrance.

The 1931 auditorium deserves special mention. The Pittsburgh History & Landmarks Foundation's National Register nomination for Prospect School called the auditorium "one of Pittsburgh's most fully realized Art Deco interiors." Tucked into the southwest corner of the building, the auditorium

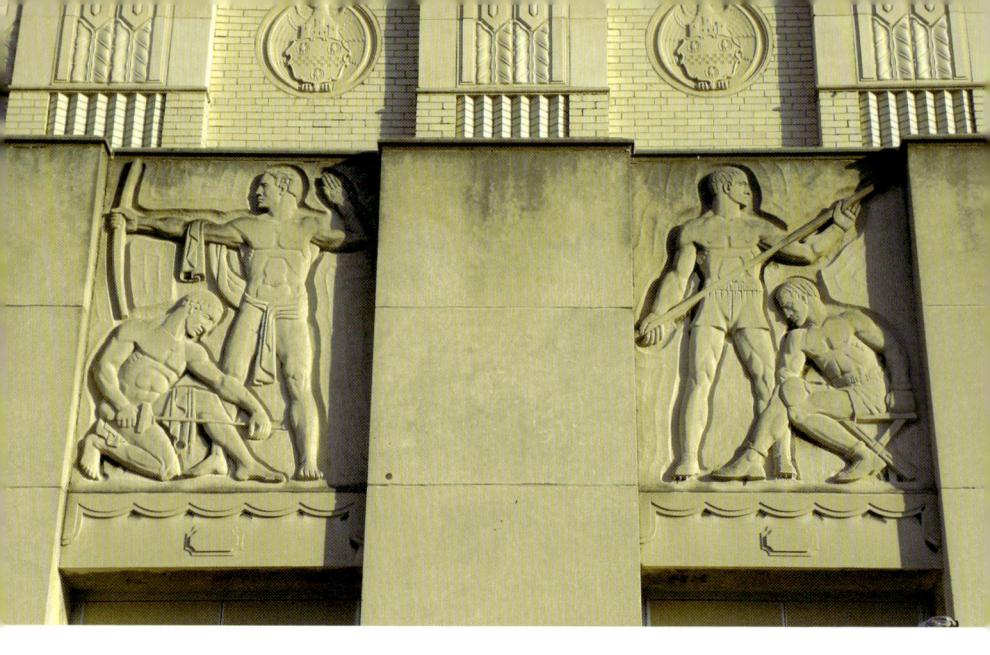

Relief panels over the gymnasium entrance (above) and auditorium entrance (bottom)

is wonderfully adorned with copper, black glass, and white metal panels depicting fish, fowl, and butterflies.

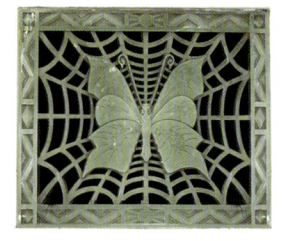

In 1936, Steen enlarged Prospect School by adding a new gymnasium at one end and auditorium at the other. The new wings, which give the building a dignified monumentality,[102] were decorated with panels of "frozen" ferns—a popular Art Deco motif— and limestone low-relief sculptures carved by Pittsburgh sculptor Charles Bradley Warren. The sculptures, completed in 1938, are rugged figures of athletes and thespians given movement and energy by "rippling raised lines surrounding them," as Marilyn Evert notes in *Discovering Pittsburgh's Sculpture*.[103] The foyer doors inside the 1936 auditorium are decorated with square metal medallions arranged in a vertical pattern. Marble, ornamented by elaborate metal grilles in a complex abstract design, covers the lower portion of the auditorium walls.

Prospect School closed in 2006; it is being converted into loft apartments and is scheduled to reopen in 2014. Since the building is listed on the National Register of Historic Places, the developer,

A. M. Rodriguez Associates, is able to take advantage of the federal twenty percent investment tax credit for the certified rehabilitation of an income-producing property.

23. Thaddeus Stevens School
822 Crucible Street, Elliott
M.M. Steen, architect, 1940
City Historic Structure;
Historic Landmark plaque

In 1940, Steen designed what may be his scholastic masterpiece in the city's West End—Thaddeus Stevens School at 822 Crucible Street in Elliott. Laid out in the tripartite plan, Stevens appears less monolithic and heavy than its siblings due to the light-colored brick and the long, incised horizontal lines that define the base. The five limestone relief sculptures by Charles Bradley Warren are unusually elegant. Art surrounded by Music and Drama identify the auditorium entrance, while athletes are portrayed over the gymnasium entrance. At the rear of the building, Discovery is symbolized by a male figure holding a globe with a Viking ship at his feet and a female figure with Pegasus at her feet; a small male figure holds a mask at the stage door entrance.

The Pittsburgh Public Schools closed Thaddeus Stevens in 2012.

The Arts

Athletics

In November 1937, an article in *Architectural Forum* called Swan Acres in Ross Township, north of Pittsburgh, "the nation's first Modern subdivision."[104] Its architect and co-planner was **Quentin Scheffield Beck** (1909–67), born in Altoona, Pennsylvania. Beck had studied architecture at Pennsylvania State College (now University), and received his Bachelor of Science degree in 1933. In 1934, Quentin and his uncle Wilbur, who was a building contractor, established Beck & Beck and built a modernist house in suburban Rosslyn Farms designed by Quentin; a newspaper article compared the house to the modern houses displayed at the *Chicago Century of Progress*:

Pittsburgh's "House of Tomorrow": 221 Puritan Road, Rosslyn Farms (now altered)

As one approaches the Beck house, the first thing that attracts the eye is the modern design. One of the Becks graduated from Penn State's architectural school with honors in modern designing, and good use of his talent is made in the present instance. Those who have attended the Fair at Chicago are more or less familiar with such designing—most of the houses on exhibition there have featured it—and those who have not been fortunate enough to see the World's Fair houses, should see Pittsburgh's example.[105]

Beck & Beck became Beck, Pople & Beck (B.P.B.) with the addition of banker Harry Pople, who oversaw financing and publicity.[106] Swan Acres opened for inspection in August 1936 with two houses under construction.[107] Two B.P.B. houses were completed first in nearby Glenshaw and opened for public tours in October 1936. Quentin Beck designed two more houses at Swan Acres and the four houses were finished in early April 1937. Beck was not yet licensed and architect Harry C. Clepper was hired to sign B.P.B. drawings.[108] Soon afterward, Wilbur Beck and Quentin—who by then had designed seven houses located in Rosslyn Farms, Swan Acres, and Glenshaw—withdrew from B.P.B.[109] A fifth Swan Acres house was completed in August 1937, designed by H. T. Lindeberg of New York. A sixth Swan Acres house was completed in March 1939, designed by Pittsburgh architect Joseph W. Hoover.[110]

After Quentin Beck left B.P.B., he managed his father's clock shop in Union Station and was later employed by the Engineering Works Division

Two of the four houses finished in April 1937: 105 (left) and 103 Circle Drive (both now altered). Swan Acres was planned with curving streets, in response to the sloped terrain, but has a typical suburban layout of detached, single-family homes and front lawns. Later homes abandoned the modern treatment.

of Dravo Engineering Corporation, working there during World War II supervising the fabrication of Landing Ships for Tanks (LSTs). He returned to architectural practice c. 1949 and established an office in Carnegie, in 1952. He designed residences, apartment buildings, and commercial buildings in the South Hills, often in collaboration with builders A. N. Young and James West. He became an advocate for mass transit and explored high-speed pneumatic transportation systems.

24. Joseph Vokral House
1919 Woodside Road, Shaler Township
Quentin S. Beck of Beck, Pople & Beck, architect, 1936
Historic Landmark plaque

In October 1936, six months before the first Swan Acres houses were completed, B.P.B. opened two houses in Glenshaw, Shaler Township, six miles southeast of Swan Acres, for public inspection. The event was heralded by a lavishly illustrated two-page spread in the *Pittsburgh Press*, October 25, 1936:

> *Two homes of new and modern design have just been completed in the Pittsburgh district and are now open for public inspection. These two homes, the first modern American homes in this section of the country,*

were designed and constructed by Beck, Pople & Beck, builders ...
and [are] representative in architecture of the type of homes now being
constructed on the company's unique and beautiful home development
plan, Swan Acres.[111]

The houses, commissioned and owned by brothers Joseph and Jerry Vokral, are not adjacent but are located on either side of Mt. Royal Boulevard. The Vokral brothers worked with their father, Czech-born Joseph Vokral, brewmaster for Fort Pitt Brewing Company, Sharpsburg, who moved to Pittsburgh in 1925 from Chicago.

The Joseph Vokral House appears to be in immaculate condition (Jerry Vokral's house has been drastically altered, as has the 1934 Rosslyn Farms house). The *Press* noted that exterior walls are "Haydite [Concrete] Block, a new fire-proof, insulating masonry" and the exterior finish is "Portland cement, painted white with waterproof cement paint." Unlike the two-story Swan Acres houses, the Joseph Vokral House is one story. Otherwise, all stylistic elements are the same.

The first four houses at Swan Acres, designed by Quentin Beck, were erected between August 1936 and April 4, 1937, and cost between $12,000 and $20,500. Two of the houses have been ineptly remodeled; the two discussed here have retained their integrity.

25. Frederick Horst House
14 Swan Drive, Swan Acres, Ross Township
Quentin S. Beck of Beck, Pople & Beck, architect, 1936–37
PHLF Historic District plaque

14 Swan Drive was the first Swan Acres model home; a perspective drawing was published in the *Pittsburgh Press* on August 23, 1936. The article noted:

> Swan Acres ... will officially open today ... Since early summer work has been in progress readying the one-time farm for home construction. ... Now under construction in Swan Acres are the first two of five exhibition homes which will set the standard for future construction.

Architect's rendering, *The Pittsburgh Press*, August 23, 1936

They will be constructed of Haydite Concrete Block walls, insulated with Therax. All equipment in them will be of the highest quality and strictly modern. … Barred too, are traditional styles of architecture. Only houses of strictly modern design—or international style—will be permitted.[112]

The house was purchased by Frederick H. Horst, vice president and secretary of the Allegheny Trust Company. Despite the use of the term "international style," the Horst House with concrete construction, rounded corners, minimal rounded window and door trim, and porthole and glass block windows is modern in the sense of *Moderne*.

26. Harry Pople House
*16 Swan Drive, Swan Acres,
Ross Township
Quentin S. Beck of Beck, Pople & Beck,
architect, 1937
PHLF Historic District plaque*

All of the elements found in the Horst House are repeated and reconfigured in the somewhat larger Pople House, which was also—at $22,500—the most expensive of the four houses. A photograph of the house was published in *Architectural Forum*, together with floor plans and construction specifications. Despite the latest construction materials and techniques, interior living spaces in all four houses were largely traditional as designed:

> *The floor plans are inclined to adhere faithfully to preconceived notions as to what relationship rooms should have with each other. The front door gives into a hall which separates the living room from the dining room and kitchen. Whether this adherence to the usual Colonial plan was done deliberately so that potential buyers would find a familiar ring inside their functional shell is unimportant: the significance is that strictly speaking these houses have Modern shells enclosing conventional plans.*[113]

American Gothic
1905–1938

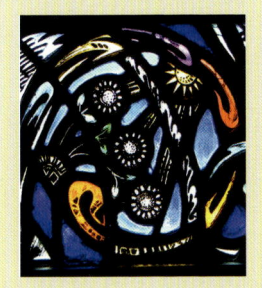

Henry Hobson Richardson began to adapt eleventh-century Romanesque architectural forms and materials in the 1870s with such skill and flexibility that his buildings created a bridge between medieval and American design and produced some of the most powerful and imaginative buildings in nineteenth-century America. Richardson's massive yet simple stone and brick buildings, with their fanciful carving and decoration, brought medieval architectural forms into the American design vocabulary for the first time in a substantial way. Richardson's Romanesque was the principal American expression of the revitalization of the art and craft of the Middle Ages championed in England by John Ruskin, William Morris, and Morris' Arts and Crafts successors.[114]

In the United States, the British Arts and Crafts movement and the medieval architectural forms explored by Richardson provided the foundation for twentieth-century American Gothic architecture and design. Modern American Gothic was inspired by twelfth-century ecclesiastical building construction innovations such as the pointed arch and the flying buttress that permitted great building height and window openings of unparalleled size. The key figures in this movement were Ralph Adams Cram (1863–1942), his partner Bertram Grosvenor Goodhue (1869–1924), architects they inspired or trained, and artists they employed and nurtured. In 1921 Ralph Adams Cram stated:

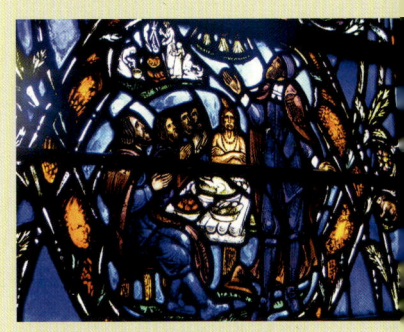

Stained glass (both), by Charles Connick, Heinz Chapel

> *Towards the end of the last century the recovery began. In France it was at first an attempt at archeological reproduction of mediaeval models; in England a revival of mediaeval principles, expressed largely through modern forms indicated by William Morris and Burne-Jones; in America it was quite a new thing altogether— new principles, materials, motives. Out of the welter has come ... old principles recovered, the old materials matched and recalled, the old craft necessarily regained, but with a certain modernism that insures vitality and contemporaneousness.*[115]

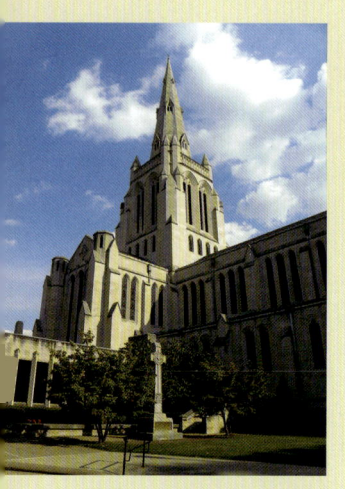

Calvary Episcopal, 315 Shady Avenue, Shadyside

British Arts and Crafts historian Peter Cormack has written: "The city of Pittsburgh is fortunate to have some of the very best Modern Gothic buildings in the USA."[116] Eleven are described here.

After apprenticing with architects Rotch & Tilden in Boston (1881–86), Ralph Adams Cram worked as art critic for the *Boston Evening Telegraph,* before establishing his own architectural firm with Charles F. Wentworth in 1889. Cram & Wentworth was succeeded by Cram, Wentworth & Goodhue (with Bertram Grosvenor Goodhue) in 1892; and by Cram, Goodhue & Ferguson (CG&F, with Frank W. Ferguson) in 1897. In 1903, CG&F opened a New York office under Bertram Goodhue's direction. Goodhue established his own firm in New York on January 1, 1914, and Cram's Boston firm became Cram & Ferguson.

Ralph Adams Cram designed **Calvary Episcopal Church** (1905–07) for Cram, Goodhue & Ferguson. When the church was completed, Pittsburgh architect John T. Comes observed:

Calvary Church is not a cut and dried study in archeology, nor a copy in any sense of the churches which inspired it; ... it is, withal, vital and modern, full of details and motives that are interesting and refreshing; it is as though one had mastered a long-forgotten language, had acquired the ideas and felt the ideals to which it gave expression, had read the meaning of an old faith and civilization and had translated them all into the speech of the day.[117]

Calvary Church is remarkable as the meeting place of two generations of ecclesiastical craftsmen. By 1910, it boasted artwork by founding members of the Society of Arts and Crafts, Boston—sculptor John Evans, tile maker William Grueby, woodcarver John Kirchmayer, and stained glass artist Harry E. Goodhue. Later, Pittsburgh-trained Charles J. Connick (1875–1945) of Boston, arguably the most important American glazier of the twentieth century, provided some seventy windows, installed between 1922 and 1939. Connick has been called "a profound advocate for the craft reform ideals articulated by William Morris."[118] [National Register of Historic Places; Historic Landmark plaque]

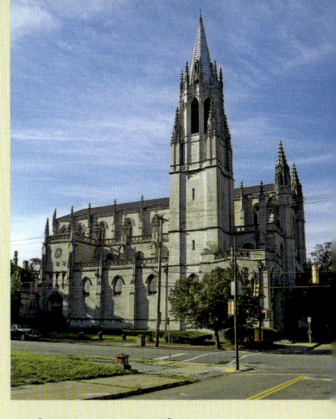

Holy Rosary Roman Catholic Church (1926–31) was designed by Ralph Adams Cram for Cram & Ferguson. It has been called "a superb city church" with an exterior inspired by late Spanish Gothic architecture: "Vastly more ornamental than was Cram's usual practice, it is perhaps the most elegantly detailed exterior he ever essayed, though the underlying strength of mass is still keenly felt."[119] The great rose window was created by Wright Goodhue (1905–31). Holy Rosary is no longer a parish church and, according to a spokesman for the Pittsburgh Roman Catholic Diocese, it is only used for special events. *[Historic Landmark plaque]*

Holy Rosary, North Lang Avenue and Kelly Street, Homewood

Spanish Gothic cathedrals also inspired **East Liberty Presbyterian Church** (1930–35), designed by Ralph Adams Cram for Cram & Ferguson. In his autobiography, published in 1936, Cram wrote about "the great church at East Liberty, Pittsburgh" as:

> one of those opportunities that come no more than once in a lifetime, and is the sort of thing an architect sees in his dreams, but hardly hopes for in realization: a church of cathedral size and general design, cruciform, with a great chancel and lofty tower

East Liberty Presbyterian Church, 116 S. Highland Avenue, with the Highland Building of 1910 (left), by D. H. Burnham

and spire over the crossing; built of solid masonry even to the high vaults, and with all manner of chapels, school, and social rooms; furthermore, an expressed desire on the part of the donors that this should be the finest example of church building the architects could accomplish and that money could buy.[120]

Commissioned by Richard Beatty and Jennie King Mellon in memory of their mothers, East Liberty Presbyterian Church provided an opportunity for Cram to oversee the design and decoration of a new "church of cathedral size" that united "Cram's love of the Gothic church and his fascination with the modernist skyscraper."[121] Seven American stained glass studios participated and more than nine firms executed stone carving, woodwork, and metal work. *[National Register District; Historic Landmark plaque]*

First Baptist Church (1909–11), by Bertram Goodhue, of Cram, Goodhue & Ferguson, is considered one of Goodhue's finest churches. An architecture critic wrote in 1912: "It is, of all the work of this firm which has so far been constructed, the most interesting and the most beautiful, and its interest is due very greatly to the fact that it is to such a slight extent traditional and to such a great extent original. ... It is genuine modern architecture."[122] The principal stained glass windows in First Baptist were designed and made by Charles J. Connick in 1911–12. The War Memorial, *St. Michael*, was designed by Goodhue and carved by Lee Lawrie; the woodwork is by Irving & Casson (New York); and the chancel floor tile came from Pewabic Pottery (Detroit, Michigan).[123] *[National Register District; City Historic District; Historic Landmark plaque]*

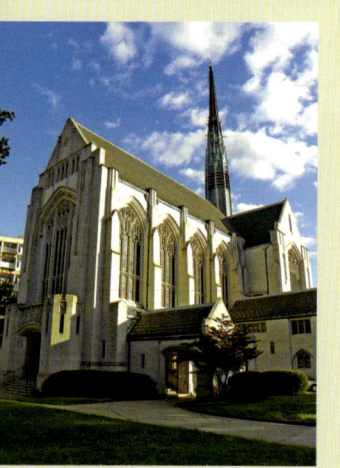

First Baptist, 159 N. Bellefield Avenue, Oakland

John T. Comes (1873–1922) was born in Luxemburg. His family emigrated to the United States and he studied architecture at Mount St. Mary's, Emmitsburg, Maryland. Comes arrived in Pittsburgh in 1894. He was the catalyst behind the organization of the Pittsburgh Architectural Club (1896) and he led a group of local Roman Catholic architects specializing in the design of churches, schools, and convents. Carlton Strong, William P. Hutchins, Albert F. Link, Leo A. McMullen, William R. Perry, and Edward J. Weber all designed highly accomplished ecclesiastical architecture. In the process, they provided work for local artists—

sculptor Franz Aretz, glaziers George and Alice Sotter and Leo Pitassi—and for professionals from the United States—glaziers Harry E. Goodhue and Wright Goodhue (Boston)—and from Europe—glazier Leo Thomas for Georg Boos (Munich). **St. Agnes Roman Catholic Church** (1914–17), now **St. Agnes Center of Carlow University**, is a variation of the Tuscan Romanesque church with red brick and stone trim favored by Comes. With its brown textured brick façade and lavishly modeled terra cotta, St. Agnes incorporates both Byzantine and Romanesque elements. The stained glass windows were designed by George Sotter and Leo Pitassi; the sculpture (and metalwork) were created by Franz Aretz. The murals were designed by Felix B. Lieftuchter of Cincinnati and painted by him and by Pittsburgh art students Helen Hartz and Ann Murray under his direction, 1930–32. The Fifth Avenue façade window is set within a splendid stone Art Moderne "Calvary group" by Franz Aretz (see *photo, page 112*). *[Historic Landmark plaque]*

St. Agnes, 3201 Fifth Avenue, Oakland, designed by Comes

Carlton Strong (1869–1931) was educated in Buffalo, then attended the University of Ottawa, Canada. He returned to Buffalo and apprenticed with architect Richard A. Waite. Strong began his own practice in Buffalo in 1888. He moved to New York City in 1900 and gained a reputation as an architect of hotels and apartment buildings. The commission to design Bellefield Dwellings (1902–04) brought him to Pittsburgh, and in 1906 he moved to Pittsburgh. Strong became a Roman Catholic in 1910 and thereafter specialized in ecclesiastical buildings. The groundbreaking for **Sacred Heart Roman Catholic Church** (1926–54) was March 7, 1924; the choir and sanctuary were dedicated in 1929, and the façade window was dedicated in 1931, the year Strong died. His successor firm, Kaiser, Neal & Reid, completed the church.

Sacred Heart, 310 Shady Avenue, Shadyside

Stone carving at Sacred Heart was done by Franz Aretz and by Angelo Lualdi of Florence, Italy, and Cambridge, Massachusetts. Woodcarving was by Xavier Hochenleitner, Oberammergau, Germany. Polish artist Jan de Rosen painted the murals in the Sacred Heart Chapel. All of the stained glass windows were designed by George and Alice Sotter and were made in Pittsburgh at Hunt Stained Glass Studios. These artists followed an iconographic program dedicated to illustrating the history of the Roman Catholic Church in America. *[Historic Landmark plaque]*

Sacred Heart depicted in stained glass

William P. Hutchins (1883–1941) was born in Neath, Wales, and was an infant when his parents came to Pittsburgh.[124] He attended night classes at Carnegie Technical Schools from 1905 to 1906, and attended the University of Pennsylvania's School of Architecture, graduating in 1908. At the outset of a practice that lasted from 1908 to 1941, Hutchins designed commercial and industrial buildings and houses. In the 1920s, Hutchins began to specialize in church architecture; especially noteworthy is **St. James Roman Catholic Church** (1928–30). The tower of St. James is reminiscent of York Cathedral in England and is decorated with winged angels and swans. The cruciform interior of the Indiana limestone building is uncluttered and open. Floors are laid with marble from Greece, Italy, Ireland, Minnesota, and Vermont. Eighty feet above, the paneled ceiling is solid chestnut. Oak was used elsewhere, most notably in the thirty-five-foot-high altar screen and canopy. The altar is backed by a twelve-foot-high Venetian marble mosaic depicting the eclipse of the sun during the Crucifixion, framed by green marble Gothic arches from Genoa; two days were needed to install the 2,700-pound mosaic. Eighty windows were designed and made by Wright Goodhue.[125]

St. James, 718 Franklin Avenue, Wilkinsburg

Details, St. James Roman Catholic Church, Wilkinsburg

119

Church of the Redeemer, 5700 Forbes Avenue, Squirrel Hill

The Episcopal Church of the Redeemer (1936–37) was designed by E. Donald Robb, of Frohman, Robb & Little, the third and final architects of the National Cathedral in Washington, D.C. Robb (1880–1942) apprenticed in Philadelphia with Theophilus P. Chandler (architect of the First and Third Presbyterian Churches in Pittsburgh) and Cope & Stewardson. In 1903, he joined Cram, Goodhue & Ferguson, working in both the Boston and New York offices. He prepared the presentation drawing for Goodhue's First Baptist Church. The Episcopal Church of the Redeemer was designed and built in 1936–37. However, the building incorporates earlier structures erected after the parish was established in 1903. According to James D. Van Trump, the principal structure, a stucco building of 1913, was "turned around, set on new foundations, encased in Gothic stone work, and a stone tower was added." The Church of the Redeemer exhibits "a fineness of scale and proportion and an amiable forthrightness of aspect that make it one of the best things of its kind in Pittsburgh."[126] The stained glass windows were designed and made between 1939 and 1962 by Howard Gilman Wilbert (1891–1966) of Pittsburgh Stained Glass Studio. *[Historic Landmark plaque]*

The forty-two-story Collegiate Gothic/Art Deco Cathedral of Learning, described by Walter C. Kidney as "an absurd but beautiful tower,"[127] forms the architectural center of what Kidney called the **University of Pittsburgh Cathedral of Learning Campus** (1926–38). Three buildings comprise the Oakland campus conceived by University Chancellor John Bowman and designed by Philadelphia architect Charles Zeller Klauder (1872–1938): the Cathedral of Learning (1926–37); the Stephen Foster Memorial (1935–37); and Heinz Memorial Chapel (1934–38). Some windows in the Cathedral and all the windows in the Foster Memorial museum and Heinz Chapel are by Charles J. Connick. *[National Register of Historic Places District; City Historic District; Historic Landmark plaques]*

Commons Room, Cathedral of Learning (above); Cathedral of Learning and Heinz Memorial Chapel (below), University of Pittsburgh, Oakland

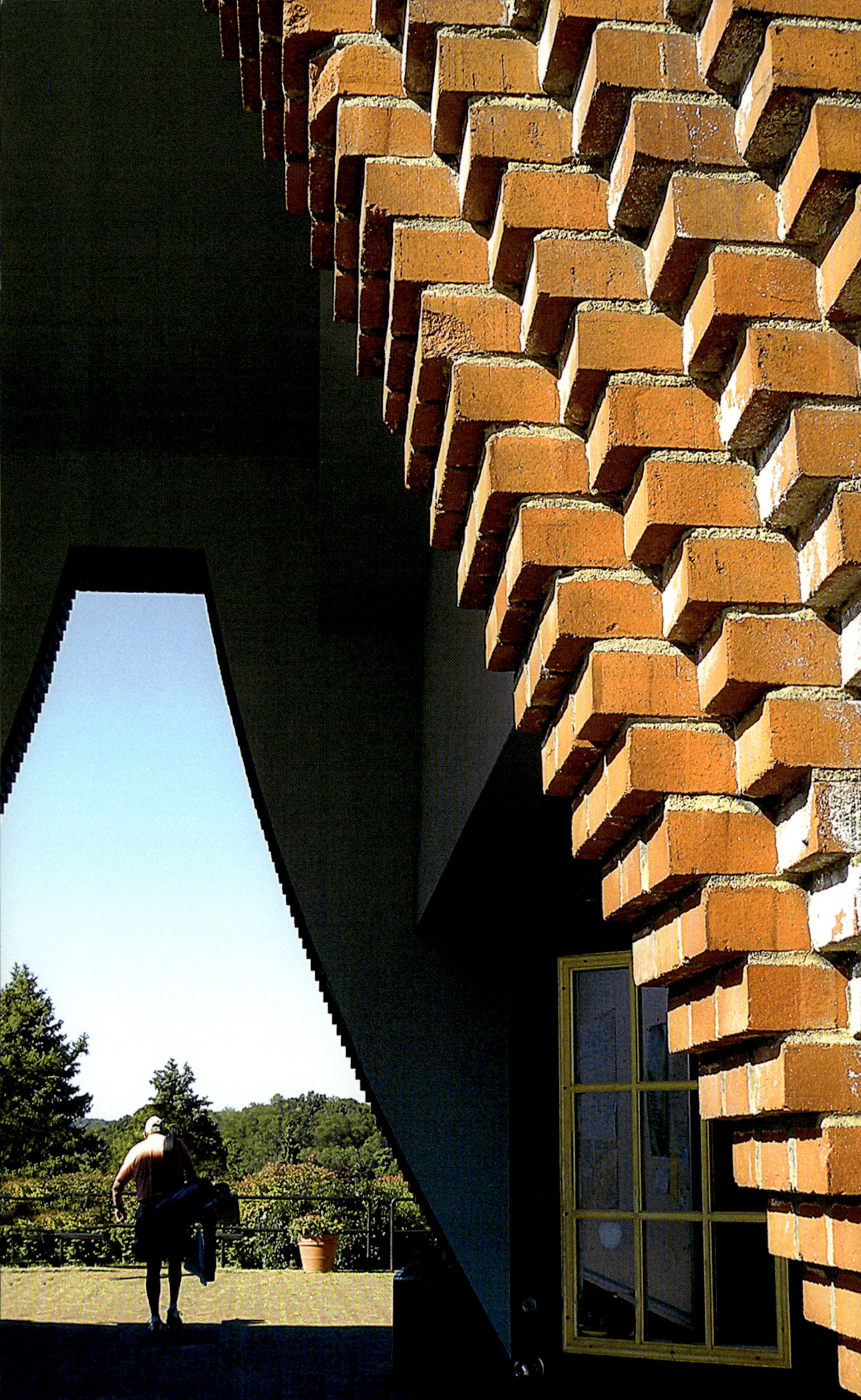

Expressionism

Expressionism has been characterized as a twentieth-century architectural movement that did not emphasize function but sought "to create free and powerful sculptural forms, often crystalline, sometimes sharply angular, and occasionally stalactitic."[128] Expressionism appears in the work of Dutch architects and designers in Amsterdam (1912–30) whose buildings "reveal a great plasticity in their forms; sculptural ornament and coloristic differentiation of the various materials (brick, tile, wood) play an essential role in the designs."[129] Expressionism also flourished in other parts of the Netherlands, Scandinavia, Germany, and Switzerland; some of the iconic Germanic Expressionist buildings include Bruno Taut's glass pavilion at the 1914 Cologne exhibition sponsored by the *Deutsche Werkbund* (an organization of German workshops established in 1907), Hans Poelzig's 1918–19 Grand Playhouse in Berlin (destroyed), Eric Mendelsohn's 1919–21 Einstein Tower in Potsdam, and Rudolf Steiner's 1924–28 *Goetheanum* in Dornach, Switzerland.[130] Eric Mendelsohn gave an illustrated lecture in Pittsburgh on October 21, 1924 to a joint meeting of the Pittsburgh Chapter AIA and the Pittsburgh Architectural Club. One spectator was unimpressed:

> American grain elevators and a few of Frank Lloyd Wright's works were shown, and the lecturer looked upon these as being of great promise. Industrial buildings in this country, however, were subject to severe criticism, and compared unfavorably with German efforts. Freakish apartments and public buildings in Holland were presented as being in step with the new expressionism.[131]

Two Pittsburgh-area buildings of the later 1930s are expressionistic in character.

Henry Hornbostel (1867–1961) was born in Brooklyn, New York. He studied architecture at the Columbia University School of Mines from 1887 to 1891. Hornbostel worked for the New York firm of Wood & Palmer from 1890 to 1894. In 1894, he attended the Ecole des Beaux-Arts in Paris (through 1897). He returned to New York City and began a partnership in the firm of Raymond & Hornbostel and later in Palmer, Wood & Hornbostel. He taught at Columbia School of Architecture from 1897 until 1903. In 1904, Hornbostel won the competition to design Carnegie Technical Schools in Pittsburgh. He established its Department of Architecture and taught there from 1905 to 1917. Hornbostel moved to Pittsburgh in 1920. In the 1930s, he served as Director of Allegheny County Parks. He retired in 1939 and moved to Connecticut.

Hornbostel designed some seventy buildings in Pittsburgh, including the Carnegie Tech campus and first buildings (1905–18); Congregation Rodef Shalom (1906–07); Soldiers' and Sailors' Memorial (1907–10); a master plan for the University of Pittsburgh and designs for five campus buildings (1908–12); the City-County Building with Edward B. Lee (1915–17); Smithfield United Church (1925–26); Grant Building (1927–30); Allegheny County Airport additions (1936); buildings at South Park (1938); buildings in North Park (1936–39); and many houses.

27. South Park Golf Club House
East Park Drive (off Brownsville Road), South Park Township
Henry Hornbostel, architect, 1938–39
Historic Landmark plaque

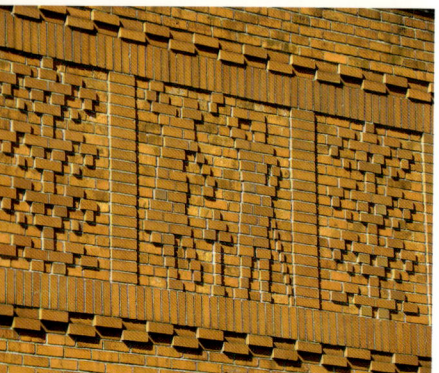

"On his eighty-eighth birthday [in 1955], Hornbostel said to a friend, 'This ultra-modern architecture is the stuff for me. Why, if I were 25 again, these young fellows of today, who think they're so progressive, would look like stuffy conservatives.'"[132]

Whatever "ultra-modern" might mean, Hornbostel did design a striking Expressionist building—the South Park Golf Club House—in 1938. Since then, dapper angular golfers have played in panels set between the second-story windows of the long, narrow, two-story brick building. Truly wonderful is the two-story opening in the center of the building—a dramatic geometric

Expressionism

gesture as well as a ceremonial triumphal arch evoking an ancient civilization (*see photo, page 122*). Hornbostel's source was a temple in Yucatan that he had seen in 1907;[133] its creative adaptation in Pittsburgh recalls Titus de Bobula's 1905 exhortation that American architects should seek inspiration in "our own archeological excavations of Yucatan and Mexico."

For a complete list of Hornbostel's works see Walter C. Kidney, *Henry Hornbostel: An Architect's Master Touch* (2002).

28. Pittsburgh Schiller
(Schiller School)
Peralta and Wettach Streets, North Side
Edward J. Weber, architect, 1939
National Register of Historic Places;
City Historic Structure;
Historic Landmark plaque

Schiller School seems to stand apart from all the other school buildings erected in the 1930s. Its modernity is that of a stark, yet fanciful, German Expressionism. Once again the plan of the building is the now-familiar tripartite one, but here the severe brick exterior rises from a stone base to a brick, diamond-patterned cornice. A series of heavy, flat-topped piers flank doorways, which are dramatically capped by five successive, stepped, triangular lintels. Even in this monochromatic design, one senses the architect's love of brickwork.

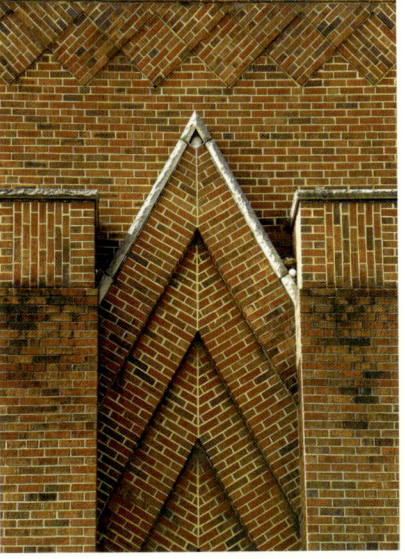

The building may have been inspired by Konrad Wittmann's design for the Great Hall of the City of Hanover Crematory, illustrated in *American Architect*, October 1928, which has a very similar use of the successive triangular lintel.[134]

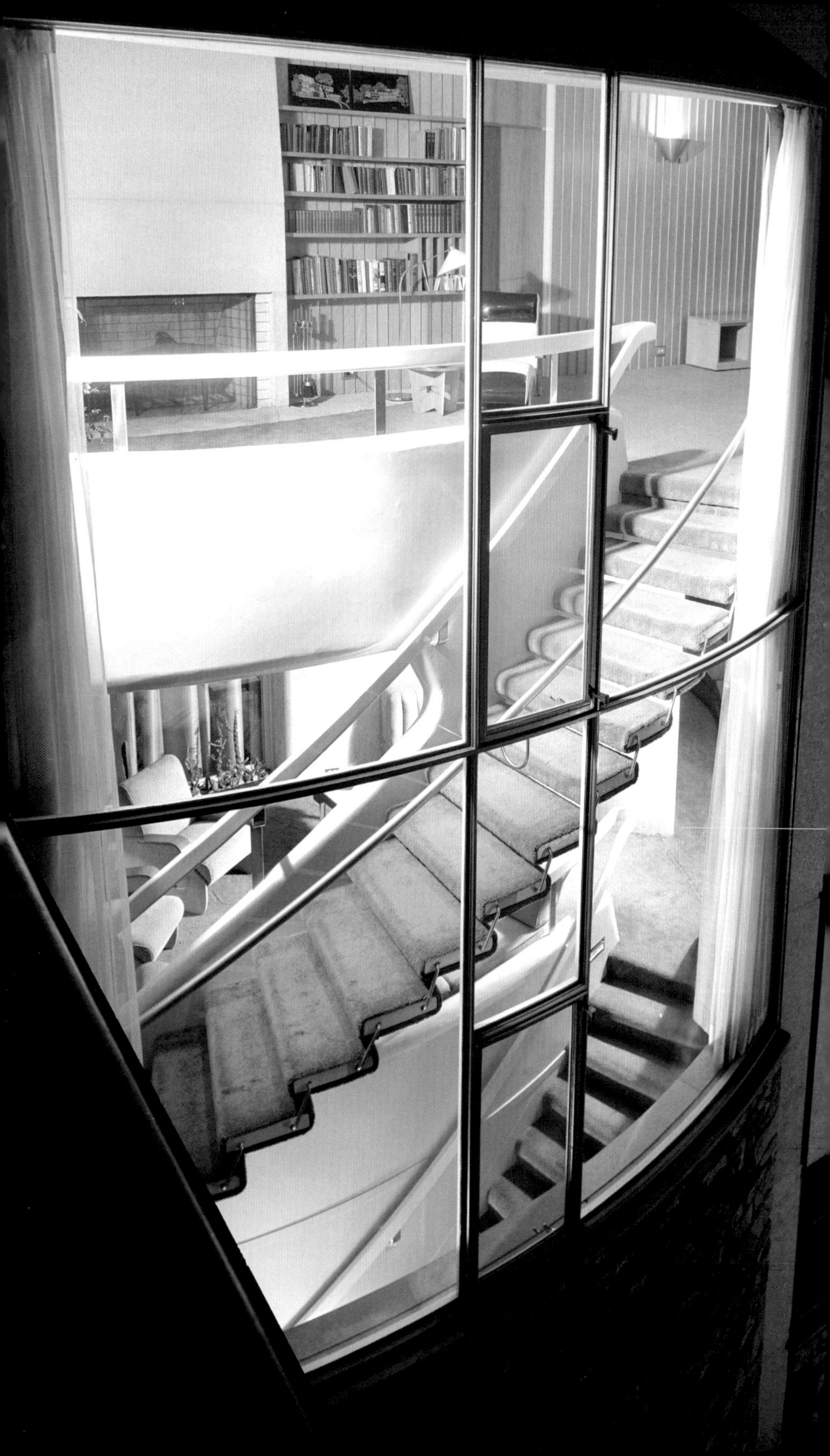

Gropius and Breuer in Pittsburgh

Walter Gropius (1883–1969) had studied architecture in Munich and Berlin, Germany, then worked for architect Peter Behrens in Berlin before establishing a partnership with Adolf Meyer (1910–c. 1925). After serving in World War I, Gropius became founding director in 1919 of the *Bauhaus* in Weimar. The Bauhaus, perhaps best translated in English as "Applied Design School," was formed by the merger of the School of Applied Arts and the Higher Institute of Fine Art. Its "most significant achievement may be its nurturing of a sustained cross-media conversation about the nature of art in the modern age. … the Bauhaus brought together artists, architects, and designers in a kind of cultural think tank for the time."[135] In 1925, the Bauhaus moved to Dessau, Germany. Gropius resigned in 1928 and moved to Berlin where he continued to practice architecture. The Nazi government closed the Bauhaus in 1933. In 1934, Gropius moved to England; his former Bauhaus colleague **Marcel Breuer** (1902–81) joined him in 1935. In 1936, Gropius was invited to join the faculty of Harvard's Graduate School of Design as professor and chairman. He accepted the position and arrived in the United States in 1937. Gropius invited Breuer to join the Harvard faculty and they established an architectural practice in 1937 that continued until 1941. (Breuer left Harvard in 1947; Gropius in 1952.)

29. Cecelia and Robert Frank House
Alan I W Frank House
96 East Woodland Road, Shadyside
Walter Gropius and Marcel Breuer
(Cambridge, MA), architects, 1939–40

Commissioned by one of Pittsburgh's oldest glass and steel manufacturing families, the Frank House was the sixth residence designed by the Walter Gropius/Marcel Breuer partnership. An article on the Frank House appeared in the March 1941 issue of *Architectural Forum*:

Marcel Breuer designed all the furniture in the Frank House: the study (left) and the dining room (right).

> *In its use of random ashlar, stone veneer, travertine and natural wood is indicated a new interest in natural materials. Also worth noting is the disintegration of the rectangle into freer shapes, as in the stairway, garden walls and entrance vestibule. If in so important an example such drastic modifications are to be seen, there is a new and impressive evidence that contemporary architecture is entering a new phase, richer, more assured, and more human.*

Inside, graceful curves soften rectilinear spaces; walls are paneled with warm pearwood, English sycamore and redwood, or are travertine or stone. Breuer designed wood, fabric, and leather furniture to express the individual character of each room. Carpets, curtains, and other furnishings were designed or chosen by the architects.

With four levels of living space, an indoor swimming pool, and a rooftop dance floor, the Frank House was the largest residence designed by Gropius and Breuer.[136]

Marcel Breuer took issue with the *Architectural Forum's* characterization of the Frank House as "International Style":

> *They used intentionally the term "International Style" which was never used by us, and which I am quite certain, is misleading. It is misleading as "international" and it is misleading as "style" and I would appreciate it very much if you would call our architecture simply "modern" or "contemporary." These are not very definite terms but we have no better ones.*[137]

Barry Bergdoll noted that the great "sensuously curved and cantilevered" interior stair (*see page 126*) "is echoed in a sculptural exterior stair of concrete taking visitors from the front to the back garden via an open terrace."

In a 2009 article on the Frank House, Barry Bergdoll, MoMA chief curator of architecture and design, noted that Gropius's 1920 commission to design a house in Berlin for industrialist Adolf Sommerfeld provided the architect with "a chance to work with a client to realize a house as a total work of art and a laboratory for technical innovations." The Sommerfeld house, destroyed in World War II, has been frequently illustrated and discussed. Bergdoll considers the less well-known Frank House in Pittsburgh "as innovative and as unusual in the Gropius and Breuer oeuvre as the Sommerfeld house." The story of the collaboration of the architects and the client, and the virtually unchanged character of the house, makes this residence "one of the best kept secrets of American Modernism." Bergdoll continued:

> *As the design was nearing its final form Gropius wrote in a letter to Robert J. Frank: "I must confess that I am deeply in love with the whole*

project and that I expect the house to be very noble in appearance."
In its myriad innovations, it was at once unique in Breuer and Gropius's career and the seedbed of much to come.[138]

Bergdoll has written on the website for the Frank House:

The Frank House is a culmination of the ideal of the complete environment long dreamed of in the European avant-gardes and the Bauhaus, which Gropius founded in 1919 and where Breuer was one of the earliest and most gifted students. In Pittsburgh they realized their masterpiece of the integration of architecture, furnishings, and landscape.[139]

The clients' son, Alan I W Frank, has established a nonprofit foundation to preserve the home and its contents as an architectural museum. The website is **www.thefrankhouse.org**.

Gropius and Breuer in Pittsburgh

Black-and-white images by Ezra Stoller; color images by Richard Pare and Richard Barnes.
All rights, including copyrights, reserved by Alan I W Frank and used with his permission.

131

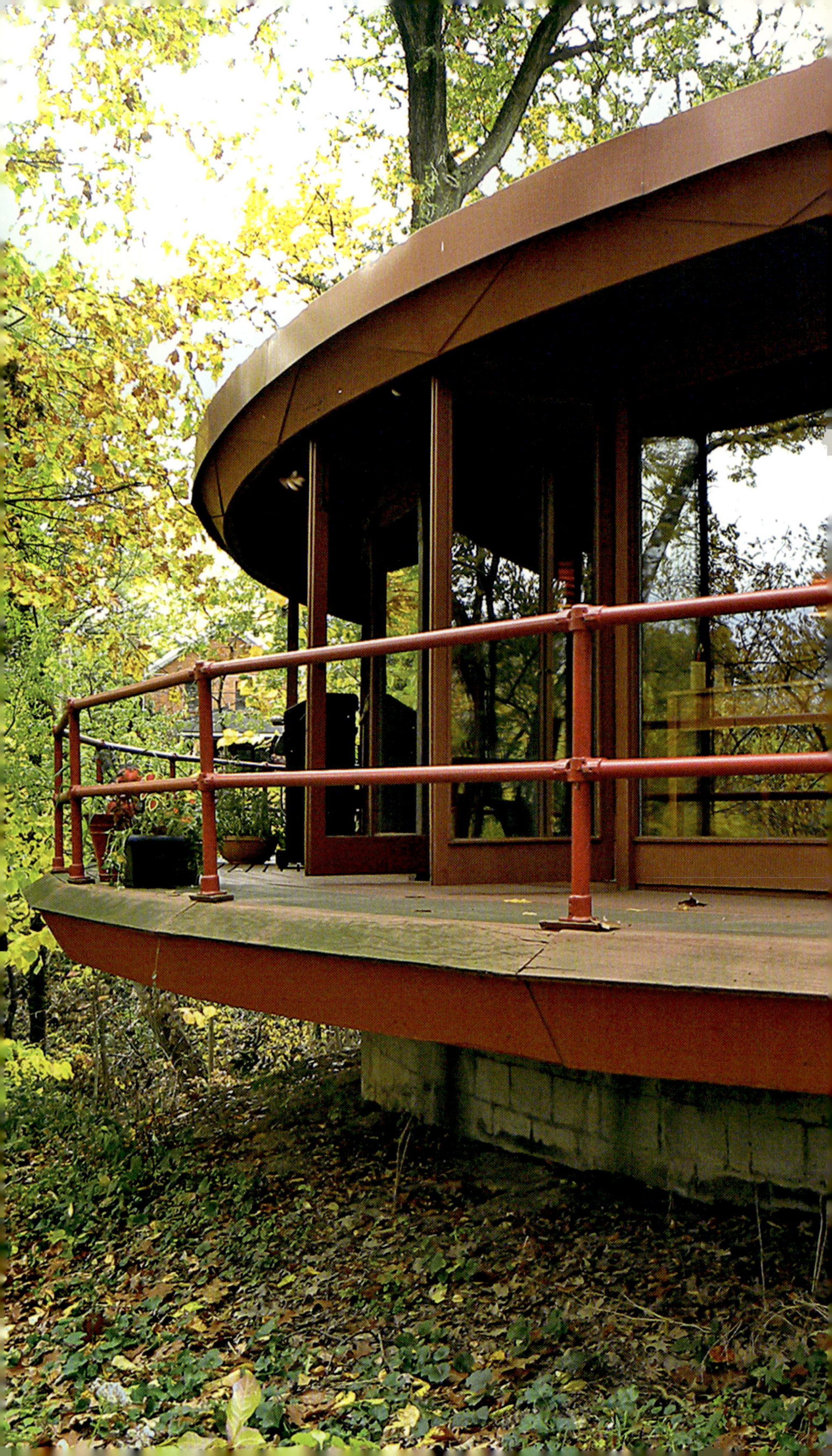

The Legacy of Frank Lloyd Wright

In 1932, Frank Lloyd Wright (1867–1959) established an apprenticeship program in Spring Green, Wisconsin, called the Taliesin Fellowship, after his Wisconsin home (the name is Welsh; it means "shining brow" and was the name of a Welsh poet). Apprentices paid a fee to work on Wright designs under Wright's direction. In addition, the apprentices maintained the Taliesin buildings, worked on the Taliesin farm, shared food preparation duties, displayed their musical and theatrical talents, and participated in a communal existence revolving around the life and work of a master architect. The Taliesin Fellowship would be an integral part of Wright's remaining twenty-seven years which saw the design of some of the most acclaimed buildings of his career: Fallingwater (1935–38), the Johnson Wax Buildings (1936/1944/1951), Wingspread (1937), Taliesin West (1937 and after), the Guggenheim Museum (1944–59), and the Marin County Civic Center (1957–70). Since Wright's death in 1959, the Taliesin Fellowship has been one of the principal heirs of his estate.

During the 1930s, Wright explored modest designs for moderately priced homes suitable for twentieth-century American lifestyles—a preoccupation of his throughout his career and one realized beginning in 1900 in his "Prairie" houses. In the 1930s, he called such houses "Usonian" (adapted from United States of America) and the house he designed in 1936 for the Jacobs family in Madison, Wisconsin, is widely considered to be the first. Although the design of Usonian houses varied, each house contained standardized elements to reduce construction costs while providing the kind of domestic environment Wright considered desirable—a carport instead of a garage, no basement, a heating system embedded in the floors, built-in indirect lighting, built-in furniture, and natural wood cladding (rather than plaster or paint). Like all Wright houses, however modest, a fireplace was essential. Brick, stone, and wood were considered desirable building materials.

Opposite: Saul and Edith Lipkind House (1954–56), Swisshelm Park, designed by Taliesin Fellows Peter Berndtson and Cornelia Brierly

In 1932, Frank Lloyd Wright published *An Autobiography*. One reader was **Cornelia Brierly** (1913–2012), a Pittsburgh-area resident and Carnegie Tech architecture student. Inspired by the book and dissatisfied with her course of study, Cornelia applied for admission to the Taliesin Fellowship; she arrived in 1934 and was there while Fallingwater and the major projects of the 1930s were designed and constructed.[140] In 1938, **Peter Berndtson** (1909–72), a Massachusetts native who had studied architecture at MIT, joined the Fellowship. Peter had worked as a painter and set designer in New York City, and later apprenticed there with an architectural firm. Peter and Cornelia were married in 1939.

In 1939, Cornelia designed Pennsylvania's first Usonian house for her aunts, Hulda and Louise Notz, in West Mifflin, eight miles south of downtown Pittsburgh. Soon after, the Berndtsons moved to Spokane, Washington, returning when possible to Taliesin. In 1946, Cornelia and Peter and their two daughters moved to Laughlintown, Pennsylvania, near Ligonier in Westmoreland County, and they established their architectural practice.

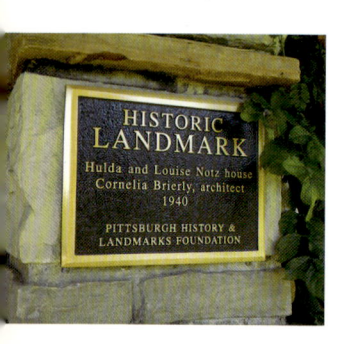

They worked together for a decade. Peter designed buildings and furniture; Cornelia focused on interior design and landscape architecture. Cornelia returned to Taliesin in 1956 and joined Taliesin Architects and became an instructor at the Frank Lloyd Wright School of Architecture.[141] Cornelia and Peter divorced in 1957. Peter moved into Pittsburgh and established an office in East Liberty, where he practiced until his death in 1972.

Together and separately, Cornelia Brierly and Peter Berndtson created some of the finest Wrightian residential architecture to be found anywhere. Beginning with the Notz House of 1939 and taking into account their ten-year joint practice and Peter's work between 1957 and 1972, almost ninety designs have been documented. Most are residential, and while buildings were erected as far east as Franconia, New Hampshire, with one in Harrisburg, one in Somerset, and three in State College, Pennsylvania, most of the constructed buildings are in Allegheny and Westmoreland counties.

30. Hulda and Louise Notz House
120 Lutz Lane, West Mifflin
Cornelia Brierly (Taliesin Fellowship, Spring Green, WI), architect, 1939–40; Cornelia Brierly and Peter Berndtson (Laughlintown, PA), architects for additions for Mr. and Mrs. Fay Bear, 1947–50; additions for Mr. and Mrs. Alan Mock, 1953
Historic Landmark plaque

The Notz House was the first of the three houses Cornelia and Peter would erect of the eight houses planned for what came to be called the Meadow Circles project in suburban West Mifflin. In 1999, Cornelia recalled the design and construction of the one-story, stone, flat-roofed Notz House and the subsequent Meadow Circles houses:

I consulted Mr. Wright who suggested the house be designed with a hexagonal unit system.

The unit system for laying out a house has had age-old success in Japan where the number of rectangular floor mats determine the placement of walls and the size of the room. Another dimension is achieved when the walls follow the lines of hexagons inscribed on the concrete floor. By emphasizing the obtuse angle a broader flow of space is achieved. Since I was a novice, Mr. Wright helped me with the plan, construction and overall design. …

Fallingwater, the Edgar J. Kaufmann house, at Bear Run, had just been completed. During the building, masons from that area were trained to lay the stonework more or less as it appears in a quarry. When we needed help these dedicated young men drove down from the mountains every day to lay the stone work for my aunts.

All went well until the young, inexperienced contractor defaulted. My husband Peter and I took over supervision. … Peter not only supervised the building but made some of the furniture. My brother-in-law Blaine Drake …, a graduate of the Carnegie Tech Art School, designed dining chairs that were made for the cost of materials in the manual training department of the school where my aunt was principal.

After my Aunt Louise died, my Aunt Hulda sold the house and 14 acres to Mr. and Mrs. Fay Bear, who hoped to develop a community. They lived in the house until Peter designed a larger house for them on the same property, then sold my aunts' house to a new couple who had us design an addition which very much extended the living space by the simple multiplication of hexagonal units and the same wall construction for a play room, master bedroom and bath.[142] On the same acreage we built another house for Mr. and Mrs. Joseph Katz, using brick masonry instead of stone.

These houses require minimal maintenance of the cypress walls and built-in furniture. There is a warmth and restful quality to the wood, providing comfort and serenity to the owners who have had the experience of living in so quiet an environment.[143]

James D. Van Trump wrote that "Peter Berndtson, while thoroughly imbued with Wrightian architectural theory has notably interpreted it through his own considerable talent."[144] In "Architecture and the Pittsburgh Land: The Buildings of Peter Berndtson," Van Trump also noted the profound impact western Pennsylvania's hills and valleys had on Berndtson's architecture.[145] Berndtson erected some houses on fairly flat terrain, but he was particularly inspired by the steep hills, siting buildings at the top or, more remarkably, descending the slopes, bringing a unique energy and dynamism to the Wrightian idiom.

31. Mr. and Mrs. Jack Landis House
2717 Mt. Royal Road, Squirrel Hill
Peter Berndtson and Cornelia Brierly (Laughlintown, PA), architects, 1947;
additions by Peter Berndtson, architect, for Dr. and Mrs. Richard P. Shapera, n.d.
Historic Landmark plaque

In 1971, Peter Berndtson described five houses he, or he and Cornelia, had designed for a Pittsburgh History & Landmarks Foundation tour. He wrote about the Landis House which he had enlarged for Dr. and Mrs. Shapera:

> The ... lot presented unusual problems. The frontage was only 25 feet, and the ground sloped steeply down from the street so that when the building line was reached, the house was already one story below the street level. The solution was to connect the house to the street through a bridge over which a car could drive to the entrance, which, in this case, was the top level. A study with fireplace, coat closet, maid's room and bath are on this level. One then proceeds **down** through the house. On the middle level are the living-dining spaces, kitchen and powder room. The living room has a fireplace and a cantilevered balcony overlooking an east view. The bedrooms, bath and utility rooms are on the lowest level opening to a small walled court. The materials used in this house are brick and wood siding, each becoming the finish of both the exterior and interior.[146]

The three-story, red-brick, flat-roofed Landis House dramatically descends down a steep and narrow Squirrel Hill slope; residents descend through the house via a vertical central stairway. If the large window on the top floor (originally a study, now a bedroom) hints at the dramatic vista, the cantilevered balcony off the second-floor living room/dining room area provides a magnificent view of the hills and valleys to the east.

32. Dr. and Mrs. Abraam Steinberg House
5139 Penton Road, Squirrel Hill
Peter Berndtson and Cornelia Brierly (Laughlintown, PA), architects, 1952
Historic Landmark plaque

Donald Miller and Aaron Sheon noted: "The design is by far the most ingenious one conceived by Cornelia and Peter."[147] The architect wrote:

The Legacy of Frank Lloyd Wright

The house, set on a steeply sloping corner lot, grows naturally out of its site. … The few materials: brick, redwood, glass and concrete carry through from the exterior to the interior, unifying them as parts of the whole. Spaces within flow into one another visually and actually as ramps lead from one level to another. … Centrally placed within the house is an outdoor garden open to the sky. With its walls completely glazed, its planting and fountain-pool reflect the season and are visible from all the major rooms. Where appropriate, furniture is built-in, using the same wood as the structure and becoming an integral part of the house.[148]

The site of the two-story, flat-roofed Steinberg House is "steeply sloping," yet less vertical than the Landis House. Its outdoor garden, located in the center of the house, is a quarter-circle and anticipates the semi-circular Lipkind House designed the following year.

33. Saul and Edith Lipkind House
1137 Onondago Street, Swisshelm Park
Peter Berndtson and Cornelia Brierly
(Laughlintown, PA), architects, 1954–56
Historic Landmark plaque

Peter Berndtson wrote about the Lipkind House:

The curved side of this lot at the edge of a wooded ravine suggested the fan shape of the plan. All major rooms face east and a continuous balcony projecting from these rooms extends their spaces into the trees of the sloping hillside.

Exterior walls of the house are light weight concrete block and glass. The roof consists of exposed wood beams radiating from a common center and covered with wood planking and a built-up roofing. The floors are of radiantly heated concrete, covered with red tile, while interior walls are of redwood plywood. Cabinets and shelves are built-in. All exposed woodwork is stained. The concrete blocks are left natural.

The rooms include a living-dining area, kitchen, utility, two bedrooms and two baths. The walk from the cobble-paved carport is under cover.

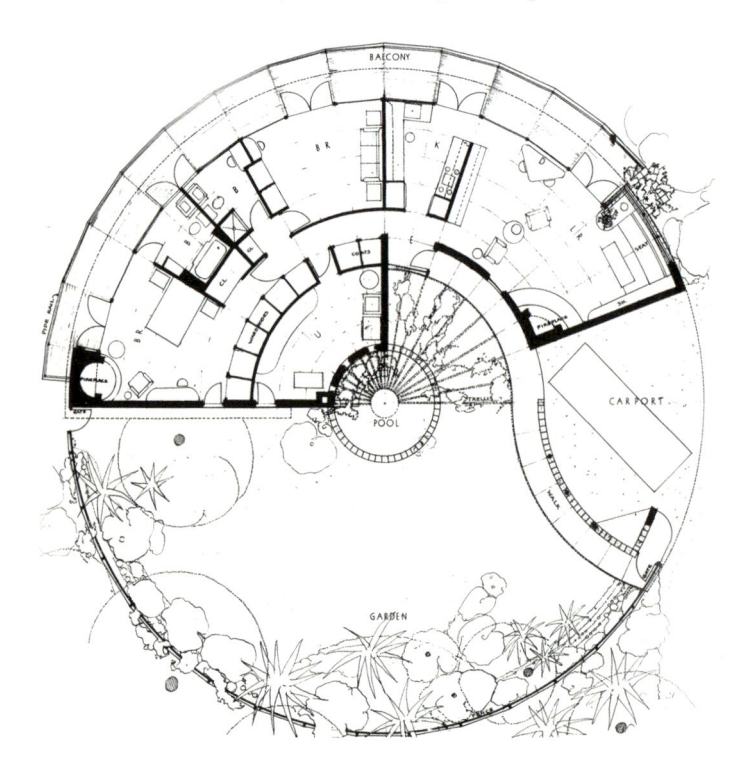

Amenities include two fireplaces, an entrance trellis, a fountain pool and concrete block wall enclosing a garden and completing the circle begun by the fan shaped plan of the house.[149]

Donald Miller and Aaron Sheon described the Lipkind House as "an innovative plan on a limited budget" and cited Edith Lipkind's affirmation that the house completely "answered her practical and psychological needs for shelter."[150] An article on the house published in 2011 stated: "The house contains only a thousand square feet, and has just two bedrooms with no attic or basement. But its placement, and layout, are spectacular."[151]

34. Dr. and Mrs. Harlan Douglas House
155 White Oak Drive, Ross Township
Peter Berndtson, architect, 1962–65
Historic Landmark plaque

The red-brick, flat-roofed Douglas House, described as "the masterpiece of Peter's architecture of the 1960s,"[152] is sited across and in the center of a sloping wooded site. Principal rooms are on the second level. Large plate glass windows overlook the woods, and cantilevered balconies provide access among and above the foliage.

Twenty-three years after Cornelia used the hexagon in the Notz House, it reappears in Peter's Douglas House. He wrote that the Douglas House:

was placed to become an integral part of the landscape. … House module is an expanding hexagon increasing in two-foot increments. … Elements of the building and their junctions work with the system, imparting unity and sense of flow. Bricks dovetailing at obtuse angle corners provide decorative patterns. … The centrally located brick core, rising through the house from the foundation through the roof, contains almost all the major utilities. All built-ins, seats, table and hassocks designed by the Architect.[153]

142

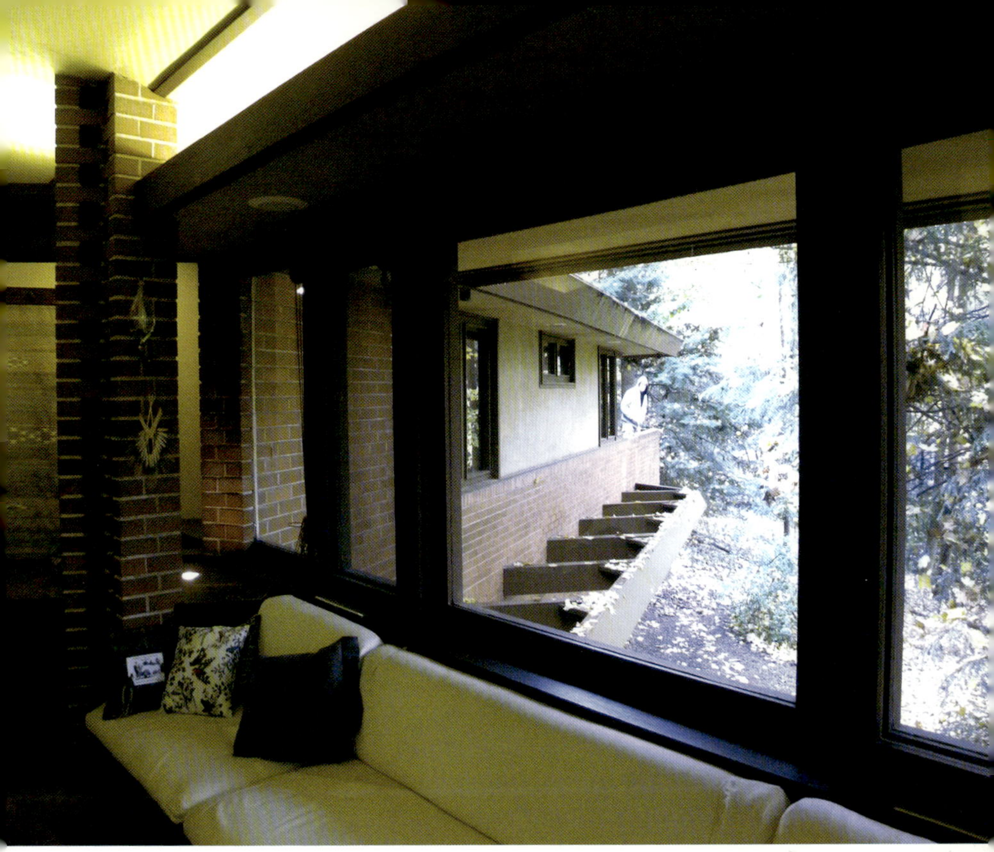

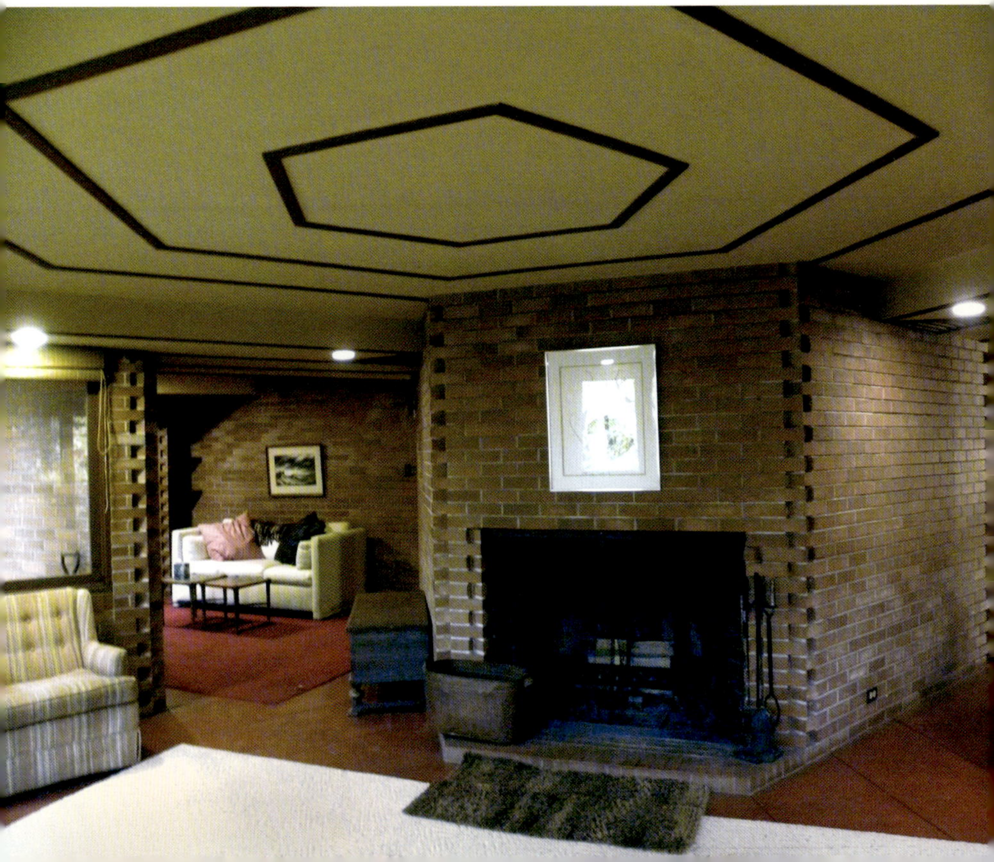

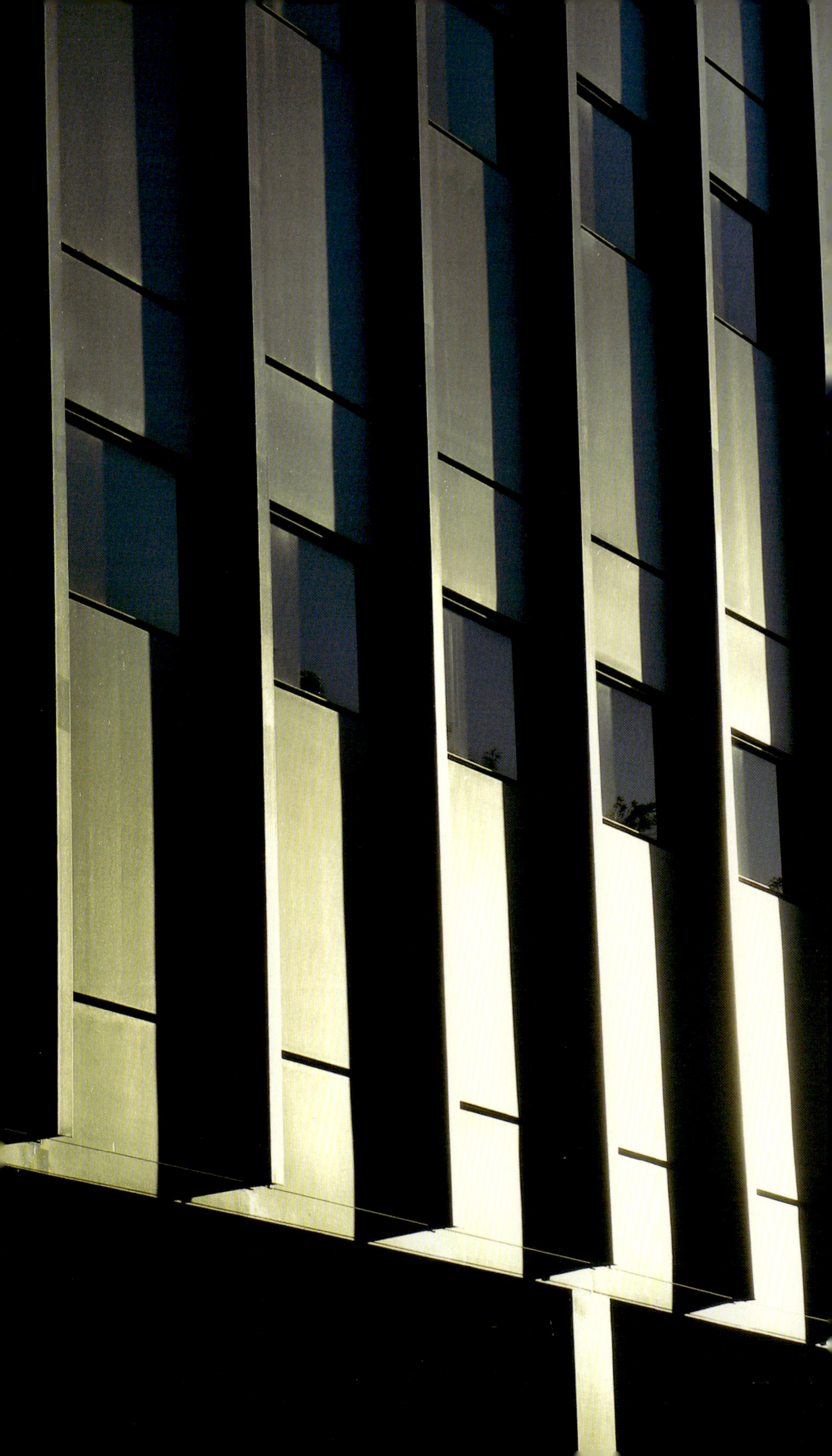

Miesian

In 1938, **Ludwig Mies van der Rohe** (1886–1969), who had been the last director of the Bauhaus in 1930–33, arrived in Chicago to head the Armour Institute, which was renamed Illinois Institute of Technology (IIT) in 1940.

> Shortly after his appointment, Mies was asked to create a new campus for the school. The result became the first entirely modern academic complex in the country. ... a three-dimensional expression of Mies's search for an architecture that was so thoroughly reduced in both form and function to its essence that it could be turned to almost any use and, he hoped, repeated with relative ease. ... Mies strove mightily for an architectural Urtyp, an essential form that would be infinitely flexible.[154]

35. Richard King Mellon Hall of Science
Duquesne University, The Bluff
Ludwig Mies van der Rohe (Chicago, IL), architect, and Paul Schweikher, supervising architect, 1962–68

Mellon Hall is a descendant of the IIT campus. The invitation to design Mellon Hall came from Mies's former Chicago colleague and friend Paul Schweikher, then Head, Department of Architecture, Carnegie Tech, at the request of Duquesne University. Early in January 1962, Mies enthusiastically accepted the commission to design his first (and only) building in Pittsburgh: "I have spent my life developing an architecture of steel and glass and now I shall have an opportunity to do a building in the steel and glass center of America."[155]

Mies authority Franz Schulze described Mellon Hall:

> the ground floor is set back from the outer wall plane, providing an arcade one bay deep around the whole structure. The plan is symmetrical,

with the auditoriums set longitudinally in the center, flanked by equipment rooms and staircases which lead to the second floor. The top three stories contain classrooms, offices, and laboratories.[156]

Vertical steel mullions on the north and south façades of the building provide support to the top three stories and draw the viewer's eyes upward, producing a visual, rhythmic counterpoint to the long, low, horizontal, four-story structure. The sense of verticality is further enhanced by the unique combination (for Mies) of solid, steel-plate walls with small window openings. Since laboratories, not classrooms, are located on the north and south sides of the upper floors of Mellon Hall, the "areas that are glazed in the standard Mies wall are infilled with steel panels for the bottom two-thirds of what would normally be glass."[157] The short east and west sides of the building have full-length windows in the center.

Academic buildings—even by distinguished architects—are often in jeopardy. The exterior and the first floor of Mellon Hall still exhibit the original, classic Miesian elements often found in his architecture, whether academic, commercial, or residential: symmetry; "crisp steel and glass";[158] and, in the interior, the use of brick, wood, and terrazzo, and spare, but elegant, stair railings.

A. James Speyer (1913–86) was born and educated in Pittsburgh. Speyer (pronounced "Spire") graduated from Carnegie Tech in architecture in 1934. After several years of study abroad, he enrolled in 1938 at the Armour Institute in Chicago (later IIT) in order to work with Ludwig Mies van der Rohe; he became Mies' first American graduate student. In 1946, Speyer joined the IIT faculty and established his architectural practice. Between 1947 and 1963, five of the houses Speyer designed were constructed—three were built in metropolitan Chicago and two were built in Pittsburgh's East End neighborhood. In 1961, Speyer became curator of twentieth-century collections at the Art Institute of Chicago.

36. Joan and Jerome Apt House
Woodland Road, Shadyside
A. James Speyer (Chicago, IL), architect, 1950–52

Joan Apt's parents were Cecelia and Robert Frank. Joan grew up in the Frank House, designed by Walter Gropius and Marcel Breuer, and studied the plans from the age of nine. Her experience living there influenced the design of this house. The Apt House—the first house Speyer designed in Pittsburgh and the third of his five executed residential commissions—is nestled in a wooded hillside sloping down toward Woodland Road, a private road. Sited on approximately two acres, this urban house is given a secluded country feeling, especially when the spring, summer, and fall foliage are in bloom. The house can only be glimpsed in the winter from a distance, beyond and above the tennis court on the lower portion of the property. However, the prominence of the architect/curator, his small body of work, and the excellence of the design requires that the Apt House be included in this Guide.

> *The volume of the house, which rests on a single long [concrete] plinth, is vintage Speyer: its steel frame encloses walls of brick [in various shades*

Pittsburgh Architecture in the Twentieth Century

of deep purple] … and floor-to-ceiling glass. … The use of glass and wood in the living room of the Apt House is, moreover, typical of Speyer. On the other hand, a brick wall encloses a fireplace framed by a round arch. … As Speyer put it, "At the time nobody was using arches, and certainly not Mies van der Rohe."[159]

To compound the heresy, Franz Schulze noted "Speyer repeated the round [Roman] arch in the three entries to the garage." Speyer showed photos of the house to Mies, who did not object to the arches, which evoke, whether intentionally or not, the arcaded brick front of H. H. Richardson's Emmanuel Episcopal Church (*see photo, page 12*).

Speyer further recollected that this divergence from a presumed norm represented a growing personal creative freedom. Certainly nothing in his work prior to the Apt House prefigures its imaginative entryway, which is located at the base of a staircase flanked by two stout brick ramparts. These abut the brick walls of the exterior of the house in a manner that brings to mind the right-angled intersections common to compositions of the Dutch De Stijl movement.[160]

Based on the roofline, the house is an efficient 100 feet by 40 feet, yet it accommodates an entry hall, living room, dining room, kitchen, gameroom, six bedrooms, five bathrooms, and ample storage. Mrs. Apt collaborated with the architect in regard to the aesthetics and asked Speyer to add a closet anywhere there was "an inch" of available space. Her husband, Jerry, provided engineering expertise. Natural light from the floor-to-ceiling and clerestory windows illuminates the oak and teak woodwork and brickwork in the elegant, spacious interior. A landscaped terrace extends beyond the main house and serves as the roof of the three-car garage.

Many mature trees were growing on the property when the house was built. The Apts planted 500 white native dogwood trees and hawthorn, white azaleas, mountain laurel, and other native trees and bushes. Mrs. Apt describes her experience of living in the house as "living outdoors, inside."[161]

37. Tillie S. Speyer House
1500 Wightman Street,
Squirrel Hill
A. James Speyer (Chicago, IL),
architect, 1963

The house Speyer designed for his widowed mother in 1963 is located at the corner of Wightman and Northumberland streets. While the Apt House is one story, the Speyer House is two stories with rooms grouped around a central atrium. "Speyer includes several references to Miesian models, juxtaposing them in a lively, inventively personal way." The house is "almost totally bordered by long low brick walls reminiscent of Mies's 1923 project for a brick country house." Inside, "a two-ramp staircase that draws upon Mies's 1951 design for the interior of the Arts Club of Chicago"[162] (and similar to the stairways in Mies's Mellon Hall under design in 1963) provides access between floors.[163] The main house is located at the northern end of the lot; a sunken garden separates it from the building that housed a studio for Mrs. Speyer at the south end.

A close friend of the Kaufmanns and Franks, Mrs. Speyer was an art mentor and collector; she began to sculpt at age 70.

The work of **Skidmore, Owings & Merrill** (SOM) "had a profound effect on the development of architecture in the USA,"[164] but their presence in Pittsburgh was minor as compared to their work in New York or Chicago. SOM's principal Pittsburgh patron was Henry J. Heinz II. In the 1950s, SOM's New York office designed three buildings for the H. J. Heinz Company, and, in the 1960s, Mr. Heinz asked SOM to prepare plans for a symphony hall similar to Philharmonic Hall at Lincoln Center, as part of a proposed Lower Hill Cultural Center (*see pages 197–201*). The plan was never realized, and in 1967, the Howard Heinz Endowment instead purchased and renovated the former Penn Theatre in downtown Pittsburgh, which opened in 1971 as Heinz Hall, the new home of the Pittsburgh Symphony Orchestra.

38. Two PNC Plaza (Equibank Building)
620 Liberty Avenue, Downtown Pittsburgh
Natalie de Blois and Myron Goldsmith of Skidmore, Owings & Merrill (Chicago Office), architects, 1973–75

Henry-Russell Hitchcock observed in *Architecture of Skidmore, Owings & Merrill, 1950–1962*, that Mies van der Rohe's 1940s Chicago architectural vocabulary was "mastered and applied by SOM's designers and technicians" in the 1950s.[165] The senior SOM designers of the elegant Miesian Equibank Building were Myron Goldsmith (1918–96) and Natalie de Blois (1921–2013). Goldsmith lists the building in his book *Buildings and Concepts* (1987), but does not discuss it. However, Goldsmith was a student at the Armour Institute in Chicago when Mies arrived—he has been called "Mies's most important student"—and he worked in Mies's office from 1946 to 1953.[166] Goldsmith joined SOM in 1955: "At SOM he used many devices, formal and structural, that recall the buildings of Mies."[167] Ms. de Blois joined SOM's New York office in 1944 and worked closely with Gordon Bunshaft until 1965 when she transferred to SOM's Chicago office; she resigned in 1974, the only woman to hitherto achieve Associate rank at SOM. In 1973, senior partner Nathaniel Owings wrote: "Her mind and hands worked marvels in design—and only she and God would ever know just how many great solutions, with the imprimatur of one of the male heroes of SOM, owed much more to her than was attributed by either SOM or the client."[168]

The building's plan is two elongated roughly hexagonal shapes, slightly shifted and joined at one side. The building's exterior is thirty-four stories of silver reflective glass with black mullions on an eight-inch-high charcoal granite base. Only the entrance doors have clear glass. An underground parking garage is topped by a pedestrian plaza designed by Simonds & Simonds.

39. Four Allegheny Center (IBM Branch Office Building)
4 Allegheny Center, North Side
Bruno P. Conterato of the Office of Mies van der Rohe (Chicago, IL), architect, 1975

Pittsburgh has one building *designed* by Mies van der Rohe (the Richard King Mellon Hall of Science) and numerous "Miesian" buildings. Architects who studied or worked with Mies were involved in the design of all four of the Miesian buildings included in this Guide. Bruno Conterato (1920–95) worked for Mies beginning in 1948; in 1969, he became one of Mies's partners, together with Joseph Fujikawa and Mies's grandson Dirk Lohan (Mies died later that year). The firm continued to practice as the Office of Mies van der Rohe until 1975.

An article on the firm, published in 1977, states that "Conterato is pretty much the firm's man in corporate work. With his longstanding relationship with IBM, he has recently completed … a 10 story tower and 300 car garage for IBM in Pittsburgh."[169]

Unlike Mies's Mellon Hall and SOM's Equibank Building, the steel exterior of the IBM Branch Office Building is white, a façade color Mies had used occasionally. The design incorporates several classic Miesian concepts. At the first floor, the building's perimeter is supported by eighteen freestanding columns, creating a colonnade on all four sides around a recessed lobby. The lobby has a high ceiling, walls of glass or pale copper-colored iron-spot brick, and a highly polished beige terrazzo floor. The tower is a flat-roofed rectangle with a repetitive window grid, with projecting vertical I-sections mounted between windows.

The adjacent poured-in-place concrete parking structure is connected to the tower by a long, low-covered sidewalk. The two short end walls of the garage are open and the edges of the parking decks are covered with precast concrete panels with an exposed aggregate finish. Its two long side walls are solid panels of pale, copper-colored brick held just short of the building's corners. The architects chose to make the side walls solid so as to conceal the sloping floors within the garage. The result is a composition of only vertical or horizontal lines with machine-made details of exact uniformity, projecting a corporate image of uncompromising consistency and efficiency.

EXIT

Brutalism

In *American Architecture Since 1780: A Guide to the Styles* (1992), Marcus Whiffen defines Brutalism as follows: "Brutalist buildings have a look of weight and massiveness. ... Windows are treated as holes in the walls or as voids in the solids of the walls, and not (as in the International Style) as continuations of the 'skin' of the building. ... Concrete is the favorite material."[170] Although Henry-Russell Hitchcock included Le Corbusier among the four leading "international style" architects in 1929, Corbusier's post-1945 buildings are considered among the first examples of Brutalism.

We include here an urban park, since its design is integrated with a six-story underground parking garage, and an educational center on Pittsburgh's North Side.

In 1939, while completing his Master's degree at Harvard University, John O. Simonds (1912–2005) designed the "First contemporary garden east of the Rockies" for the Pittsburgh Garden Center.[171] A native of North Dakota, Simonds received his landscape architecture degrees from Michigan State University (1935) and Harvard (1939). He established the firm of **Simonds & Simonds** with his brother Philip in Pittsburgh in 1939. In 1970, Simonds & Simonds became EPD: Environmental Planning & Design. (The Simonds were also partners in the firm of Collins, Simonds & Simonds, 1952–70, based in Washington, D.C.) John Simonds was influential as a practitioner and as a teacher. His book, *Landscape Architecture: The Shaping of Man's Natural Environment* (1961), has been called the "major textbook used in landscape architecture and planning education during the latter half of the 20th century."[172]

James A. Mitchell (1907–99) moved to Pittsburgh when he was a child. He received his architecture degrees from Carnegie Tech (1932) and Columbia University (1933). He apprenticed with several Pittsburgh firms. In 1938, he formed a partnership with Pittsburgh native Dahlen K. Ritchey

(1910–2002), who received his architecture degrees from Carnegie Tech (1932) and Harvard (1934). In 1939, **Mitchell & Ritchey** worked with Simonds & Simonds to design the structure (apparently demolished) for the first contemporary garden east of the Rockies. Mitchell was the designing partner of the firm, which was dissolved on August 30, 1957.[173] Mitchell & Ritchey and Simonds & Simonds collaborated on the design of Mellon Square.

40. Mellon Square
Bounded by Smithfield Street, Oliver Avenue, William Penn Place, and Sixth Avenue, Downtown Pittsburgh
James A. Mitchell of Mitchell & Ritchey, architect, 1948–55;
Simonds & Simonds, landscape architects, 1948–55
National Register District; Historic Landmark plaque

The idea for an urban park on this site was inspired by the impression Union Square in San Francisco had made on Richard King Mellon. In 1948: "On a Labor Day week-end at his home, James Mitchell drew up the basic concept of a park and underground garage. His sketch, which incidentally visualized the two new skyscrapers not yet planned, won approval of Mr. Mellon and two top aides, Wallace Richards and Park H. Martin."[174] On April 22, 1949, three Mellon family foundations—Andrew W. Mellon Educational and Charitable Trust, the Richard King

Mellon Square, c. 1955–56, flanked by the towering Alcoa Building (left) and Mellon-U.S. Steel Building (top center), now 525 William Penn Place

Mellon Foundation, and the Sarah Mellon Scaife Foundation—initially pledged $4,000,000 and later contributed $300,000 more toward the project. The Mellon family donated a square block of buildings between Smithfield Street, William Penn Place, Oliver Avenue, and Sixth Avenue.

Mellon Square is a one-acre surface park over a six-story underground parking garage with retail space along Smithfield Street. The principal material is reinforced poured-in-place concrete. The visible parts of the structure are faced with granite and the surface pavement is polychromatic Venetian terrazzo in a triangular pattern.

Simonds & Simonds designed the landscaping. John O. Simonds wrote:

> *the average cityscape is a conglomerate aggregation of metal, glass, and masonry cubes on a dreary base plane of asphalt and oil-spattered concrete. … In the oppressive and barren cityscape a park must be— perhaps most of all—a cool and refreshing oasis. In contrast with the sharp building profiles and the hard surface and dull hues of pavement, building stone, and brick, it must give the welcome relief of foliage, shade, splashing water, flowers, and bright color.*[175]

Unlike most urban parking garages, Mellon Square has succeeded in maintaining an active streetscape by having its plaza at grade on William Penn Place and storefronts along Smithfield Street, downhill from and parallel to William Penn Place.

The Pittsburgh Parks Conservancy began restoring Mellon Square in 2011. Under an agreement with the City of Pittsburgh, the Parks Conservancy will manage and maintain Mellon Square.

Tasso Katselas (b. 1927) was born in Pittsburgh and received his Bachelor of Arts degree in 1950 and Master of Arts in Architecture from Carnegie Tech in 1953. He apprenticed with several Pittsburgh firms, including Mitchell & Ritchey and Ingham, Boyd & Pratt. He established his own practice in 1956. His best-known building is arguably the Pittsburgh International Airport (1981–92), but he has designed many apartment buildings and several educational campuses, such as the Community College of Allegheny County. His own residence is illustrated in Marcus Whiffen's *American Architecture Since 1780* as an example of Brutalism. Katselas's house (1962) combines concrete and brick "in a manner that was first seen in Le Corbusier's two Jaoul houses of 1952 at Neuilly-sur-Seine."[176]

41. Manchester Bidwell Corporation Headquarters
1815 Metropolitan Street, Chateau (North Side)
Tasso Katselas, architect, 1985–86; 1989

One of the finest of Tasso Katselas's projects—often overlooked in discussions of his work—is this masterful, indeed magical, community arts center and job training complex set in a gritty, industrial neighborhood. Manchester Bidwell is a multi-purpose, L-shaped, two-story building of brick, concrete, and glass. There are dramatic two-story spaces—the lobby and corridors spanned by second-floor bridges, an auditorium (home to a regular jazz series), and classrooms—as well as one-story workshops, an art gallery, a library, a cafeteria, an adult career training center, and offices. All receive natural light from large windows in the first floor and arched clerestory windows on the second; there the windows look out on the rooftops of industrial neighbors and beyond to city towers and to the distant, dramatic landscape of Mt. Washington.

Inside, warm brick and golden oak woodwork, geometric forms, and colorful décor predominate: one passes through Roman arches and under circular and semi-circular openings and windows. In the light, the adobe-colored brick varies its tones. Art is everywhere: hanging quilts, photographs, paintings, prints, and ceramics; some furniture was made by Japanese-born Pittsburgh master craftsman Tadao Arimoto.

Bill Strickland, the client and founder and CEO of the Manchester Craftsmen's Guild and Bidwell Training Center, worked closely with the architect. He wrote that Katselas "turned my vision into a tangible reality."[177] Strickland stated:

> *Everything about the place—the sculptural dimensions of the exterior design; the interior rhythms of proportion and scale; the color and texture of the walls, floors, and fabrics; and that uplifting quality of light—was exactly what I had hoped it would be. ... an environment that had the power to transform lives.*[178]

159

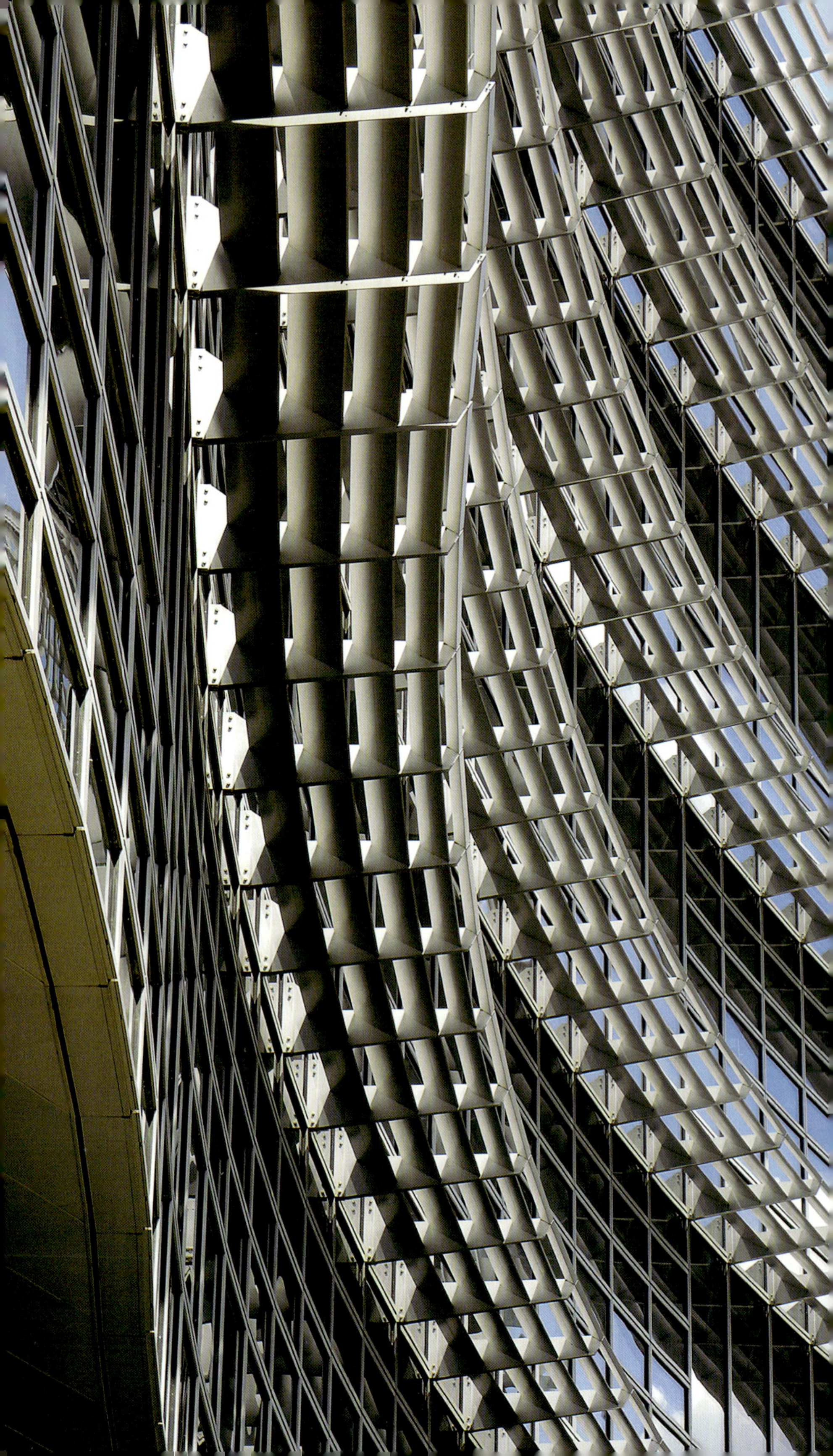

Corporate Industrial Design

After World War II, several Pittsburgh industrial corporations began to explore new products, new uses for their principal products, and better ways of advertising those products. Between 1950 and 1967, several Pittsburgh firms—Alcoa, United States Steel, and Westinghouse Corporation—erected corporate headquarters that attracted national attention. In the case of Alcoa and United States Steel, their industrial products—aluminum and steel—became key visual elements in their new skyscraper headquarters in downtown Pittsburgh, overlooking Mellon Square. The innovations in the Westinghouse Building at Gateway Center were internal.

These three corporate skyscrapers were designed by the New York architectural firm of **Harrison & Abramovitz**. Wallace K. Harrison (1895–1981) and Max Abramovitz (1908–2004) were well known to the New York business community and often employed by Nelson Rockefeller. Their best-known projects include the South Mall in Albany, New York, and the United Nations and Lincoln Center complexes in New York City. The firm designed seven corporate/educational buildings in Pittsburgh between 1950 and 1974. In Pittsburgh, Harrison & Abramovitz occupied a similar place to that of SOM in New York and Chicago. Harrison designed the firm's first Pittsburgh building, the Mellon-U.S. Steel Building (now 525 William Penn Place); they worked jointly on the second, the Alcoa Building; and Abramovitz designed the remainder.[179] Abramovitz also worked as a consultant to the University of Pittsburgh. John Harwood, in the first critical study of Abramovitz's work, wrote:

> *Corporate headquarters, which form the vast majority of his projects, provide us with perhaps the most fertile ground for exploring Abramovitz's architectural approach. Although any number of his other buildings would suffice, two projects in particular—headquarters*

for two of the great industrial giants of the twentieth century, the Aluminum Company of America (Alcoa) and United States Steel (USS)—stand out for their radical reformulation of received traditions in tall office building.[180]

42. 425 Sixth Avenue (Alcoa Building, Regional Enterprise Tower)
425 Sixth Avenue, Downtown Pittsburgh
Harrison & Abramovitz (New York, NY), architects, 1950–52
National Register District; Historic Landmark plaque

In 1946, Max Abramovitz was hired by the Aluminum Company of America (Alcoa), which after World War II "had begun to eye the potential demand for end products, particularly in the largest individual market for the material: the rapidly expanding building industry."[181] His studies produced the first aluminum curtain wall building system, first used in a tall building in Pittsburgh's Alcoa Building. Abramovitz designed the thirty-story office tower and Harrison designed the lobby, "a triple-height 'bird cage' of aluminum-sheathed steel and glass to be filled with aluminum sculptures, adventurous lighting fixtures, and circular fountains."[182] Mary Callery (born in New York City and brought up in Pittsburgh) designed the aluminum lobby sculpture, *Three Birds in Flight*.

"Upon its completion the *Architectural Forum* hailed the Alcoa headquarters as 'America's most daring experiment in modern office building,' its skin, 'the beginning of true industrial design in architecture.'"[183] Indeed, John Harwood noted:

> the experimental technologies evident everywhere in the building ... all functioned normally; and per square foot, it was the lightest tall office building ever built. Its dimpled façade suggested something of both the flexibility and potential strength of aluminum as a building material, as well as a sense of the ornamental possibilities that it offered—a high

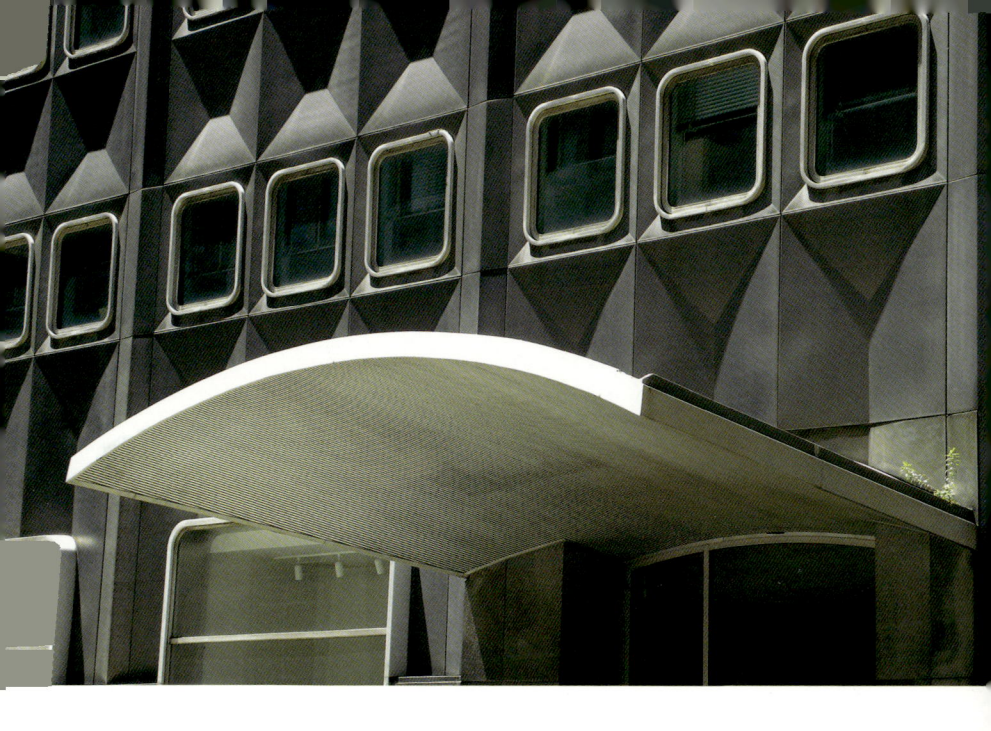

priority on Alcoa's agenda. It was hardly lost on contemporary observers that the building was as much a trade catalogue of architectural aluminum applications as it was a work of architecture.[184]

It is interesting to compare the Alcoa Building to its contemporary near neighbor—Harrison & Abramovitz's first Pittsburgh commission, designed by Harrison for U.S. Steel and now called 525 William Penn Place (1950–51): "as conservative as the Alcoa was daring, and as costly as Alcoa was economical: the verticality of its limestone ribbon piers flanked by stainless steel fins recalls the RCA and Empire State buildings."[185] If 525 looked back, Alcoa looked ahead, although in retrospect the Alcoa Building was very much a building of the 1950s; its windows, which pivot to allow cleaning, have:

rounded corners and relatively small size evoking the windows of modern jet aircraft. Indeed, sitting at their desks in the finished building, Alcoa employees would have the distinct impression that they were in a massive aluminum-clad vehicle, gazing out portholelike windows as the building taxied toward the runway.[186]

In 1998, Alcoa moved to the Alcoa Corporate Center on the North Shore (*see pages 171–173*) and donated their former headquarters building to the Southwestern Pennsylvania Corporation, a nonprofit involved in regional planning and development. It became the Regional Enterprise Tower until it was sold in 2012 for residential, office, and retail development.

43. Four Gateway Center
444 Liberty Avenue, Downtown Pittsburgh
Max Abramovitz of Harrison & Abramovitz (New York, NY), architect, 1958–60

The Plaza at Gateway Center (Equitable Plaza)
400 Liberty Avenue, Downtown Pittsburgh
Schell & Deeter, architects; Simonds & Simonds, landscape architects, 1961–62
National Register District

Four Gateway Center, a steel-and-glass commercial office tower financed by Equitable Life Assurance, is significant for two reasons: it exhibits an architectural sophistication missing from the three earlier Gateway Center buildings, and it is the first in a group of distinguished Gateway Center buildings on Stanwix Street, including the former IBM Building at Gateway Five.

The *Architectural Record* described Gateway Four, as it is commonly called, when the building was completed in 1960:

> A 22-story, free-standing tower clad in glass and stainless steel, the building occupies a corner site and adjoins a landscaped plaza that forms the roof of a 750-car underground garage. A separate tower ... containing elevators and most of the mechanical equipment and services is joined to the building on the Stanwix St. side, so that the office space itself is virtually uninterrupted.[187]

The pedestrian-friendly Equitable Plaza, landscaped by John O. Simonds, shares some design elements with its predecessor Mellon Square—here the geometrically patterned paving is gray-and-white Venetian terrazzo—and a similar "rich variety of trees (many are flowering trees), shrubs, and flowers animate the space."[188] It is, however, a two-acre park, roughly L-shaped. The short side of the L faces Liberty Avenue; the long side runs behind the Gateway buildings on Stanwix Street between Liberty Avenue and the Boulevard of the Allies. Some garden paths meander, unlike Mellon Square's symmetrical grid. John Simonds stated:

> Equitable Plaza marks a striking transition-point between the rigid and cold array of cruciform buildings which form the original Golden Gateway group in Pittsburgh's Golden Triangle. Here the street bends, the giant building forms shift from cruciform to slab, the plaza level rises above the street, the eye rests comfortably upon irregularity and color. Still under the shadow of giants, the pedestrian is partially set free from the heavy 'project' environment of much of the Gateway Center.[189]

Gateway Four is the most elegant of Harrison & Abramovitz's Pittsburgh buildings, and with U.S. Steel Tower, it represents the firm's best work here.

Curtis & Davis was established in New Orleans by Nathaniel C. Curtis, Jr. (1917–97) and Arthur Q. Davis (1920–2011). Both Curtis and Davis, New Orleans natives, attended Tulane University. Davis also attended the Harvard Graduate School of Design during the Gropius era, receiving a Master's degree in Architecture in 1946. They practiced together from 1947 to 1978. Karen Kingsley noted the firm's "commitment to modernist aesthetics and to employ and express the new technologies and materials."[190]

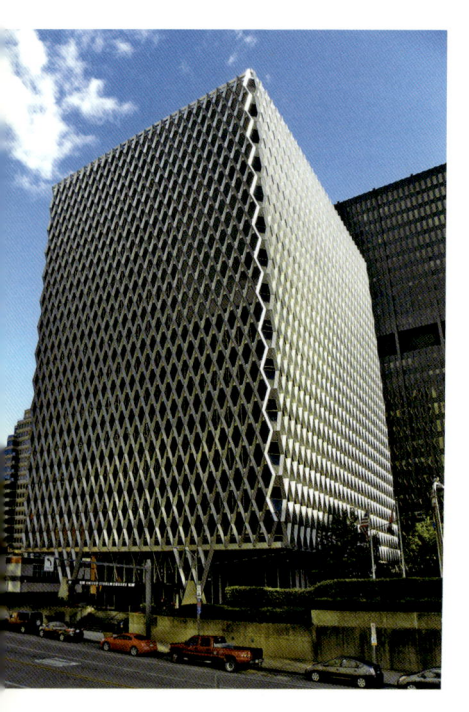

44. United Steelworkers (IBM Building, Five Gateway Center)
60 Boulevard of the Allies, Downtown Pittsburgh
Curtis & Davis (New Orleans, LA), architects, 1962–63
National Register District

Regarding their Pittsburgh building, Arthur Davis recalled: "The original design was conceived in prestressed concrete. When we presented this to IBM we were reminded that we were building in the steel town of Pittsburgh—there was no question that it should be done in steel." Davis noted that the key element of the building is "the principle of no columns in the exterior structural system supporting the building."[191]

The Charette reported in 1962 that the thirteen-story building "represents a marked departure in design. … The other Gateway buildings are of curtain wall construction, in which a thin wall of steel, aluminum or glass is applied over a structural frame."[192]

As built, the building has no exterior columns, no corner columns, and no interior columns. This remarkable feat is achieved by supporting the floors on steel beams which span fifty-four feet from the bearing walls of the elevator core to the exterior wall trusses. The entire perimeter is supported by eight concrete piers—which is quite a balancing act. Three different steels—A-36, T-1, and Tri-Ten—were used in the trusses to resist the increasing loads from the top down. The trusses were then clad with uniform-sized stainless steel covers and diamond-shaped windows were set into the openings. Karen Kingsley observed that the building "used less steel than the traditional skeleton frame construction and directed all wind loads to eight points at ground level."[193]

In 1968, architectural historian Carl Condit found the IBM Building's exterior structural system intriguing and suggested an eighteenth-century precursor: "Curious forms of rigid-frame trusses appear in the walls of the International Business Machines building in Pittsburgh—welded steel lattice trusses that bear a surprising resemblance to the original ancestor invented by Ithiel Town in 1820."[194] Condit noted that Town's wooden lattice patterned truss was the "first truss to be free of arch action and to exert only a vertical load on its supports."[195]

The lobby retains its original finishes and includes an amusing detail: the metal radiator covers are punctured with patterns derived from IBM computer punch cards.

167

45. U.S. Steel Tower (United States Steel Building; USX Tower)
600 Grant Street, Downtown Pittsburgh
Max Abramovitz, Charles H. Abbe, Harrison & Abramovitz (New York, NY), architects, and United States Steel Innovations Committee, 1965–71

Max Abramovitz was the lead designer in a unique collaboration:

> *In a long and productive career, [Abramovitz] developed radical new uses for modernism's standard repertoire of materials—concrete, steel, glass, aluminum. He consistently proved himself capable of finding elegant architectural solutions to complex organizational issues. More than almost any other architect, he is linked by his list of powerful clients to the political, cultural, and corporate history of postwar America.*[196]

The U.S. Steel Tower is 841 feet high, sixty-four stories, and has a gross area of 3,080,000 square feet (including parking). When completed in 1971, it was the largest commercial high-rise office building in the world. The shape is triangular with notched corners:

> *[A]fter calculations involving every possible contingency, plus tests of a model in a wind tunnel, the engineers determined that a triangular shape would provide the most efficient solution. ... The architects and engineers argued that the triangular plan ... neatly echoed the shape of the city, the wedge of land bound by the Monongahela and Allegheny Rivers.*[197]

The core of the triangle contains building services, including elevators, with offices located on each of the three rectilinear sides of the triangle. The eighteen exterior supporting box columns, six per side and attached at every third floor, are fabricated of USS Cor-Ten plate steel. Originally developed for steel surfaces that could not be painted, Cor-Ten is intrinsically resistant to atmospheric corrosion, and had been used extensively for rail cars, bridges, and transmission towers. The columns are located three feet from the curtain wall and are:

> filled with 400,000 gallons of water treated with an antifreeze of potassium carbonate, with potassium nitrate added to prevent corrosion. The fireproofing solution … was vented at the roof … propelled solely by changes in temperature.[198]

Box columns had been used before, but their use as fire-protection conduits at the United States Steel Building was the first in the nation.

The Penn Central railroad tunnel, which passed underground through the site before construction, was replaced by a steel-framed, X-braced railroad trestle, encased in concrete fireproofing, and isolated from the surrounding substructure of the building.

On the interior, handsome Palladiana marble in terrazzo wall panels and dramatic steel support columns and diagonal bracing in the first- and second-floor lobbies are clearly visible through large, exterior, plate glass windows.

Since 2008, the letters "UPMC" have been mounted to the top of the skyscraper on three sides, since the University of Pittsburgh Medical Center (UPMC) is a major building tenant.

The design process for this Pittsburgh landmark was unusual. In May 1965, United States Steel (USS) Corporation established an Innovations Committee to work with architects Harrison & Abramovitz, who had

U.S. Steel Tower (UPMC)
with 525 William Penn Place
(middle right)

designed what is now 525 William Penn Place for USS in 1950. The committee was composed of experts from within various USS divisions, including American Bridge Division, as well as outside consultants in engineering, climate-control, lighting, security, construction, and fabrication. One consultant was structural engineer Leslie E. Robertson, who had worked on the innovative steel façade of Curtis & Davis's Pittsburgh IBM Building in 1962.

In 2013, two USS members of the Innovations Committee, structural engineer Ronald L. Flucker and architect Robert Hossli, recalled that the purpose of the committee had been to develop "innovative design concepts, not only in terms of shape and façade, but also for construction and operating systems." Committee members were to explore "new, even weird, ideas." The collaborative process led to an innovative building design, new construction techniques, and advances in various building systems such as air conditioning and fire proofing.[199] USS understood that "the building of a major structure was a unique commercial opportunity. It could be a valuable proving ground to evaluate the merits of steel used in many building products—old and new—and in several innovative ways."[200]

Speaking about the USS Building commission in 1967, Max Abramovitz said:

> [I]t isn't often that an architect has the opportunity to approach a special problem with an open mind, and is encouraged to search out the best of professional talent for exploring the full potential of the client's program as to space, structure and the many technical systems that must be closely coordinated in a modern building today. It is a unique and rare chance.[201]

Much larger commercial skyscrapers have been erected world-wide since 1971. However, U.S. Steel Tower remains a Pittsburgh classic, the tallest building in the region and visible for many miles. It is about twice as high as the surrounding hills, and the sight of it often catches you by surprise.

Corporate Industrial Design

In 1987, Paul O'Neill became Alcoa's chairman and decided that the downtown headquarters building was inadequate. It had just 11,000 square feet of usable space per floor, low ceilings, long corridors, and small windows. "There were light limitations and structural wall limitations that went along with the 1950s idea that space should be associated with position—more space for higher level people, the least desirable interior space for his assistants." O'Neill believed that the building contributed to inefficiency and rigidity in the way the company functioned.[202] He commissioned **The Design Alliance**, founded in Pittsburgh in 1977, and **Rusli Associates** (1989–99) to design a new headquarters across from downtown Pittsburgh, on the North Shore of the Allegheny River.

46. Alcoa Corporate Center
201 Isabella Street, North Shore
The Design Alliance Architects, architects, with Rusli Associates, design consultants, 1996–98

The principal façade of the six-story aluminum-and-glass building faces the Allegheny River between the Andy Warhol (Seventh Street) and Rachel Carson (Ninth Street) bridges. The dramatically curving southeast curtain wall, with its projecting sun screens, suggests the rippling movement of the river, and the rough stone foundation of the building echoes the stone piers of the bridges. A handsome terrace provides outdoor seating and overlooks a section of the Three Rivers Heritage Trail.

Agus Rusli, principal of Rusli Associates and a faculty member at Carnegie Mellon during the period this building was designed, described

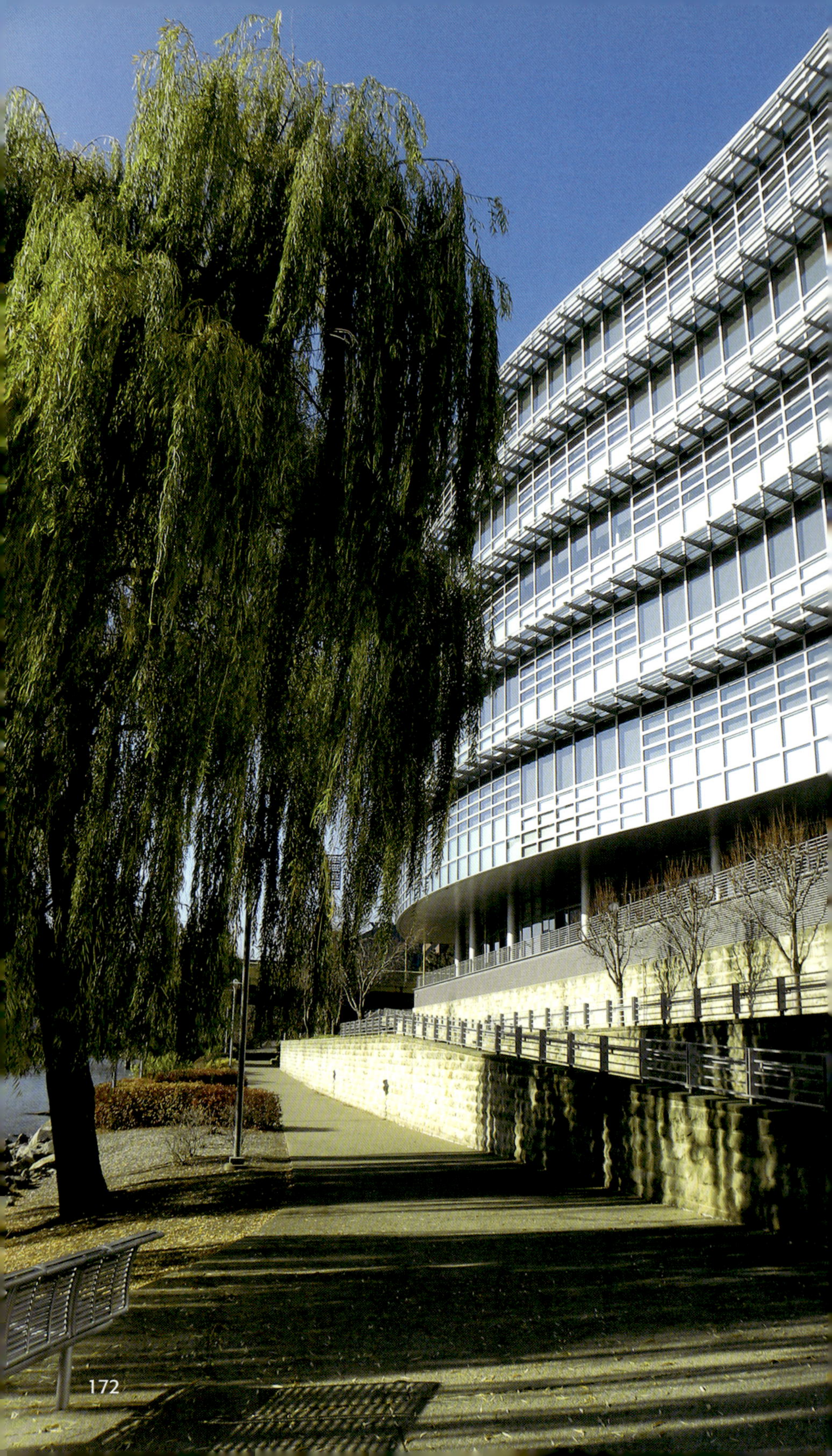

the interior in which offices open onto a central atrium as "non-hierarchial" which encourages "impromptu interaction, spontaneous communication, and ubiquitous access for all to all at all times."[203]

    Paul O'Neill stated: "We went from a building with 31 floors and hundreds of private, closed-door offices to a much more open environment. … The entire building is your office, and within the building everyone works collaboratively."[204]

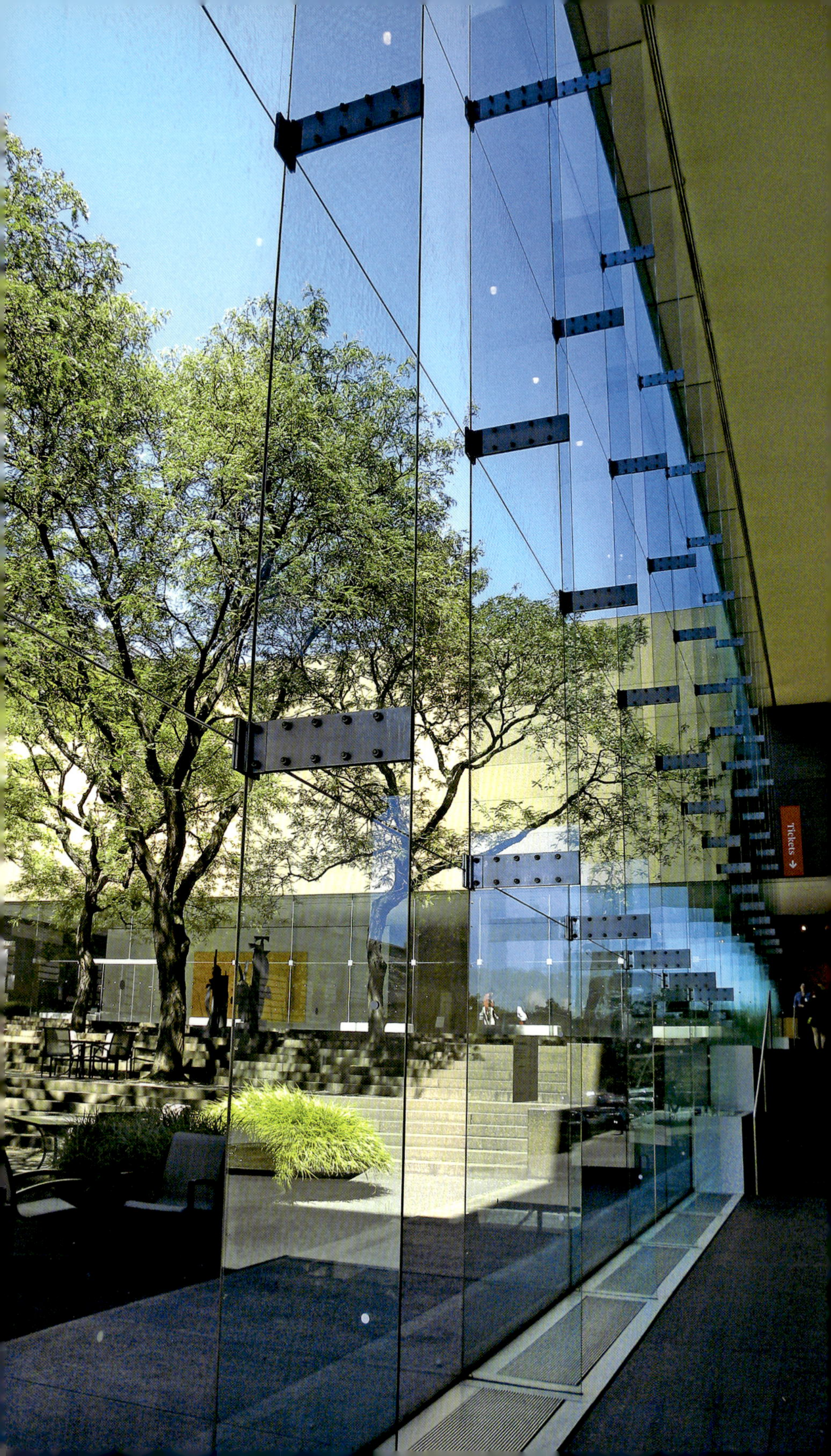
Tickets

The Legacy of the International Style

Edward Larrabee Barnes (1915–2004) was born in Chicago. He attended Milton Academy in Milton, Massachusetts, and Harvard University (Bachelor of Science, 1938). After teaching English and Fine Arts at Milton Academy for two years, he returned to Harvard and the Graduate School of Design (Bachelor of Architecture, 1942). Barnes worked in the office of Gropius and Breuer, with whom he studied at Harvard, before serving as a naval architect in San Francisco for the remainder of World War II. He opened an office in New York City in 1948. Concerning his training he wrote:

> At Harvard, Le Corbusier was the hero, but he was one step removed, and we saw the International Style at first hand through Breuer's work. … I admired the sureness of his touch—his ability to combine totally dissimilar elements and materials and yet not crowd the space. … The Harvard training with its strong functional base, later ridiculed for being too narrow, was actually a good approach—a good discipline in combination with vital aesthetic and formal considerations.[205]

Barnes' entry in the *Oxford Dictionary of Architecture* noted that "he was one of the first architects of the Modernist tendency to become a proponent of contextual design [*see page 176*]. … His museum interiors are treated as simply as possible, but the exteriors are given a civic presence."[206]

47. Sarah Mellon Scaife Galleries, Carnegie Museum of Art
4400 Forbes Avenue, Oakland
Edward Larrabee Barnes (New York, NY), architect, 1970–74

Designing a major late-twentieth-century addition to a grand early-twentieth-century building such as the American Renaissance-style Carnegie Institute (Longfellow, Alden & Harlow, 1895; Alden & Harlow, enlarged 1907) was indeed a challenge and had to address different needs of a later time. The 1970s addition, for example, had to include two primary entrances: one facing Forbes Avenue and another equally important one, on the opposite side, opening onto a parking area. While the historic building was designed

The Forbes Avenue entrance (above) and details (below)

with many windows so natural light could supplement the limited wattage of the incandescent bulb, the 1970s building was designed to protect and properly light the artwork, while avoiding direct sunlight and extreme heat or cold, by using florescent lighting and air conditioning to control temperature.

Contextual design is "architecture that responds to its surroundings by respecting what is already there."[207] The Scaife Galleries addition intentionally aligns its street façade with the existing building, nearly matches its height, approximates its color, and expresses the same massive feel of the older stone walls. The addition has been described as a "severe though grandly proportioned wing [that] transforms the classicism of the main block into the abstraction of the late International Style."[208]

The Forbes Avenue elevation of the two-story Scaife Galleries is joined to the principal façade of the 1907 building, but is slightly recessed in deference to the twin projecting pavilions of the older building. The addition's wall is not flat but is "sawtooth" (*middle photo, above*); this eases the transition and permits tall, narrow windows to face east, providing natural light which does not shine into the galleries. Further east is the street entrance. Large, recessed, one-story plate glass windows and doors reveal the lobby and museum restaurant which look onto a wide, granite-paved plaza with a fountain and sculptures.

From the opposite side of the building, visitors can appreciate the

The entrance facing the parking lot (above) and the Sculpture Court (above and below)

artfulness, practicality, and beauty of Barnes' design. A two-story plate glass façade with reinforcing glass mullions (*see photo, page 174*) provides an unobstructed view to the outdoor Sculpture Court and fills the entrance lobby with natural light. A granite-paved staircase leads to the Forbes Avenue lobby, and an open, monumental stair, rising alongside Sol LeWitt's 1980s wall drawings, leads to the Carnegie Museum of Art's second-floor Scaife Galleries.

   The Forbes Avenue lobby overlooks the Sculpture Court and serves as both a reception hall and the principal corridor connecting the museum offices, the restaurant, the gift shop, and the modern art galleries to the 1907 building, with its Hall of Sculpture, Hall of Architecture, Heinz Architectural Center, Carnegie Museum of Natural History, and Carnegie Music Hall. The entire complex is a cultural palace for the people, just as founding benefactor Andrew Carnegie had envisioned.

Richard Meier (b. 1934) received his Bachelor of Architecture degree from Cornell University (1957), then apprenticed with Skidmore, Owings & Merrill and with Marcel Breuer. He opened his own firm in New York City in 1963.

48. Frank Giovannitti House
118 Woodland Road, Shadyside
Richard Meier (New York, NY), architect, 1979–83

Meier has called the Giovannitti House a "gem."[209] In 1984, the year after the house was completed, Martin Filler wrote in *House and Garden*:

> *Meier's originality is crystal clear in his Giovannitti house in Pittsburgh. … This is a work of exceptionally high quality, and though at first sight it might appear to be more reiteration than origination, a closer look shows just how great this extraordinary architect's capacity for variations on a theme can be. He is the Mozart of late Modernism, working within a rigid formal system that nonetheless seems for him the perfect stimulus*

The Legacy of the International Style

to invention. … There is not an extraneous gesture nor a wasted movement in the Giovannitti house. …[210]

This tiny, yet highly sculptural, three-story, flat-roofed house has white-painted exterior walls, white metal window mullions, white metal pipe railings, and a white, free-standing colonnade, all attesting to the architect's interest in the abstract, formal qualities of design. The house is built into the side of a hill. In 1996, critic Paul Goldberger considered it among Meier's six best house designs.[211]

Frank Giovannitti is often asked to describe what it is like to live in an all-white house. He immediately replies that he does not live in an all-white house:

I consider the house to be a canvas, the palette is light, and the artist Meier. He controls his brush by strokes of transparency and massing. He paints with light, directly, indirectly; with natural light, artificial light with the infinite changes of light during the day: early morning, late morning, afternoon, early evening, dusk, moonlight. There are also the infinite reflections of the seasons. Therefore, the house is never white.

So then, how do I describe living in a Richard Meier house? The answer is light, light, light, light.[212]

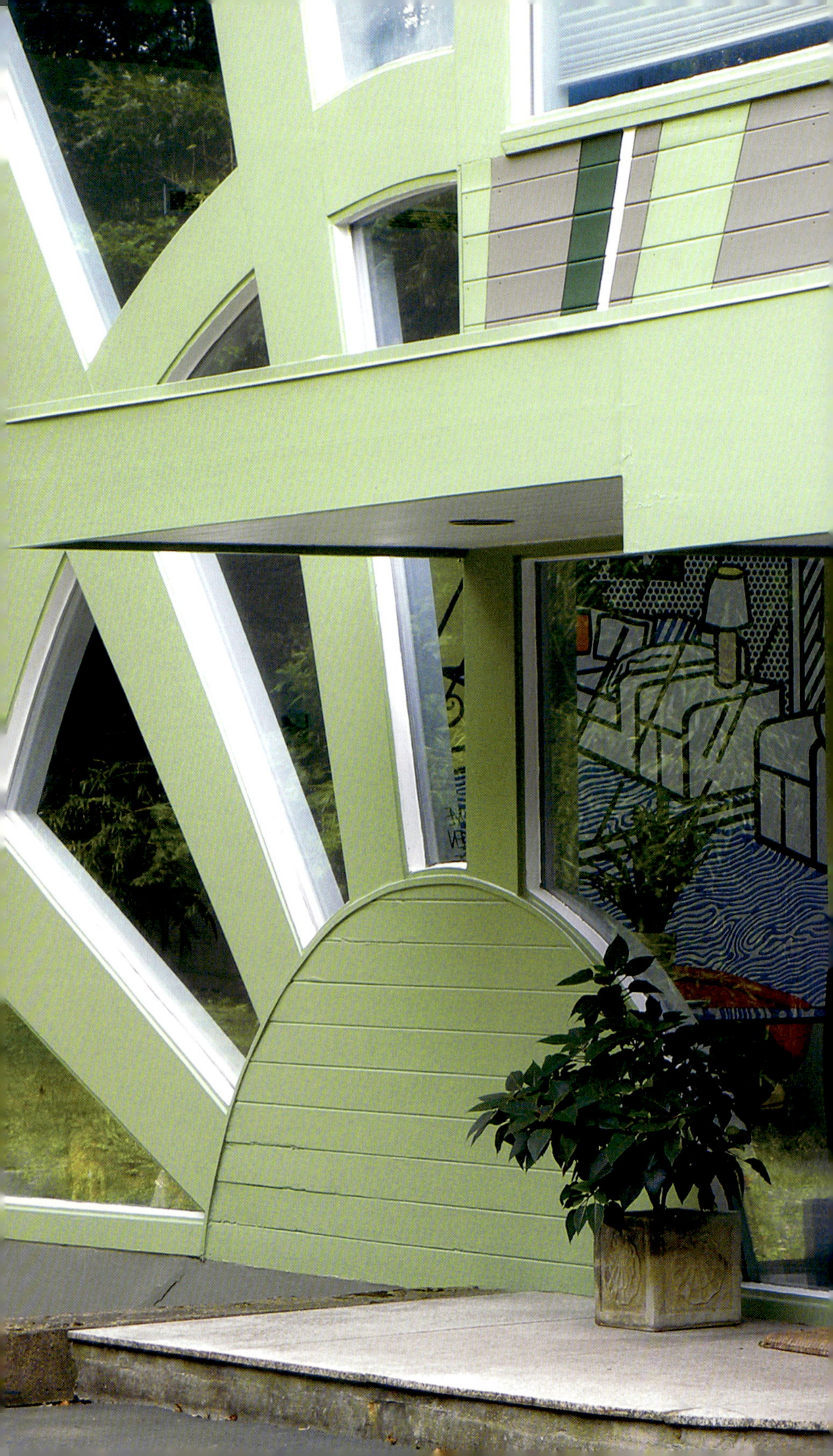

Postmodernism

Robert Venturi (b. 1925), an architectural historian, writer, and architect, led the 1960s challenge to the definition of modernism prevailing since the 1930s. What came *after* modernism was contemporary design that was "allowed" to draw upon historical architectural forms and materials; it came to be known as Postmodernism. Venturi received his undergraduate (1947) and graduate (1950) degrees in architecture from Princeton University. He apprenticed with Eero Saarinen and Louis Kahn. He taught at the University of Pennsylvania (1954–65) and later at Yale and Harvard universities. Venturi established his architectural practice in 1960, working with various partners—in particular with John Rauch (1964–89)—and with his wife, Denise Scott Brown (1969–2012). The firm became Venturi, Scott Brown & Associates. Venturi retired in 2012 and his firm continues as VSBA.

49. Betty and Irving Abrams House
118A Woodland Road, Shadyside
Robert Venturi of Venturi & Rauch (Philadelphia, PA), architect, 1979–82

When Betty Abrams visited the Frank House as a teenager, she knew she wanted to live in a modern home. In 1979, she commissioned Robert Venturi to design her home. The relationship between architect and client was not passive, but interactive and somewhat confrontational, and the finished house was not included in the firm's list of works.

British architectural historian Richard Pain had known of the commission but thought that the Abrams House had not been built. He visited Pittsburgh in 2002 to attend "Out of the Ordinary: The Architecture and Design of Robert Venturi and Denise Scott Brown and Associates," an exhibition at the Carnegie Museum of Art.[213]

Pain learned that the Abrams House had, in fact, been built. He visited it and subsequently wrote about the house in the British architectural journal *Blueprint*, calling it "a secret masterpiece."[214]

In his article, Pain reviewed the birth of the house from the purchase of the property in 1979; the Abrams' preliminary search for an architect, beginning with Philip Johnson, followed by Robert Stern, Michael Graves, Luis Barragán, and finally the choice of Robert Venturi. According to Pain:

> *The first drawings from May 1979 show a very different house to the one that was eventually built. ... Venturi and Scott Brown were interested in the house as a generic building that would adapt and support many lives and occupiers, rather than being restricted to a tight and unique means of operation.*"[215]

Betty Abrams—"a strong willed client who knew what she wanted and was determined to have it"[216]—requested changes. Plans were revised by July 1979: the stairs to the second floor were relocated away from the front door; the kitchen opened to the living/dining space; a proposed fireplace was removed from the plans; and the large north window combined the original "sunburst" design with a "rising stepped orthogonal window."[217] The window, as executed, is dramatic, indeed magical. Through the south window, one sees the century-old stone bridge that inspired the shape of the house.

Betty worked with New York designer Noel Jeffrey on the interior; the three shades of blue on the walls and ceiling are subtle elements in the main room, while the Roy Lichtenstein graphic provides polychromatic pizzazz.

The Abrams House demonstrates a masterful organization of space. It is a small house with adjacent living, eating, and sleeping spaces, yet feels spacious and open, both internally and in relationship to its wooded site.

Robert Venturi and Denise Scott Brown visited the house, which they had never seen in its completed state, in November 2002, and Venturi wrote to Betty Abrams:

> *You should know that via Richard Pain's recent and current focus on the Abrams house in general and then our visit to the house last November and my reviewing Richard's distinguished manuscript on the house and our original drawings currently, I am now considering the project one of the best that has come out of our office which I am very, very proud of.*[218]

Philip Johnson (1906–2005) moved from the curatorial world to the practice of architecture; he graduated from Harvard's Graduate School of Design in 1943 and opened a New York City architectural office in 1945. From 1967 to 1991, Johnson collaborated with architect John Burgee (b. 1933).

Johnson's initial work reflected the influence of Mies van der Rohe, but Johnson would subsequently admit:

> *The International Style had a longer life, it seems to me now, than ever it deserved. ... The Style lasted clearly through the 1950s, but then I got bored with it. My reaction was an anti-father one. Anti-Mies. Anti-Modern. I joined in with what Robert A. M. Stern and Robert Venturi were doing, putting forth the continuity of history as something that could be learned from.*[219]

50. PPG Place
Stanwix Street (between Boulevard of the Allies and Market Square), Downtown Pittsburgh
Philip Johnson of Johnson & Burgee (New York, NY), architect, 1979–84

In 1994, Philip Johnson declared that he considered PPG Place his favorite building, and discussed its design and character in detail:

> *The client was very interested in showing off glass since that was part of their business. They practically refused to build it. So I suggested we mock up a big enough piece, and then we both go across the river [Monongahela] to look at it, and that persuaded them.*
>
> *The tower idea came from the Cathedral of Learning, the famous Gothic Tower at the University of Pittsburgh. The idea of the series of towers came from Richardson's Allegheny County Courthouse.*
>
> *... it's a village idea. A cathedral and the low buildings around its base*

PPG's grid-like glass-and-aluminum façade provides an effective contrast to the historic buildings (c. 1850–90) on Fort Pitt Boulevard, facing the Monongahela River.

make a square. Well, the truth was that they had five acres. What the heck was I going to do with five acres? I suggested that we build a plaza and the lower buildings, which could be rented out.

I like the idea of PPG, because there's no detail. Detailing is where you get into trouble. Why is PPG Gothic? It's just this pointed thing. It's just decoration. And somehow I can defend that as better. In the AT&T building, I used Romanesque-cushioned capitals. Well, they weren't very good, because there's something in the air of proportion of detail that simply will not translate. … A copy just doesn't do it.[220]

According to Eli Attia, a senior designer on the PPG project, the pinnacles of the neighboring St. Mary of Mercy Church (William P. Hutchins, architect, 1936) inspired the design of the pinnacles on PPG Place.[221] (*See photo, pages 44–45*)

The forty-story PPG tower has a large glass Wintergarden with exposed, clear span structural trusses in a one-story wing facing Stanwix Street. PPG Place includes five more buildings—four are six stories and one is fourteen

Postmodernism

stories—and a plaza. Initially, the plaza only featured a central, pink granite obelisk, but has since been enlivened by a fountain in the summer and an ice skating rink in the winter.

PPG Place may seem cold and uninviting during the day, due to the silver *Solarban* reflective glass, but the faceted façade dramatically reflects the light, especially when the sun sets or a storm approaches. At night, when the tower spire lights are illuminated, the building sparkles.

Kohn Pedersen Fox was formed in 1976 by A. Eugene Kohn (b. 1930), who received his Bachelor of Architecture (1953) and Master of Architecture (1957) degrees from the University of Pennsylvania; William Pedersen (b. 1938), who received his Bachelor of Architecture (1961) and Master of Architecture (1963) degrees from MIT; and Shelton Fox (1930–2006), who received his Bachelor of Architecture (1953) degree from the University of Pennsylvania.

51. EQT Plaza (Allegheny International Tower, CNG Tower, Dominion Tower, and 625 Liberty Avenue)
*625 Liberty Avenue, Downtown Pittsburgh
William Pedersen of Kohn Pedersen Fox (New York, NY), architect, 1984–87*

This thirty-two-story skyscraper is illustrated and discussed in *Kohn Pedersen Fox: Buildings and Projects 1976–1986*:

> the building is divided into three 60-foot bays. … The surfaces are sheathed in two different-colored granites. …

Overlayed onto the composition is the reference to three distinct scales. The traditional height of old Pittsburgh is articulated in the base and piano nobile [principal floor, usually located above the ground floor]. The intermediate 200-foot height of the [neighboring] Midtown Tower and the predominant streetwall is threaded through the fabric of the building skin at its midsection. At the top, the height of the more recent skyscrapers is met, and, in this case, the vaulted truss roof is symbolic of the importance and proximity of the converging waterways and the many bridges which transverse the Allegheny River.[222]

The building was intended as the headquarters of Allegheny International, the successor to Allegheny Ludlum Steel Corporation. Although two towers were designed—like bookends they were to mirror one another—"only the first tower will be built in the initial phase."[223] Ultimately, only one tower and the adjacent plaza were built.

Traditional forms appear on the Postmodern façade: arches, cornices, keystones, columns, finials, and circular moldings. The roof is both arched and flat. The quality of building materials and contextual design delight the eye.

Postmodernism

A display in the lobby commemorates the Pittsburgh Agreement of May 31, 1918, that lead the way for the founding of Czechoslovakia. That document was signed in the 1915 Moose Building, located on the northeast corner of the site, which was demolished in 1984 prior to the construction of the Allegheny International Tower.

Arthur Lubetz (b. 1940) was born and reared in Pittsburgh. He attended weekly classes at the Arts and Crafts Center (now Pittsburgh Center for the Arts) and subsequently attended Carnegie Tech where he received a degree in architecture. He later taught a studio class at Carnegie Mellon University. The catalog of a 1989 exhibition of his work at the University of Pittsburgh cites sculptors Richard Serra and Claes Oldenburg, pop artist Andy Warhol, the Russian artist and architect El Lissitzky, and the aesthetic theories and practices of Russian Constructivism among his influences. Lubetz also acknowledges the importance of Pittsburgh as a source of inspiration:

> I noticed that the architecture that held up over time, against this background of mills and powerful geography, is strong bold architecture. … Therefore our buildings have exposed ducts, exposed steel structure, and corrugated metal, simple concrete masonry and other very basic materials.[224]

52. Fort Couch Tower
180 Fort Couch Road, Bethel Park
Arthur Lubetz Associates, architects, 1984–85

The Fort Couch Tower office building, roughly H-shaped in plan, is sited on a slightly sloping suburban lot used mostly for parking. The building is five stories facing Fort Couch Road and four stories at the rear. The lower story walls and the freestanding rectangular piers are made of eight-inch by eight-inch concrete block with red mortar. The three upper stories have alternating bands of light-beige and medium-beige stucco-like exterior insulation and finish systems, and a flat roof. The square windows are located within the medium-beige bands. The four outside corners of the H-plan have larger glass block windows at each floor and glass block caps extending above the roof. At the center of the H-plan is a four-story-high cylinder of glass block set in red mortar, containing two elevators and a small lobby. The glass block cylinder is surmounted by a tall, open steel-framework crown made up of vertical pipe columns and three horizontal rings of I-beams and miscellaneous cross bracing.

Arthur Lubetz explained:

> *A building is split to reveal its essence and the limited vision of its suburban context. The split defines a mute urban space in which a tower/silo recalls the site's past as farmland and the tower is transformed into an urban monument. The split exposes the present day process of construction and the building's entrance. The silent, empty urban spaces look forward to the future ripening of the suburban context. The split of the building and the thrust of the tower are physical forces that energize the building and its surroundings.*[225]

Professor M. F. Hearn of the University of Pittsburgh characterized the design of the Fort Couch Tower office building as "witty." Many of Arthur Lubetz's buildings exhibit not only a profound sense of place, but also a sophisticated sense of humor.

Postmodernism

Michael Graves (b. 1934) is a native of Indianapolis, Indiana. He is a graduate of the University of Cincinnati and received a Master of Architecture degree from Harvard University. He opened his architectural firm in Princeton, New Jersey, in 1964 and has taught architecture at Princeton University.

53. O'Reilly Theater, Theater Square, Katz Plaza
621 Penn Avenue, Downtown Pittsburgh (Pittsburgh Cultural District)
Michael Graves & Associates (Princeton, NJ), architects, 1996–99

Architecture critic Cynthia Davidson "reviewed" the O'Reilly Theater building in 2001:

> *The new building is distinctly Graves, a product of his own iconoclastic language of architecture: a cylinder; a barrel vault; Kasota stone; an exaggerated running bond pattern on a side elevation; extensive use of curly maple inside. It is elegant, a little bit precious, and somewhat overstated; the latter quality, according to Graves, is to help the small*

Theater Square (above) and Katz Plaza (opposite) on Penn Avenue, downtown

building (53,000 square feet) hold its own in a neighborhood of large loft buildings.[226]

She observed that:

Graves repeats the circle as a motif, in both plan and section, throughout the O'Reilly: the barrel-vaulted roof protrudes slightly out over the street; the lobby is formed in plan by two concentric circles. At night, the lobby's two levels are clearly visible through a customized, curved curtain-wall system.[227]

The O'Reilly Theater was the first element in a three-part commission designed by Graves in 1996. The commission also included Agnes R. Katz Plaza, by landscape architect Daniel Urban Kiley (1912–2004) and sculptor Louise Bourgeois (1911–2010). Both the O'Reilly and Katz Plaza opened in 1999. The third element, Theater Square—a multipurpose ticket office, broadcasting studio, cabaret performance space, restaurant, and parking garage—was completed in association with Pittsburgh architects WTW in 2003.[228] The nine-story Theater Square building is made of poured-in-place concrete. Some of the walls are covered with brick, glazed tile, metal louvers, and brightly colored columns.

The O'Reilly Theater, Katz Plaza, and Theater Square—completing our selection of notable extant sites in this Guide—were developed by the Pittsburgh Cultural Trust. Envisioned by Henry J. Heinz II, the Cultural Trust was established in 1984 to transform a fourteen-block downtown area, that included many significant twentieth-century buildings, into an arts and entertainment/mixed-use neighborhood. In 1987, the Cultural Trust oversaw the listing of the Penn-Liberty National Register and City of Pittsburgh historic districts. The City Historic District was expanded in 1999 and the National Register Historic District was expanded in 2013. Now managing seven theaters, eight public parks and art installations, and a dozen art galleries, the Pittsburgh Cultural Trust has become a national model for urban revitalization through the arts.

Modern Landmarks— Relocated, Concealed, Unfinished, or Demolished

Over time, it is not unusual for buildings—or parts of buildings—to be demolished, remodeled, not completed as designed, or even moved to another location. Here are ten, twentieth-century, architecturally distinctive Pittsburgh structures, spaces, and architectural elements that are all—in some sense—gone.

(1) Titus de Bobula's first Pittsburgh building was **Holy Ghost Greek Catholic Church** (1903) in Allegheny City (now Pittsburgh's North Side), dedicated August 9, 1903. Its central feature was less a spire and more a four-story tower: the cube-shaped first story supported the upper cylindrical tower, framed by four bullet-shaped engaged columns, and a dome-covered belfry. The church was partially destroyed by fire in 1925 and was demolished shortly thereafter.[229]

(2) Richard Kiehnel's **City of Pittsburgh Hospital at Marshalsea** (1909), known later as the Medical Building at Mayview State Hospital, was Kiehnel's third, and one of his largest, Secessionist buildings. It was demolished between 2011 and 2013. Two, two-story wings extended from a three-story central pavilion. The shape of the building—rectangular blocks with overhanging low-hipped roofs—was typical of turn-of-the-century medical and educational facilities. The

building's distinctive character came from the ornamentation. The great arched doorway was crowned with a border of sinuous vines forming almost symmetrical triangles, topped with small flowers. Below this, an Austrian "Imperial Banner" decorated the pilasters on either side of the door, with long ribbons joined by rows of rings suspended from a row of five egg-shaped spheres framed by luxuriant foliage. The ribbons varied in length, from the shortest in the rear to the longest in the front.

(3) Janssen & Cocken's **Kaufmann's Department Store Main Floor and Mezzanine** (1927–30) is described in the Introduction (*see pages 24–28*). In 1946, Kaufmann's was sold to the May Department Stores Company; Edgar Kaufmann, Sr., remained president and continued to manage the Pittsburgh store. When Kaufmann died at the age of 69 on April 15, 1955, one obituary ranked the 1930 remodeling with its "now familiar black glass columns and murals"[230] among his major achievements. Five months after Kaufmann's death, an article in the store's employee newsletter dated September 27, 1955, declared:

> "First Floor Redecorated—Famous Black Glass Columns Lightened": Kaufmann's famous First Floor columns of marble and black Carrara glass have been enclosed in wood, painted and covered with vari-colored fabrics in pastel shades including pink, natural, turquoise, grey and off-white. The elevator banks and walls surrounding the central Service Desk have been covered with grey fabric. This vast redecoration plan conforms with the rest of our expansion program, creating a light, spacious atmosphere. Existing fixtures on the First Floor were refinished and the top ledges have been covered with white rubber.[231]

(4) The design and fabrication of Frank Lloyd Wright's **Office for Edgar Kaufmann, Sr.** (1935–38) dates roughly from the same period as the design and construction of Fallingwater. The office was installed on the northwest corner of the store's tenth floor. The walls are cypress-veneered plywood. A prominent feature is an abstract geometric wood mural, incorporating a triangular lighting fixture, on the wall behind the desk. Wright designed a desk/conference table, chairs, and a set of stools for extra seating. He also designed the upholstery fabric and carpeting, which was woven by Loja Saarinen, master weaver and wife of architect Eliel Saarinen. Christopher Wilk stated: "easily lost sight of within the full range and extent of Wright's work … [the Kaufmann office] is an excellent example of Wright's ability as a designer of interiors."[232] The office was dismantled and moved to the fifteenth floor of the First National Bank Building at 511 Wood Street (now demolished) and reassembled as the office of the Edgar J. Kaufmann Charitable Foundation and Charitable Trust. In 1963, the office was again dismantled and placed in storage where it would remain for a decade. Edgar Kaufmann, jr., gave the office to the Victoria & Albert Museum in London; it arrived there in 1974 but was not installed until 1993 (it is currently in storage).

Heinz Vinegar Plant, before (above) and after re-siding (left)

(5) In 1988, Carol Krinsky wrote that the reputation of the **Heinz Vinegar Plant** (1950–51) [Gordon Bunshaft (1909–90), for Skidmore, Owings & Merrill, New York Office];

> rests upon Bunshaft's exterior design and artistic use of materials in solving practical problems. While thirty years of use have taken their toll—modern caulking materials and special glass thickness did not exist around 1950—writers at the time of completion called the façade "the handsomest wall in Pittsburgh, the most sophisticated steel and glass curtain Skidmore, Owings & Merrill have yet put up."[233]

The Vinegar Plant is located on South Canal Street on Pittsburgh's North Side. The building façade is now covered with mustard-colored corrugated metal panels.

(6) The **Lower Hill Cultural Center** (1954–61) was only partially realized and its most notable element—the Civic Arena (later Mellon Arena)—was demolished in 2012. Conceived by philanthropist Edgar J. Kaufmann, Sr., and funded as an innovative public-private partnership, the Lower Hill Cultural Center was intended to be a grand contribution to the region. In 1947, plans were published for major demolition and new construction in downtown Pittsburgh at the Point and in the Lower Hill east of Grant Street. Pittsburgh architects Mitchell & Ritchey described the anticipated key buildings in the Lower Hill development: "a large, circular exhibition hall where sporting events, conventions, and industrial exhibits are conducted; a symphony hall; and an open-air amphitheater where future seasons of civic light opera will be presented."[234] Historian Roy Lubove noted:

Civic Arena

> Although the City Planning Commission had certified the 95-acre Lower Hill for redevelopment in 1950, uncertainties over financing the planning delayed

The Civic Arena in 1961, just before its dedication on September 17, with its 415-foot-wide dome, the widest in the world when built.

council approval until 1955. Demolition began in 1956, displacing 1551 (mostly Negro) families and 413 businesses.[235]

Ultimately, only a multipurpose civic auditorium, designed by James Mitchell of Mitchell & Ritchey in 1954, was erected in the Lower Hill. (Mitchell invented and patented the retractable dome.) Completed and altered as an entertainment/sports arena by Deeter & Ritchey in 1961, the Civic Arena was a daring, contemporary design and an extraordinary feat of engineering with the world's largest retractable roof. (The construction of the Civic Arena between 1958 and 1961 by Dick Corporation is documented in the William V. Winans Jr. Photograph Collection [http://digital.library.pitt.edu/images/pittsburgh/winans.html].)

By agreement with the Sports & Exhibition Authority of Pittsburgh and Allegheny County (SEA) in 2007, the Pittsburgh Penguins, a principal tenant of the arena, was given an option to purchase the

The Civic Arena c. 1963, with its retractable roof fully open during an event. The Washington Plaza Apartments is under construction (top right).

twenty-eight-acre property, including the site of the Civic Arena, for redevelopment. The Penguins constructed a new arena across Centre Avenue, and opened their 2010–11 season in the Consol Energy Center.

On September 16, 2010, the SEA board voted unanimously to demolish the Civic Arena, in order to clear the way for a mixed-use development proposed by the Penguins that would re-establish an urban street grid in the Lower Hill. After much public debate, demolition of the Civic Arena began in September 2011 and was completed in June 2012.

In order to preserve and honor the memory of the Civic Arena, the SEA prepared a Historic American Buildings Survey (HABS PA 6780) and filed copies with the Pennsylvania Historical and Museum Commission, Library of Congress, Carnegie Library of Pittsburgh (Main Branch, Oakland), and Pittsburgh History & Landmarks Foundation.

The Carnegie Library has videos pertaining to the Civic Arena and electronic files containing scans of architectural plans for the Civic

Dahlen K. Ritchey (left) and James A. Mitchell were photographed with a scale model of the Civic Arena on February 22, 1950. Mitchell & Ritchey was the leading Pittsburgh architectural firm during the city's Renaissance.

Arena. Many original plans are housed at the Carnegie Mellon University Architecture Archives, thanks to DRS Architects. The Senator John Heinz History Center received a significant collection of objects and archival materials. The photo above is from the Historic American Buildings Survey report archived at the Pittsburgh History & Landmarks Foundation.

(7) Paul Rudolph (1918–97), New Haven, Connecticut, collaborated with *Woman's Home Companion* to design a model house. **Companion House for Family Living**, **No. 1** (1956)—one of five adaptations of the plan—was erected in suburban Allison Park.[236] The house still stands but has been completely remodeled. (Current address: 9474 Northgate Drive.)

Five Companion House No. 1 models were erected in 1956— one in Pittsburgh, one in the St. Louis, Missouri, suburb of Warson Woods (shown), and three in Indianapolis.

Modern Landmarks—Relocated, Concealed, Unfinished, or Demolished

(8) **Washington Plaza Apartments** (1958–64), 1420 Centre Avenue in the Lower Hill, is the only Pittsburgh building by I. M. Pei (b. 1917), for developer William Zeckendorf, Webb & Knapp, New York, but it is unfinished. Only one of the three connected buildings planned for the site (1,000 apartments were envisioned) was completed.[237] When Washington Plaza Apartments opened, the public was invited to tour four model apartments furnished by Kaufmann's Department Store.

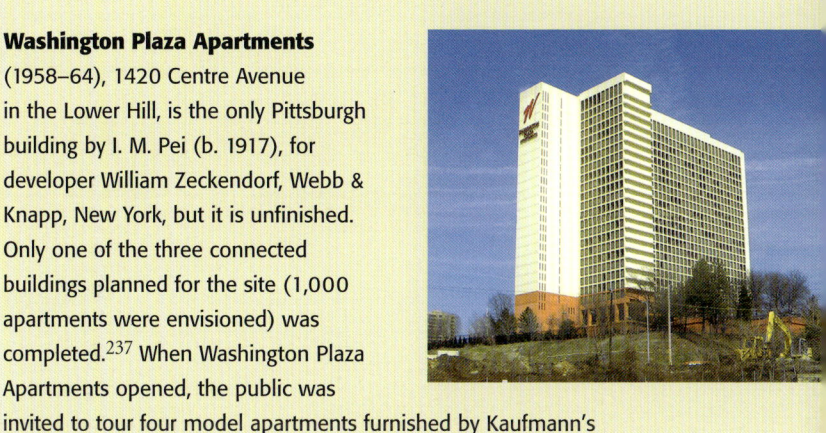

The proposed plan for the Lower Hill, including Washington Plaza Apartments (1), a performing arts hall for the symphony (6), and the Civic Arena.

(9) **"Point Counterpoint II,"** the American Wind Symphony Orchestra (AWSO) barge (designed 1964–67; completed 1975) was commissioned by AWSO founder and music director Robert Boudreau of Mars, Pennsylvania, and was designed by Louis I. Kahn (1901–74). The barge, made of welded steel plates, is painted a metallic silver. It features oversized circular openings and a folding roof which opens to serve as an acoustic shell. The barge—which has traveled throughout the Mississippi River system, and to Cuba, Britain, and Europe—was anchored on the Allegheny River, alongside Point State Park, from 1976 to 1996. Because of periodic flooding at the Point, the barge was moored elsewhere.[238] In 2012, Point Counterpoint II returned to its Point State Park dock and presented two evening concerts on July 14 and 21. Beginning in 2014, the barge will be moored along the Erie Canal.

(10) William Lescaze (1896–1969) is best known for his Philadelphia Savings Fund Society Bank (1929–32), called by William Jordy "the most important tall building erected between the Chicago School of the 1880s and 90s and the metal and glass revival beginning around 1950." He had left Philadelphia to practice in New York City when

Modern Landmarks—Relocated, Concealed, Unfinished, or Demolished

he was hired to design One Oliver Plaza (1968), a thirty-eight-story steel-and-granite skyscraper at the corner of Wood Street and Liberty Avenue in downtown Pittsburgh. As designed, the North Lobby was dominated by a thirteen-foot-high by twenty-foot-wide **mural by celebrated French artist Pierre Soulages** (b. 1919). Lescaze commissioned Soulages, as the architect later noted, "to work with me right from the beginning of the concept of the whole building. The mural in ceramic tile is a welcome and powerful feature in the main lobby."[239] Lescaze often added modern artwork to his buildings, but this was the only time he collaborated with an artist during the design process.

The mural was removed in 2009 when the lobby was remodeled to reflect the corporate image of the building's new principal tenant, K&L Gates, the law firm for which the building is now named. The mural is now in Ohio at The Butler Institute of American Art, Trumbull branch.

Pierre Soulages' mural in The Butler Institute of American Art, Trumbull branch

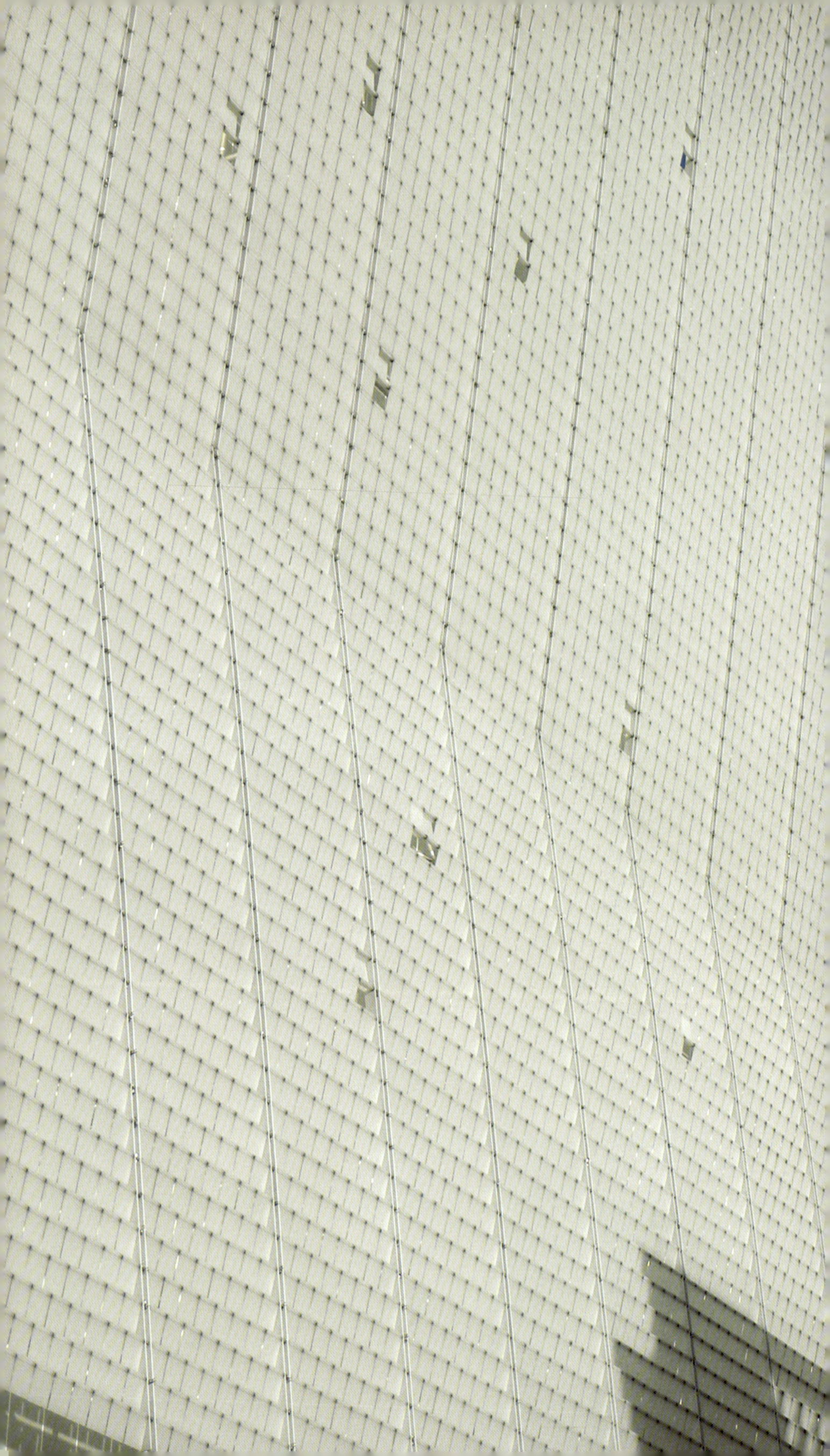

Epilogue

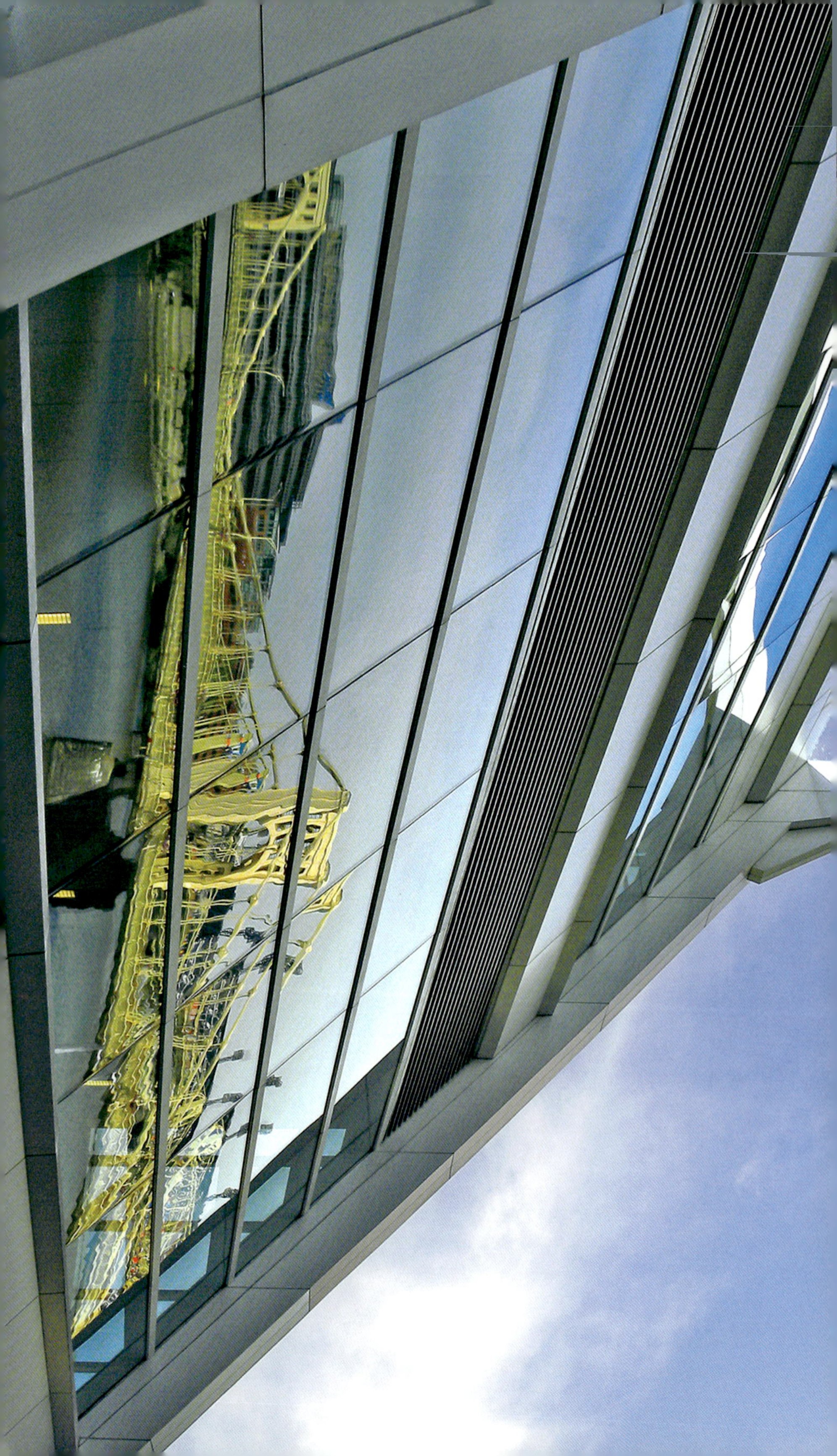

Twenty-first Century Architecture in Pittsburgh

Charles L. Rosenblum, PhD

The twenty-first century and its architecture have arrived with powerful computing technologies as driving forces. Just as the structural and aesthetic possibilities of the Industrial Revolution's innovative engineering techniques and new materials drove much of the avant-garde architecture of the twentieth century, so too do the advancing digital design techniques promise the same cutting edge role in the twenty-first. Works from Frank Gehry and Zaha Hadid, for example, are computed as much or more than they are actually drawn, and the trend will only increase. But just as the Bauhaus alone would have made for a very bland twentieth century, today's digital avant-garde on its own would give us an over-boiled twenty-first. Preservationists and historians know better than avant-gardists that the decades and centuries do not succeed each other; they actually coexist. Our lasting buildings are not relics, but rather artifacts of persistent values in what we hope is a healthy dialogue with the new and experimental. Indeed, the twentieth century showed varying approaches to architecture with roots in different historical eras coexisting fruitfully at the same time. Thus far, so does the twenty-first.

The avant-garde is not an exclusive lock on appropriate approaches to architecture, but it is one current in a much larger stream of relevant ideas and responses which invariably intermingle. In the twenty-first century, Pittsburgh has a few examples of computer-driven avant-garde architecture, and perhaps it could use a few more adventurous clients demanding more. Nonetheless, the scene here is lively and substantive, with some healthy strains of Modernism also playing prominent roles. Issues of sustainable design loom significantly for increasing numbers of architects.

The best approach for Pittsburgh architecture is to examine what has been visible and well-received. Prominent among these has been the David L. Lawrence Convention Center, by Rafael Viñoly Architects. The result of a well-publicized competition among several renowned architecture firms, this scheme won in part because of the architect's compelling initial concept to evoke both the historic bridges and the dramatic topography

The David L. Lawrence Convention Center connects with the Allegheny River via a riverfront trail and a path at Tenth Street winding between walls of water.

of Pittsburgh in a sweeping, largely cable-suspended roof structure that uses colossal, cantilevered trusses rising from the street level to support the floors and roof on the river side. Bucking the trend of convention centers at the time of its design, the building makes extensive use of daylighting, in addition to a roster of other advanced sustainable design features.

A pedestrian connection to the Allegheny River, along with extensive views from inside and out of the building, have proved advantageous, though some unfriendly blank walls at the street level and a troubled construction process have been shortcomings. Overall, this is a building of iconic, experiential, and urbanistic successes that has defined a significant corner of downtown Pittsburgh as well as the image of the greater city at the dawn of the millennium. Its willful recollection of twentieth-century bridges and its inevitable comparison with Eero Saarinen's mid-century Modern classic Dulles airport suggest that structurally heroic Modernism is alive and well at the beginning of the twenty-first century.

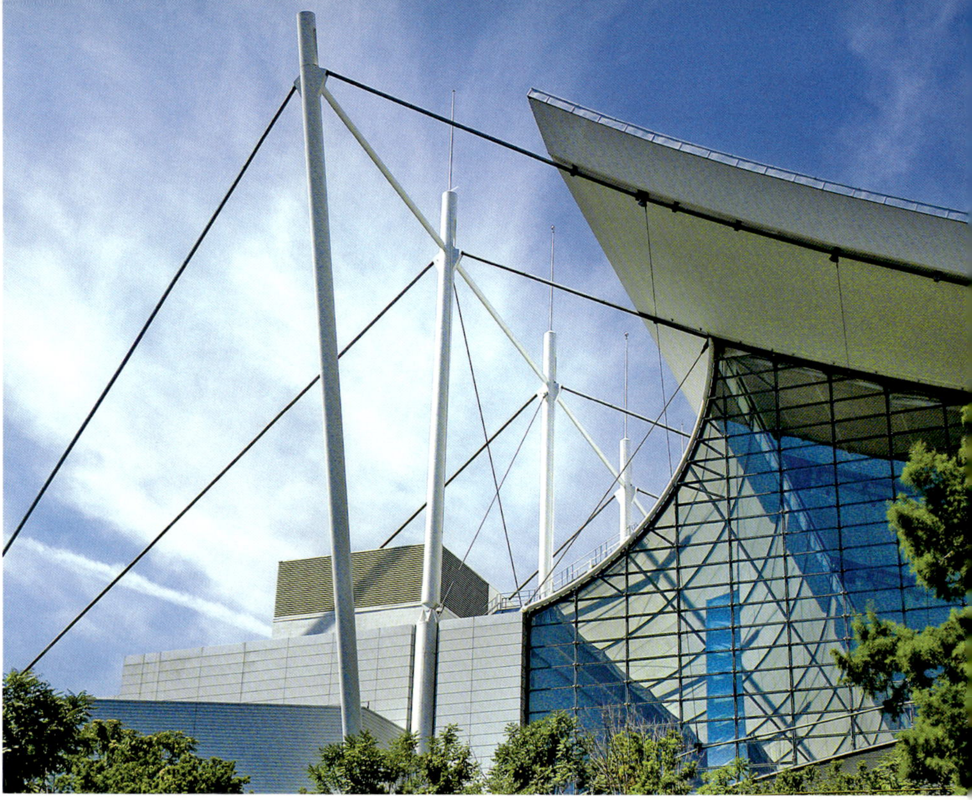

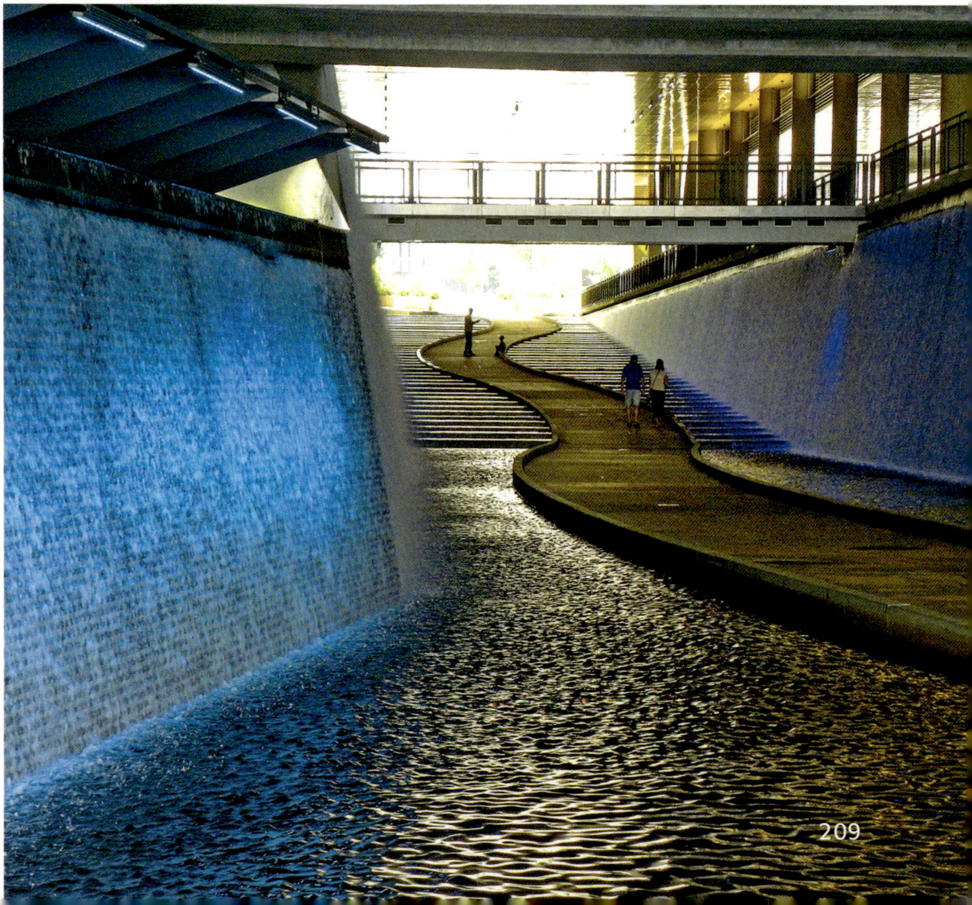

The Children's Museum on Pittsburgh's North Side occupies buildings from three centuries: the nineteenth, twentieth, and twenty-first.

Across the Allegheny, Children's Museum of Pittsburgh includes another of the millennium's noteworthy new works in the city. Like the Convention Center, this building is also a nationally published design that was the result of a design competition, which Santa Monica-based architects Koning Eizenberg won. The project also has won national awards from the American Institute of Architects (AIA), the National Trust for Historic Preservation, and the American Association of Museums. It is a combination of renovation and reuse of the historic Allegheny Post Office (1897) and Buhl Planetarium (1939) connected by a contemporary, nearly cubic, multi-story wing for museum exhibitions. Its exterior walls are a collaborative work, designed by the architects with environmental artist Ned Kahn. Made of outward-canted steel screens and small translucent shingles hinged only at the top, Kahn's "Articulated Cloud" reflects light and shadow and ripples in the wind. At night, the sculpture is illuminated.

As an icon, Children's Museum of Pittsburgh has in its new construction the requisite creases in its thinly expressed skin that could place it in at least one formal category of contemporary architecture. "Folding" was identified in prominent 1990s publications and beyond as a significant movement of the avant-garde, with concomitant developments in computer design technology (which has gained influence) and cultural theory (which has not). Yet, while the Children's Museum possesses a hint of the fashionable form, its architectural emphasis lies elsewhere. The building resulted from a community-oriented process of meetings and information gathering, and includes office space for several nonprofit partners. It works socially and architecturally to make connections among individuals and institutions as well as between new and historical architecture. These qualities are as noteworthy as its formal design. They speak to a continuing humanism that is necessary in architecture of any period.

Probably the most formally ambitious and visually exciting piece of contemporary architecture in Pittsburgh—another winner of a national AIA design award—is the Gates Hillman building by Mack Scogin Merrill Elam Architects, located at Carnegie Mellon University. This home of the School of Computer Science is incongruously tucked into a less than ideally visible site on campus, visible (but not prominent) on Forbes Avenue. Its design reflects both the complexity and aspirational nature of computer science, as well as the software-driven processes of design and construction. It is a building for the digital age. A driving desire for a view from every

The Gates Center for Computer Science and Hillman Center for Future-Generation Technologies at Carnegie Mellon University, as seen from within the campus

office, combined with a healthy variety of classrooms, lecture halls, conference rooms, and breakout spaces, encouraged a complex floor plan, which the architects emphasized on each floor and between levels. The multiple cantilevered building appears like a massive stack of differently shaped jigsaw puzzle pieces, whose divergent shapes lead to a multiplicity of balcony and outdoor spaces on an already-precipitous site.

The sense of individuality among faculty members corresponds to an articulation of exterior skin in which every window treatment, with creased zinc panels, is slightly different than the others, adding constant variety to a dynamic black-shingled skin. A major interior organizing device in the building's lower floors is a spiraling staircase, perhaps a superfluous element in such a complex structure, whose interlocking multi-level interior spaces would be more than sufficiently articulated without the spiral. This building, in its formal zealousness, even with some flaws that are as prominent as its achievements, is a welcome addition to Pittsburgh's frequently conservative architectural culture. It is the most decisively avant-garde building in the city and the only one this large.

Numerous other Pittsburgh buildings reached completion in the first years of the twenty-first century, but very few, if any others at a large scale by nationally known architects, reached the level of either overall quality or ambitiousness as these preceding three. The local firms that build at a large scale do not usually gain recognition for aesthetic design alone. Conversely, the most consistently achieving local design firms, while earning some significant design recognition, tend to do so with smaller projects.

The most avant-garde building by local architects in Pittsburgh may paradoxically be a fairly subtle one, but it is admirable and clear in its embrace of current approaches. The Gateway T Station is the work of six architects who were at the time members of the firms EDGE Studio and Pfaffmann + Associates. What might look, at an unknowing glance, like a pleasantly straightforward glass enclosure is actually a mathematically complex exercise in multivariable geometries of curves, seams, and facets, made possible only by parametric design. The building is also infrastructurally complex, as it resolves the competing needs and rights of way of current mass transit and defunct passenger rail lines, as well as a slew of structural and utilitarian incursions and building and fire codes. It creates an unusual visual connectivity from the lower level transit platform through the glass to the ground level downtown, enhanced by a dramatic escalator procession. What seem like fashion-

The Gateway T Station is located on Stanwix Street between Penn and Liberty avenues in downtown Pittsburgh. "Pittsburgh Recollections" (1984), a ceramic-tile mural by African American artist Romare Bearden, is on the track level of the station.

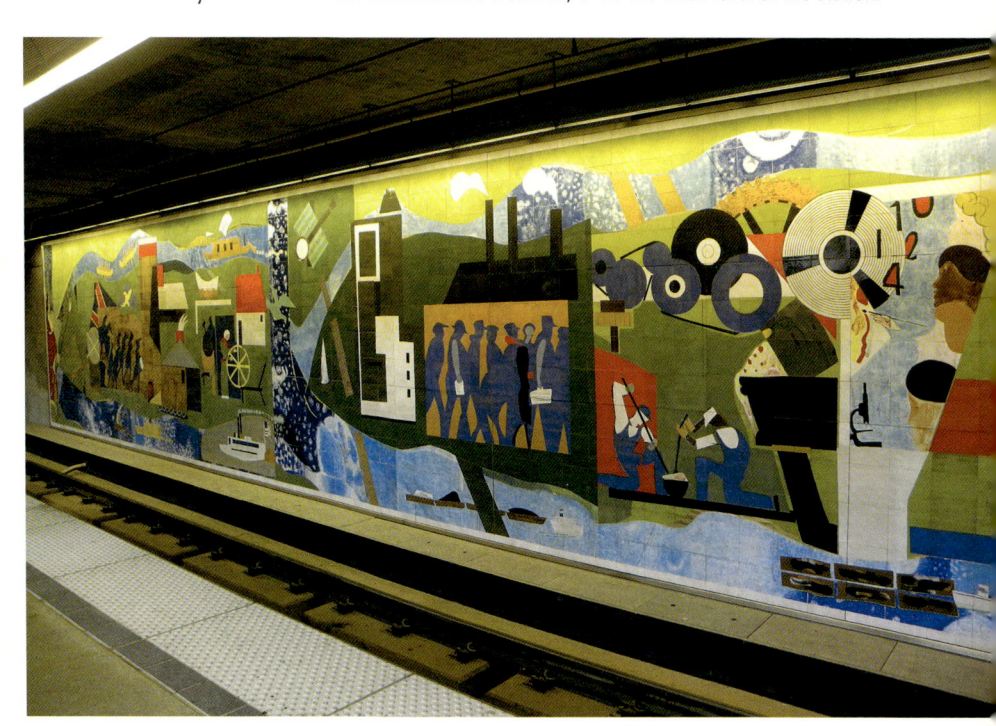

ably canted columns actually take their shape from structural necessity. This building is erudite and accomplished; it is simply moderate rather than overdone.

At the much more visually strident end of the avant-garde is the Glass Lofts project by Arthur Lubetz Associates, now known as Front Studio Architects, after the New York-based firm of former Lubetz students with whom he merged his practice. A moderate-cost, multi-unit housing project for Friendship Development Associates, the Glass Lofts engages a willfully angular geometry of offset volumes on spindly supports in a palette that includes both raw concrete block and fluorescent green walls. Lubetz has decades of architectural practice using unfinished materials and broken geometries to convey a sense of intensified architectural experience, in buildings around Pittsburgh and further afield. The ideology has some intellectual roots in the conceptual art of the 1970s. Similarly, to trace some formal elements to movements relating to deconstruction in the late 1980s and early 1990s is to trace the lineage of architectural approaches that, when well implemented, still have relevance and aesthetic power. Lubetz and his more recent collaborators are Pittsburgh's version of architects such as Coop Himmelb(l)au and Thom Mayne.

One could engage the cantilever as an evergreen architectural element in similar fashion. What Fallingwater embodied as a culmination of the art in 1937, perhaps as an echo of earlier speculative works of Russian Constructivism, is experiencing a resurgence as an architectural trend, brought to completion in works nationally by practitioners including Steven Holl and Schwartz and Silver. Architectural ambition in a private residence can still be expressed with the largest cantilever possible. Eric Fisher's structure for Emerald Art Glass, which projects a large cantilevered residential space over a South Side warehouse, landed on the pages of the *New York Times*. Fisher is an unapologetic Modernist, whose primarily residential projects blend sensibilities of mid-century California breeziness with up-to-date Pittsburgh grit.

Glass Lofts, 5491 Penn Avenue, Garfield

Emerald Art Glass, 2300 Josephine Street, South Side

Epilogue

Live/Work Studio (with door detail, right), 139 South 22nd Street, South Side

   In fact, the South Side is one of Pittsburgh's foremost neighborhoods for prominent high design architecture. Studio d'ARC, with no local project bigger than three stories, has generated interest in its buildings from publications and books around the globe. Foremost among these is the Live/Work Studio, a consistently rectilinear study in Cor-Ten steel and weathered mahogany that absorbs the sensibilities of Pittsburgh's material palette and landscape topography, implementing them with precise tectonic expression. The building façade hints at the three dimensional flow of skylit and walkway-connected spaces inside. Studio d'ARC's nearby Muriel Street house makes reuse of a pre-existing garage and urban courtyard to create an interlinked series of outdoor courts and indoor spaces. It was named *Pittsburgh Magazine's* House of the Year for its artifice. The studio d'ARC

Muriel Street residence, 56 South 16th Street, South Side.

48th Street Row, Lawrenceville

aesthetic is, for the most part, resolutely orthogonal, keeping early- to mid-century Modernism alive and well. The visual parallels are with practitioners as diverse as Marlon Blackwell in Arkansas and Glenn Murcutt in Australia.

Moss Architects plays a similar role of bringing high design to the newly redeveloping Lawrenceville neighborhood, balancing historic preservation with Modernist new construction. An early project to renovate an unadorned two-story brick storefront surmounted the otherwise-unassuming Butler Street building with a dramatic butterfly roof containing two residential units. While the architect's own residence in that neighborhood is a confident essay in additions and erosions of corrugated metal—a suitably industrial palette—some of the firm's best work in Lawrenceville comes from new incursions made into historic buildings, such as their 48th Street Row, done for Botero Development.

Architect's residence (left) at 221 38th Street and 4209 Butler Street, Lawrenceville

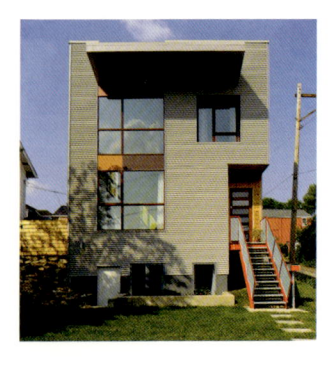

Epilogue

A building campaign of the new Carnegie Library of Pittsburgh branches, begun in 2003 and still ongoing, resulted in the closing of several architecturally distinguished late-nineteenth and early-twentieth-century buildings, the abolition of the Art and Architecture Library, and the removal of hundreds of important architecture and design books and journals to a limited access off-site storage facility. Nonetheless, it is still important to recognize the general excellence of the moderately sized renovations and new constructions throughout the city by a representative roster of ambitious local firms: Arthur Lubetz in Squirrel Hill; EDGE Studio in East Liberty; Pfaffmann + Associates in the Hill District; and Loysen + Kreuthmeier in the North Side, Brookline, and Woods Run.

A discussion of twenty-first-century architecture in Pittsburgh would be incomplete without a mention of sustainable design. Phipps' Center for Sustainable Landscapes touts itself as one of the world's most environmentally conscientious buildings as a participant in the International Living Building Institute's Living Building Challenge. Houses designed by Thoughtful Balance pay particular attention to building envelope insulation and performance of mechanical systems to reduce energy consumption drastically. The forthcoming Tower at PNC, designed by Gensler, promises to be one of the most environmentally conscientious buildings of its kind. There is no doubt that sustainability is a requirement, rather than an option, for architecture on a warming planet. Yet, architects should pursue, rather than abandon, the effort to intermesh their aesthetic ambitions with the possibilities and requirements of environmental design.

Allegheny Branch, North Side

Phipps' Center for Sustainable Landscapes, Schenley Park

Rendering, Tower at PNC, downtown

The prevailing architectural mode in Pittsburgh in the twenty-first century is a solid, elegant Modernism which embraces community input and responds with a proud regional identity and a slow absorption of the comparatively frenetic avant-garde. The current architecture consists of achievements worthy of pride, but they should not prevent designers and patrons from diving into the present with more adventurousness.

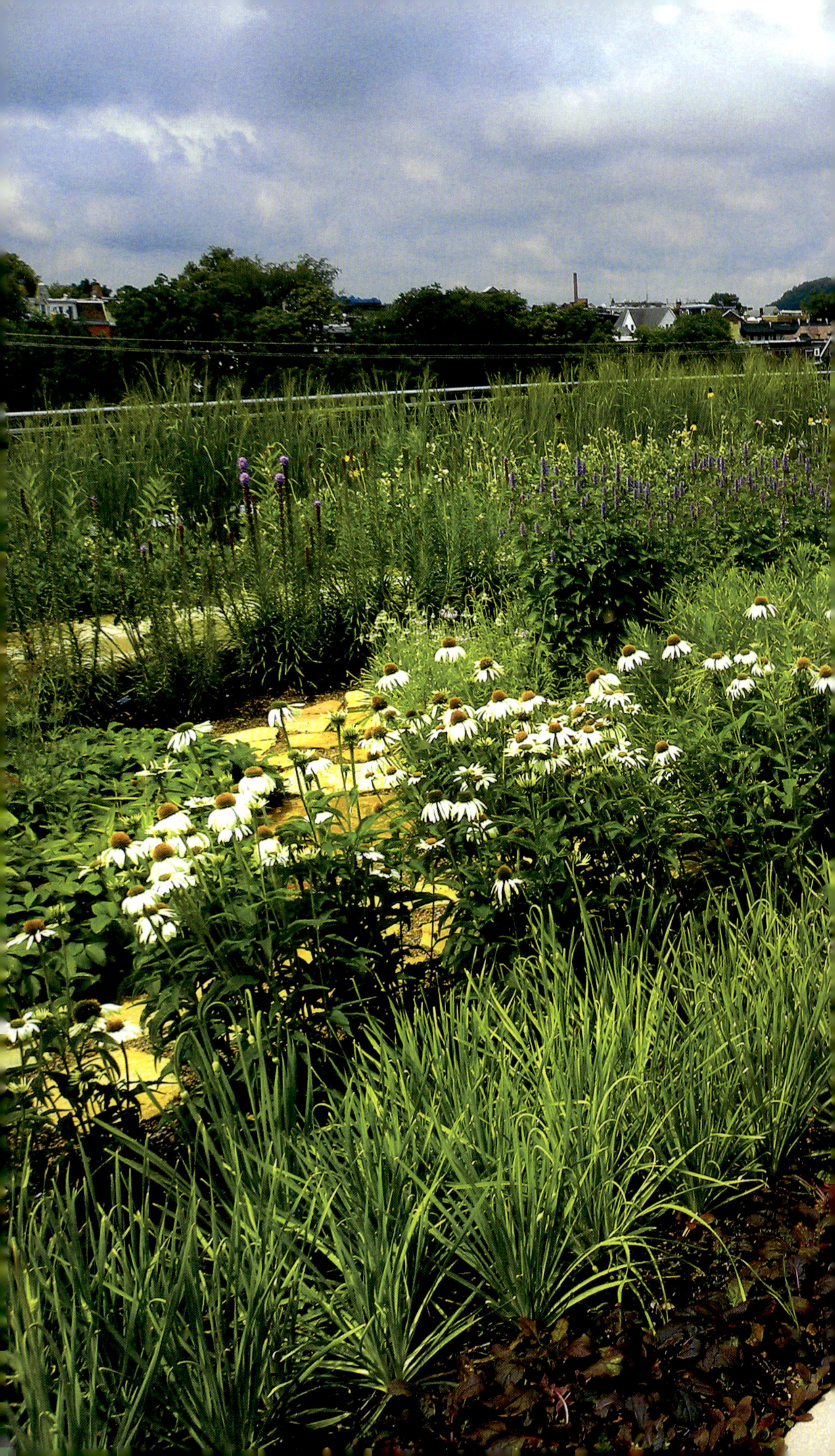

Appendices

340
HIGHLAND
TOWERS

Illustration Sources

All photographs are from the Pittsburgh History & Landmarks Foundation unless otherwise noted. We thank the following:

Courtesy of Joan Apt: 148, 150

Avery Architectural and Fine Arts Library, Columbia University: 192

Carnegie Library of Pittsburgh: 10–11, 12–13 (top), 14, 20, 39, 60, 193 (top), 194 (bottom), 200 (bottom)

Carnegie Mellon University Architecture Archives: 24 (top middle), 30, 36

Carnegie Museum of Art, Pittsburgh: 29 (bottom)
—Frank Lloyd Wright, architect, American, 1867–1959; Allen Lape Davison, delineator, American, 1913–1974; *Twin Bridges Project for Point Park, Pittsburgh, Pennsylvania*, 1947; graphite, colored pencil and ink on paper; H: 30 in. x W: 58 in. (76.20 x 147.32 cm). Gift of the Women's Committee Carnegie Treasure Room Cookbook Fund, 86.24. © *2013 Frank Lloyd Wright Foundation, Scottsdale, AZ/Artists Rights Society (ARS), NY*

Thomas & Katherine Detre Library and Archives, Senator John Heinz History Center: 156

Courtesy of Alan I W Frank: 126–131 (also see credits on page 131)

Gensler: 217 (bottom)

Ed Massery, Massery Photography, Inc.: 215 (top right and bottom)

Greg Pytlik, Pytlik Design Associates: 90

Photo by Joseph P. Rudinec, courtesy of The Butler Institute of American Art, Ohio: 203

William Rydberg, PHOTON: xiii, xvii, 26, 27 (top left, bottom left, bottom right), 79 (top and bottom left), 81 (left), 87 (bottom), 106 (middle), 107 (bottom left, bottom right), 119 (top), 179 (bottom left, bottom right), 193 (bottom), 194 (top)

Sally Siegel: 77 (bottom right)

Susanne Slavick: 110 (top)

Jason Snyder: 216 (bottom left)

© Ezra Stoller/Esto: 196 (top)

Joseph Urban Collection, Rare Book and Manuscript Library, Columbia University: 97 (top)

Albert Vercerka: 216 (top)

Courtesy of the Western Pennsylvania Conservancy: 24 (bottom), 29 (top; © *2013 Frank Lloyd Wright Foundation, Scottsdale, AZ/Artists Rights Society [ARS], NY*), 195

THIS ROOM IS DEDICATED
TO THE MT LEBANON CITI-
ZENS WHO SERVED IN THE
WORLD WAR

Acknowledgements

A lead grant from the Sports & Exhibition Authority of Pittsburgh and Allegheny County made it possible for the Pittsburgh History & Landmarks Foundation (PHLF) to concentrate its efforts on creating this guidebook during the past two years, but I have been interested in architecture from the late-nineteenth and twentieth centuries ever since I began working for the Department of Special Collections, University of Chicago Library, in 1969. When I moved to Pittsburgh in 1990 and joined PHLF's staff as Historical Collections Director, I began to focus my research on the Pittsburgh region.

Since that time, many people have contributed to the story of twentieth-century architecture in the Pittsburgh region that is told here. My thanks especially to the following architects, architectural critics, curators, historians, building owners (and their heirs and their representatives) who have shared information, insights, and memories, or introduced me to interesting communities and remarkable buildings, and helped me better understand talented and visionary architects, builders, and craftsmen: Sondra Goetz Abrahamson, Betty Abrams, Samuel Albert, Terence and Faith Alcorn, Joan Apt, Drew Armstrong, Martin Aurand, Angelique Bamberg, the late Ruth Beck and Karen Beck Bock, Martha Berg, Barry Bergdoll, Indira Berndtson, the late Cornelia Brierly, Richard Cleary, Peter Cormack, Val M. Cox, Alan Crawford, Lu Donnelly, Mimi Goetz Fleming, Ronald L. Flucker, Alan I W Frank, Gregory R. Fuhrman, Michael and Alison Gimbel, Frank Giovannitti, Scott Gordon, Robert Hossli, Thomas A. Josephi, David and Jeree Kiefer, Karen Kingsley, Reverend Ilona Komjathy, Carol H. Krinsky, Fr. David Lesko, the late Edith Lipkind, Patricia Lowry, Marcia Mastrangelo, Jason and Sara McClelland, Edward Mitchell, Gerald Lee Morosco, Tracy Myers, Paulo Nzambi, Janet Parks, Clinton Piper, Nicholas and Dorothy Rescher, Eric K. Rueter, Raymond Ryan, Steve Salvador, John Schalcosky, Ann Scheid, Elaine Schotting, Franklin Toker, Fred Watts, J. Dustin Williams, and Scott Wise and Robert Moore.

Opposite: Lobby, Mt. Lebanon Municipal Building

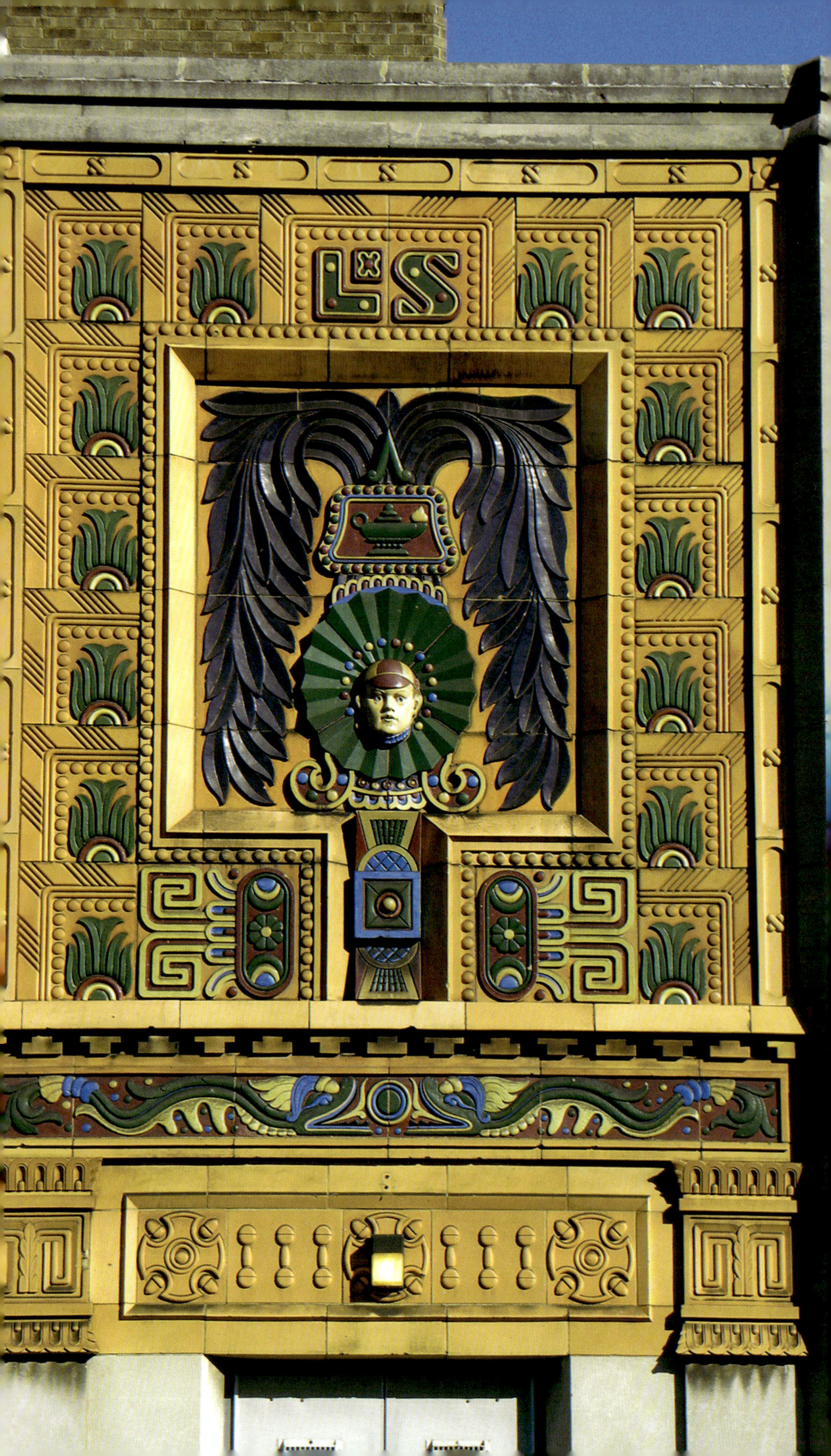

Acknowledgements

I am indebted to librarians and curators at the Avery Architectural and Fine Arts Library, Columbia University, New York City; Boston Public Library Fine Arts and Microtext Departments; Carnegie Library of Pittsburgh; Carnegie Mellon University Architecture Archives; the Library of Congress; Los Angeles Public Library; Rotch Library of Architecture and Design, Massachusetts Institute of Technology; and the University of Pittsburgh Library.

The following people thoughtfully reviewed various drafts of the manuscript and provided valuable comments, corrections, and insights: Martin Aurand, Michael Cahall, Richard Cleary, Laurie Cohen, Lu Donnelly, Karen Kingsley, Charles L. Rosenblum, Jeff Slack, and David J. Vater. Louise Sturgess, Executive Director of PHLF and project director for this book, worked closely with Mr. Vater and others in editing the publication and took many of the photographs credited to PHLF. Frank Stroker, assistant archivist at PHLF, provided valuable help in obtaining historical images and in verifying site information. Other PHLF staff members and college interns took part in this team effort.

Greg Pytlik and Beth Buckholtz of Pytlik Design Associates worked skillfully to produce a handsome guidebook—the *fifth* in PHLF's series featuring significant landmarks, artists, and architects in this region.

Many PHLF members and friends have provided essential financial support for our series of guidebooks, and I thank them for their continuing generosity and interest in discovering more about and exploring this region's significant architectural history.

—Albert M. Tannler
October 2013

Opposite: Detail of the Mezo-American polychrome terra cotta at the former Lemington School, now Destiny International Ministries

219

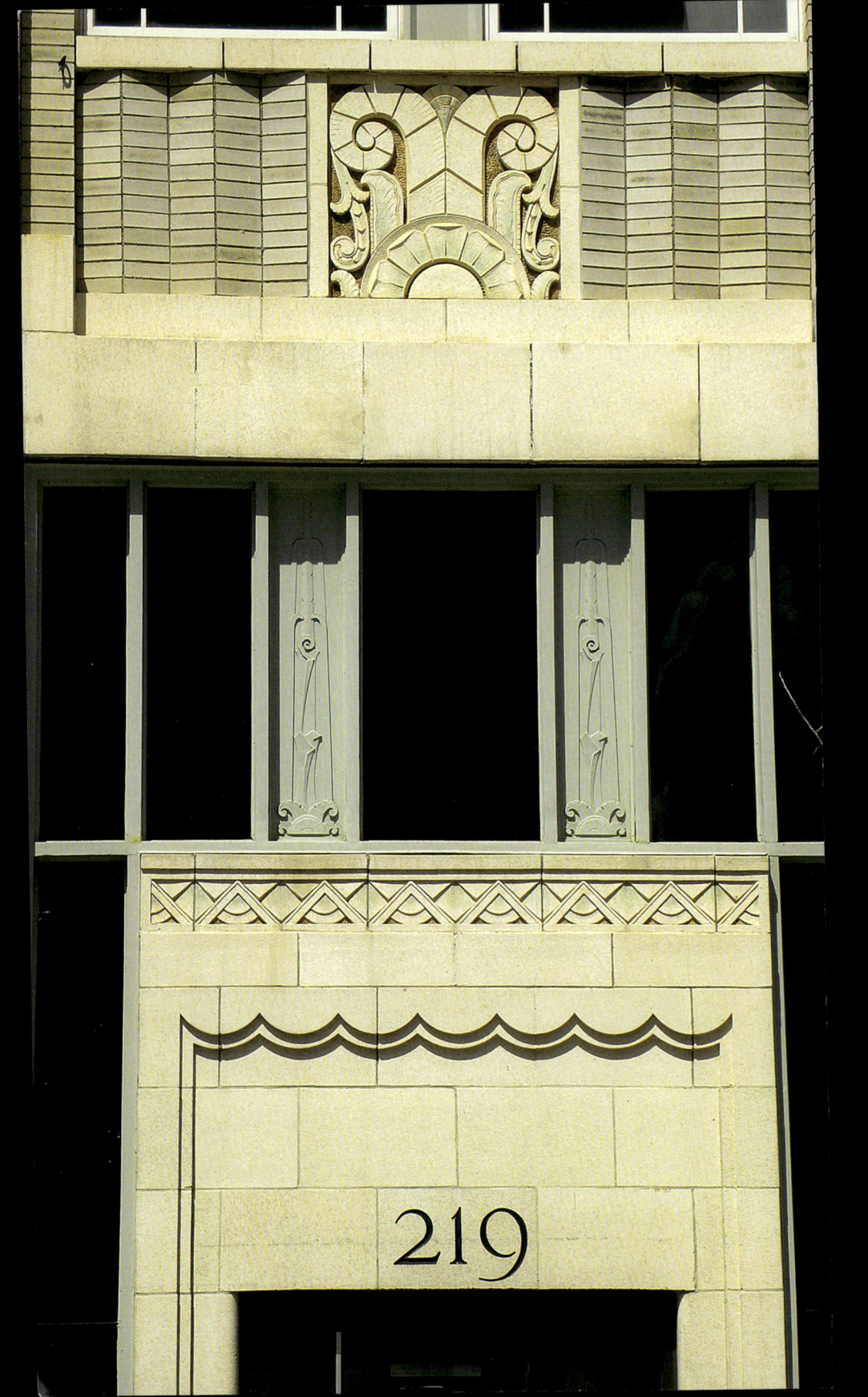

Notes

Preface

[1] C. R. Ashbee, *American Sheaves and English Seed Corn: Being a Series of Addresses Mainly Given in the United States*, 1900–1901. (London: Edward Arnold and New York: Samuel Buckley & Co., 1901), 84–85. The "one little landmark" saved by the Ladies was Bouquet's Redoubt, built in 1764, and now called the Fort Pitt Block House. Open to the public since July 15, 1895 thanks to the Fort Pitt Society of the Daughters of the American Revolution, the Block House is the city's oldest, continuously operating museum.

[2] Even before the twentieth century, Carnegie Company steel supported Chicago skyscrapers. See Andrew Saint, *The Architect and the Engineer: A Study in Sibling Rivalry* (New Haven: Yale University Press, 2007), 170–172. See also Thomas J. Misa, *A Nation of Steel: The Making of Modern America 1865–1925* (Baltimore: Johns Hopkins Press, 1999).

[3] Martin Aurand, http://dli.library.cmu.edu/charette/

[4] Henry-Russell Hitchcock to James D. Van Trump, November 17, 1963, in the James D. Van Trump Papers, James D. Van Trump Library, Pittsburgh History & Landmarks Foundation. The quotation was published in *PHLF News* 140 (October 1995), 1. A longer excerpt was published in *The Charette* 44:1 (January 1964), 2.

Definitions of Modern Architecture

[1] *Webster's New International Dictionary of the English Language*, W. T. Harris, editor-in-chief (Springfield, MA: G. & C. Merriam Company, 1923), 1389.

[2] *Chambers 2-in-1 Dictionary & Thesaurus* (Edinburgh: Chambers, 1995), 587.

[3] William T. Comstock, *Modern Architectural Designs and Details Containing Eighty Finely Lithographed Plates, Showing New and Original Designs in the Queen Anne, Eastlake, Elizabethan, and Other Modernized Styles* (New York: William T. Comstock, 1881).

[4] Comstock, "Preface," [no page]

Opposite: Suave Art Deco brickwork and terra cotta on the former G.C. Murphy Company entrance, now part of Market Square Place, downtown Pittsburgh

[5] "The Big Event: Great Preparation for the Architectural Exhibit; Work Now Being Placed in Position. Manager T. M. Walker Pleased With the Outlook—Many Visitors Expected," [Allegheny City] *Evening Record*, September 15, 1897, 1.

[6] *Catalogue of the Architectural Exhibition of Pittsburg, Pa. Held at Carnegie Art Rooms, Allegheny, From Thursday, September 16 to Saturday, September 25, inclusive. 1897.* Supplement to *The Builder* (Pittsburgh).

[7] Louis H. Sullivan, "The Modern Phase of Architecture," subsequently published in *The Inland Architect and News Record* 33 (June 1899) and reprinted in *Louis Sullivan: The Public Papers*, ed. by Robert Twombly (Chicago: University of Chicago Press, 1988), 121–122.

[8] Albert Kelsey, ed., *The Architectural Annual 1900*, Vol. 1 (Philadelphia: The Architectural Annual, 1900), 15.

[9] Russell Sturgis, *A Dictionary of Architecture and Building: Biographical, Historical, and Descriptive*, 3 Vols. (New York: MacMillan & Company, 1902), Vol. 1, 774.

[10] Frank Lloyd Wright, "In the Cause of Architecture," *Architectural Record* 23 (March 1908), quoted *In the Cause of Architecture: Essays by Frank Lloyd Wright for Architectural Record 1908–1952*, edited by Frederick Guthem (New York: McGraw-Hill, 1975), 59.

[11] C. Matlack Price, *The Practical Book of Architecture* (Philadelphia: J. J. Lippincott & Company, 1916), 203.

[12] Price, 204. Mention should be made of the Catalan style *Modernista*, which has been compared to *Art Nouveau*, but which appeared in Barcelona in the work of Antonio Gaudi and his peers in the 1880s, a decade before *Art Nouveau* originated in Belgium. *Modernista* did not receive widespread critical attention in the United States until the 1970s.

[13] Price, 205.

[14] Price, 207.

[15] Grace Glueck, "Design Review: When Americans Awoke to Modern Styles," *New York Times*, May 19, 2000.

[16] Richard Guy Wilson, "Machine Aesthetics," *The Machine Age in America*, 49. The term "Art Deco," derived from *arts décoratifs*, began being used in the 1960s.

[17] Patricia Bayer, *Art Deco Architecture: Design, Decoration and Detail From the Twenties and Thirties* (New York: Abrams, 1992), 7.

[18] Vincent Scully, "Foreword to the De Capo Edition," Henry-Russell Hitchcock, *Modern Architecture: Romanticism and Reintegration* (New York: De Capo Press, 1993), vii.

[19] Hitchcock, *Modern Architecture*, 160.

[20] Hitchcock, *Modern Architecture*, 160.

[21] Hitchcock, *Modern Architecture*, 162.

[22] Franz Schulze, *Philip Johnson: Life and Work* (Chicago: University of Chicago Press, 1994), 71. See also "MoMA, Russell, and the New Style," 58–64; "The American Invasion," 70–74; and "The 1932 Show: The Revolution Goes Uptown," 75–86.

[23] The contents and layout of the exhibit are documented in Terence Riley, *The International Style: Exhibition 15 and The Museum of Modern Art* (New York: Rizzoli, 1992).

[24] Henry-Russell Hitchcock and Philip Johnson, *The International Style: Architecture Since 1922* (New York: W. W. Norton, 1932). Revised and reprinted 1966 and 1995.

[25] Alfred H. Barr, Jr., "Preface," *The International Style*, 29.

[26] Rudolph Schindler, who had studied with Otto Wagner and Adolf Loos in Vienna, came to the United States in 1914 and worked for Wright before settling in Los Angeles in 1920, initially as project architect at Wright's Barnsdall house. Schindler opened his own practice in Los Angeles. Neutra came to the United States in 1923, worked briefly for Wright in 1924, and moved his family to Los Angeles in 1925 at Schindler's invitation; the Neutra family shared Schindler's home until 1930. Hitchcock found Schindler's work "extreme" and he was not included in the 1932 exhibit. Judith Sheine, in *R. M. Schindler* (Phaidon, 2001) writes of the 1932 exhibit (*Modern Architecture—International Exhibition*): "Neutra was in; Schindler was out; and Wright was included, but in a way that made him seem like a has-been." (70)

[27] John Stevens Curl, *Oxford Dictionary of Architecture and Landscape Architecture* (Oxford: Oxford University Press, 2nd ed., 2006), 607.

[28] Scully, "Foreword to the De Capo Edition," viii–ix.

[29] Carter Wiseman, *Shaping a Nation: Twentieth-Century American Architecture and Its Makers* (New York: W. W. Norton, 1998), 220.

[30] Robert Venturi, *Complexity and Contradiction in Architecture* (New York: Museum of Modern Art in association with the Graham Foundation for the Fine Arts, Chicago, 1966), 22.

[31] Richard Longstreth, "Chapter 50: North America 1900 to 1950," *Sir Banister Fletcher's A History of Architecture*, 20th edition, edited by Dan Cruickshank (London: Architectural Press, 1996), 1483–1484.

The Eve of Modernism / How Modern Architecture Came to Pittsburgh

[1] Walter C. Kidney, *H. H. Richardson's Allegheny County Courthouse and Jail* (Pittsburgh: Allegheny County Bureau of Cultural Programs, 1981), [no page]

[2] Kidney, *H. H. Richardson's Allegheny County Courthouse and Jail*, [no page]

[3] Christopher Monkhouse, "The ABC's of an Architectural Library in Pittsburgh: Anderson, Bernd and Carnegie," *Carnegie Magazine* 63:2 (March/April 1996), 20–26. See also K. Salome Stamm, "Architectural Books in the Carnegie Library: The Bernd Collection," *The Charette* 5:5 (May 1925), 1–3.

4 [Monthly feature on architectural books acquired by the Carnegie Library of Pittsburgh; title varies] *The Charette*, 5–29 (March 1925 through October 1949).

5 *Construction Record* has been digitized and is searchable on the Carnegie Library of Pittsburgh website. Carnegie Mellon University Architecture Archives has hard copy of the *Builders' Bulletin* 1916–27; Carnegie Library of Pittsburgh has hard copy of the *Builders' Bulletin* 1922–2005.

6 *Catalogue of the Architectural Exhibition of Pittsburg, Pa. 1897.* From 1891 to 1911, Pittsburgh was officially spelled without the "h". Allegheny City was annexed by Pittsburgh in 1907.

7 "The Big Event," [Allegheny City] *Evening Record*, September 15, 1897, 1.

8 Pittsburgh Chapter, AIA. *Catalogue of the First Annual Architectural Exhibition by the Pittsburgh Chapter American Institute of Architects Held at the Carnegie Art Gallery, Pittsburgh, Pa., May 2nd to 31st.* (Murdoch-Kerr Press, 1898).

9 Henry M. Kropff, "Recollections of Some of the Old Timers," *The Charette* 12:3 (March 1932): "From St. Paul came John T. Comes, an active enthusiastic draftsman, to settle in Pittsburgh and discovering that we had no Architectural Club began to interest the draftsmen he met in organizing one," 1.

10 *Catalogue of the First Annual Exhibition of the Pittsburgh Architecture Club 1900* (Erie: Herald P. & P. Co., 1900). Regarding the exhibition, Kropff, "Recollections of Some of the Old Timers," wrote: "In 1900 we held our first exhibition in the Carnegie Galleries and it required some effort by the Exhibition Committee of the Club to convince the Trustees that architects make artistic drawings of interest to the public; their idea of an architectural exhibition was a lot of blue prints, but after they saw the Exhibition we had little difficulty securing the galleries for future exhibitions," 1–2.

11 Only the Philadelphia architectural club catalog illustrated many of the English exhibits—seventeen of the thirty on display—but other buildings were published in contemporary magazines and books, thus allowing us to see much of what was shown in 1900. Some of the English exhibits traveled to architectural clubs in Philadelphia, New York, Chicago, St. Louis, Detroit, Cleveland, and Pittsburgh, from December 17, 1899 through July 1, 1900.

12 "Would Preserve Beauty Spots of Pittsburg: London Man Will Endeavor to Organize Society Here With That Object in View." *Pittsburgh Dispatch*, November 21, 1900, 13.

13 Alan Crawford, *C. R. Ashbee: Architect, Designer and Romantic Socialist* (New Haven: Yale University Press, 1985), 96.

14 Albert M. Tannler, "C. R. Ashbee Visits Pittsburgh," *PHLF News* 172 (April 2007), 16. Ashbee's opinion of Pittsburgh is found in *American Sheaves and English Seed Corn*, 83–87; 104–106; 115; 125; 130, and *Where the Great City Stands: A Study in the New Civics* (London: The Essex House Press, 1917), 70, 130.

15 Pittsburgh Architectural Club, *Fourth Exhibition at The Carnegie Institute Galleries, November 1907.*

[16] Christopher Monkhouse, "A Century of Architectural Exhibitions at The Carnegie: 1893–1993," *Carnegie Magazine* 61 (November/December 1993), 32.

[17] *Dekorative Vorbilder* (Stuttgart: Verlag Julius Hoffmann). Volumes 17 through 19 (1906–08) published numerous designs by J. K. Becker-Gundahl, Walter Caspari, G. M. Ellwood, Remigius Geyling, Joseph Goller, M. J. Gradl, Frantisek Kupka, Valentin Mink, and Franz Waldraff. Their work was exhibited in Pittsburgh in 1907.

[18] In 1911, C. R. Ashbee would include Möhring among the Austrian and German architects having a "certain kinship" to Wright: "Frank Lloyd Wright: A Study and an Appreciation," *The Early Work of Frank Lloyd Wright* (New York: Bramhall House, 1958), 7. Bruno Möhring (1863–1929) is discussed in Anthony Alofsin, *Frank Lloyd Wright: The Lost Years, 1910–1922—A Study in Influence* (Chicago: University of Chicago Press, 1993), 12–14, 326; John Heskett, *German Design 1870–1918* (New York: Taplinger, 1986), 76, 77. Some of Möhring's buildings are illustrated in *The Architecture of the Early 20th Century: Journal of Modern Architecture*, ed. by Ernst Wasmuth, reprinted in *Architecture of the Early 20th Century*, ed. by Peter Haiko (New York: Rizzoli, 1989).

[19] Frank Lloyd Wright and a number of his office staff were among the midwestern architects who visited the Austrian and German exhibits at St. Louis. Irving Pond reviewed the German exhibit for *Architectural Record*. He approved of the designs and was happy to find them free of the excesses of Art Nouveau: Irving K. Pond, "The German Exhibit of Arts and Crafts," *Architectural Record* 17 (February 1905), 118–125.

[20] Petr Wittlich, *Prague: Fin de Siécle* (Paris: Flammarion, 1992), 265. See Serge Fauchereau, *Kupka* (Barcelona: Ediciones Polígrafa, S.A., 1989).

[21] Fritz Schumacher (1869–1947) was born in Bremen and was educated in Munich; he co-founded the German *Werkbund*. He was Chief Architect, City of Hamburg 1909–33, and a specialist in school design. For the 1906 Dresden exhibition, see Ludwig Eisenlohr, Carl Weigle, and Carl Zetzsche, eds. *Architektionische Rundschau: Skizzenblätter aus allen Gebieten der Baukunst* (Stuttgart: J. Engelhorn Verlag, 1906), 73–77. Fritz Schumacher's work is illustrated on 73, 77, and plate 74; a living room and a Protestant church exhibited in Pittsburgh in 1907 are illustrated. See also Heskett, *German Design*, 106–118. For an overview of Schumacher's career and discussion of his later work see Alfred C. Bossom, "German Municipal Architecture: Illustrating the Work of Fritz Schumacher, Municipal Architect, Hamburg," *American Architect* 132:2534 (December 5, 1927), 709–714. Also John Zukowsky, ed., *The Many Faces of Modern Architecture: Building in Germany Between the Wars* (New York: Prestel, 1994), 112–115, 120–121. Wilhelm Kreis and Max Kühne were among the 1906 Dresden exhibitors who exhibited in Pittsburgh in 1907.

[22] The following "progressive" midwestern architects exhibited in Pittsburgh between 1898 and 1916: S. S. Beman (1903), Lawrence Buck (1907, 1910, 1912), George Dean (1898) and Dean & Dean (1907), Frost & Granger (1898), Elmer Grey (1898, 1900), Walter Burley Griffin (1900, 1907, 1910, 1912, 1913), Marion Mahony Griffin (1912 for Hermann von Holst), Jens Jensen (1907, 1910, 1911), George W. Maher (1898, 1907, 1910, 1911, 1912), William K. Fellows (1898)

and Nimonds & Fellows (1905, 1910), Dwight H. Perkins (1898, 1900, 1907, 1910, 1911, 1912, 1913), Pond & Pond (1900, 1910, 1912), Howard Van Doren Shaw (1898, 1907), Richard Schmidt (1898), Hugh Garden (1907, 1912), Robert C. Spenser (1911, 1913), Louis H. Sullivan (1898, 1907 in Northwestern Terra Cotta Company advertisements, 1911, 1912), Vernon S. Watson (1900, Talmadge & Watson, 1910, 1912, 1913, 1915), and Frank Lloyd Wright (1907, 1913).

[23] "Letter from Stanley L. Roush," *The Charette* 12:3 (March 1932), 4–6. Kiehnel remained a member of the exhibition committee for subsequent exhibitions, which ended in 1916.

[24] *Western Architect* 11:1 (January 1908), 12. See also "To Show the City Beautiful: Forthcoming Exhibition of the Pittsburgh Architectural Club in the Carnegie Galleries Will Typify the Improvement of American Cities," *Ohio Architect & Builder* 10:3 (September 1907), 46–48; G. B. Ford, "The Pittsburgh Architectural Club Exhibition, 1907," *American Architect* 92:1666 (November 30, 1907), 179–81; "The Great Pittsburg Architectural Exhibition," *The Inland Architect & News Record* (December 1907), 70.

[25] http://dictionary.reference.com/browse/charrette

[26] http://dli.library.cmu.edu/charette/

[27] Van Trump wrote for *Carnegie Magazine, Western Pennsylvania Historical Magazine, The Pittsburgher*, and other regional publications.

[28] The catalogue is *A Classified Collection of Kunstgewerbe Arranged by the Deutsches Museum für Kunst im Handel und Gewerbe, Hagan, i. W., and Oesterreichen Museums für Kunst und Industrie in Vienna: For Exhibition in the American Art Museums of Newark, Chicago, Indianapolis, Pittsburgh, Cincinnati and St. Louis* (1912). See also John Heskett, *German Design 1870–1918* (New York: Taplinger, 1986), 127.

[29] "A Selected Collection of Objects from the International Exposition of Modern Decorative and Industrial Art, Paris, 1925," exhibition catalog, American Association of Museums, 1926.

[30] *The Charette* 6:11 (November 1926), 9.

[31] Robert Schmertz, "International Architecture: A Review of the Current Exhibition of Modern Architecture," *Carnegie Magazine* 6 (June 1932), 69–71. Riley, *The International Style*, includes Pittsburgh in "Appendix 4: Subscribers Memorandum by Philip Johnson," 222, but it was omitted from "Appendix 5": the "list of institutions at which [the] International Exhibition of Modern Architecture was shown."

[32] Schmertz, "International Architecture," 70.

[33] "Kaufmann's Supplement," *Pittsburgh Sun-Telegraph*, May 11, 1930, [no page] Quotations describing Kaufmann's first floor are taken from the "Supplement" unless otherwise noted. See Albert M. Tannler, "'Utility is Beauty:' The Kaufmann Legacy in Pittsburgh." *Pittsburgh Tribune-Review, Focus* 22:21 (March 22, 1998), 8–9; "Special Places: Kaufmann's 1930 First Floor Revisited." 22:47 (September 27,

1998), 11; "Two Interiors Destroyed: The May Company Déjà Vu," *PHLF News* 155 (August 1999), 16.

[34] Richard Cleary, *Merchant Prince and Master Builder: Edgar J. Kaufmann and Frank Lloyd Wright* (Seattle: Heinz Architectural Center in Association with the University of Washington Press, 1999), 21.

[35] Edgar J. Kaufmann, jr., *Fallingwater: A Frank Lloyd Wright Country House* (Abbeville Press, 1986), 34. Kaufmann notes that Urban was a visitor to the family home in Fox Chapel. The black columns topped by electrically illuminated abstract geometric capitals in Urban's 1926 design prefigures Janssen & Cocken's design of 1927. For Urban's 1926 design for Kaufmann's see John Loring, *Joseph Urban* (New York: Abrams, 2010), 174–175.

[36] James D. Van Trump, *Life and Architecture in Pittsburgh* (Pittsburgh: Pittsburgh History & Landmarks Foundation, 1983), 111.

[37] Other unspecified white metal alloys or steel were apparently used for the entranceway doors, grilles, drinking fountains, and Arcade furniture. The Boardman Robinson murals are in the collection of the Colorado Springs Fine Arts Center.

[38] Kaufmann, *Fallingwater*, 34. Janssen & Cocken also designed the Art Deco Cork Bar and barber shop in the Duquesne Club Annex (1930–32) and Deco decoration and furnishings in the Mellon Institute (1931–37). See Mark M. Brown, Lu Donnelly, and David G. Wilkins, *The History of the Duquesne Club* (Pittsburgh: The Duquesne Club, 1989), 78, 81, and Miller, 140–151.

[39] Richard Cleary, *Merchant Prince*, and "Edgar J. Kaufmann, Frank Lloyd Wright and the 'Pittsburgh Point Park Coney Island in Automobile Scale'," *Journal of the Society of Architectural Historians* 52:2 (June 1993), 139–158.

[40] The Kaufmann office is now in the Victoria & Albert Museum, London. See Christopher Wilk, *Frank Lloyd Wright: The Kaufmann Office.* (London: Victoria & Albert Museum, 1993), 72–79. For the unrealized designs see Cleary, *Merchant Prince*, 174–193.

[41] Cleary, *Merchant Prince*, 27.

[42] Howard Saalman, "Architectural Education at Carnegie Tech: 1905–1990," typescript, Carnegie Mellon University Architecture Archives, 19.

[43] Walter Sobotka also taught at Carnegie Tech from 1941 to 1948, and perhaps later. Information from Martin Aurand and J. Dustin Williams.

[44] Saalman, 23. Saalman also mentions industrial designer Peter Müller-Munk from Berlin, who came to the United States in 1929; he joined the Carnegie Tech faculty in 1935, but left in 1944 to practice privately in Pittsburgh.

[45] Cleary, *Merchant Prince*, 27.

[46] Nina Stritzler-Levine, ed., *Josef Frank: Architect and Designer* (New Haven: Yale University Press, 1996). See also "Speaking Frankly," *The Charette* 29:4 (April 1949), 16.

[47] Martin Aurand, *The Spectator and the Topographical City* (Pittsburgh: University of Pittsburgh Press, 2006), 57.

[48]Roy Lubove, *Twentieth-Century Pittsburgh: Government, Business, and Environmental Change* (New York: Alfred A. Knopf, 1969), 1.

[49]Lubove, 2.

[50]Lubove, 2.

[51]Lubove, 15.

[52]Lubove, 8. In addition to Lubove, see John F. Bauman and Edward K. Muller, *Before Renaissance: Planning in Pittsburgh, 1889–1943* (Pittsburgh: University of Pittsburgh Press, 2006) and Maurine W. Greenwald and Marge Anderson, eds., *Pittsburgh Surveyed: Social Science and Social Reform in the Early Twentieth Century* (Pittsburgh: University of Pittsburgh Press, 1996).

[53]Lubove, 10.

[54]Bauman and Muller, 271.

[55]Bauman and Muller, 85–86.

[56]Lubove, 114.

[57]Quoted in Aurand, *The Spectator and the Topographical City*, 65.

[58]Lubove, 113–114.

[59]Robert C. Alberts, *The Shaping of the Point: Pittsburgh's Renaissance Park* (Pittsburgh: University of Pittsburgh Press, 1980), 154. Alberts' discussion of the Portal Bridge is on pages 154–162.

[60]Michael Cannell, *I. M. Pei: Mandarin of Modernism* (New York: Clarkson Potter, 1995), 109.

[61]Lubove, 123.

[62]"Equitable Builds a Gateway" (Ben Rosen Associates, 1964). Other Gateway buildings mentioned in the booklet and in this chapter, but not discussed in the Guide, are the former Hilton Hotel, designed by Hilton Hotel architect William B. Tabler, Jr. (New York); Gateway Towers, designed by Emory Roth & Sons (New York); the former State Office Building, designed by Altenhof & Bown; the former Bell Telephone Building, designed by Dowler & Dowler; and the former Allegheny Towers Penthouse Apartments, designed by Tasso Katselas. The former Westinghouse Corporate Headquarters at Gateway Six was not mentioned since it was designed by Harrison & Abramovitz after the booklet was published. Martin Aurand, *The Spectator and the Topographical City*, notes that Mitchell & Ritchey's *Pittsburgh in Progress* (1947), commissioned by E. J. Kaufmann, Sr., had advocated green spaces as an element in downtown redevelopment, 60–61.

[63]"Gateway Center," *The Charette* 31:4 (April 1951), 12.

[64]"Pittsburgh Renaissance Historic District," *National Register of Historic Places Registration Form* (Skelly & Loy, Inc./Pittsburgh History & Landmarks Foundation, 2012), Section 7, Page 3.

[65]"Pittsburgh Renaissance Historic District," Section 8, page 8. See also "Gateway Center," (April 1951), 12.

[66]Email from Martin Aurand to Albert Tannler, January 4, 2013. For an illuminating discussion of Le Corbusier's concept and Gateway Center see Aurand, *The Spectator and the Topographical City*, 54–61.

[67]Alvin Rosensweet, "3 Architectural Experts Criticize Point Buildings," *Pittsburgh Post-Gazette*, April 14, 1960, 1, 4.

[68]Jane Jacobs, *The Death and Life of Great American Cities* (New York: Random House, 1961), 223.

[69]Lubove, 139–140.

[70]Lubove, 138.

[71]Nick Stamatakis, "Bipartisanship not always a cure-all," *The Pitt News*, October 22, 2012.

Notes on the Language of Architecture / Guide

[1]Cyril M. Harris, *American Architecture: An Illustrated Encyclopedia* (New York: W. W. Norton, 1998), viii.

[2]Richard Guy Wilson, "Machine Aesthetics," *The Machine Age in America* (New York: The Brooklyn Museum in association with Harry N. Abrams, 1986), 47. Jugendstil is derived from *Jugend* (Youth) magazine, published in Munich, Germany, beginning in 1896.

[3]Maria Makela, *The Munich Secession: Art and Artists in Turn-of-the-Century Munich* (Princeton: Princeton University Press, 1990); Peter Paret, *The Berlin Secession: Modernism and Its Enemies in Imperial Germany* (Cambridge, MA: Harvard University Press, 1980).

[4]Harry F. Millgrave, "General Introduction," *Modern Architecture*, by Otto Wagner (Santa Monica, CA: The Getty Center, 1988), 1. General recommendations for further reading: Carl Schorske, *Fin-de-Siécle Vienna: Politics and Culture* (New York: Random House, 1981); Franco Borsi and Ezio Godoli, *Vienna 1900: Architecture and Design* (New York: Rizzoli, 1986); and Iain Boyd Whyte, *Three Architects from the Master Class of Otto Wagner: Emil Hoppe, Marcel Kammerer, Otto Schönthal* (Cambridge, MA: MIT Press, 1989). Readers are also directed to books about Otto Wagner, Joseph Olbrich, Josef Hoffmann, Jože Plečnik, Joseph Urban, and Adolf Loos.

[5]Wright scholar Paul Kruty, in *Frank Lloyd Wright and Midway Gardens* (Urbana: University of Illinois Press, 1998), states that "Wright was greatly affected by what he saw in St. Louis" (214). The World's Fair was Wright's "first direct encounter with modern German and Austrian architectural sculpture" and influenced his design of sculpture in the Dana House (Springfield, IL) and in the Larkin Building (Buffalo, NY): "These two designs are … the first indications of Wright's attraction

to the European Secessionists," 194. The patterned walls of the Avery Cooley House in Riverside, Illinois (1907–09) are a later legacy of the 1904 World's Fair. Secessionist influences are also evident on the façades of Unity Temple (1905–09), Oak Park, Illinois, and City National Bank (1909), Mason City, Iowa, designed prior to 1910 when Wright first visited Vienna, Darmstadt, and Berlin.

[6] C. Matlack Price, "Secessionist Architecture in America," *Arts and Decoration* 3 (December 1912), 52, cited by Anthony Alofsin, *Frank Lloyd Wright: The Lost Years, 1910–1922* (Chicago: University of Chicago Press, 1993), 347. See also Price, *The Practical Book of Architecture* (Philadelphia: J. J. Lippincott, 1916), 207.

[7] Frank Lloyd Wright, "Style in Industry," *Modern Architecture, Being the Kahn Lectures for 1930* (Princeton: Princeton University Press, 1931), 32.

[8] Albert M. Tannler, "Architecture with a Dash of Paprika: Titus de Bobula in Pittsburgh," *New Rusyn Times* 13:5 (September/October 2006), 6–10. Martin Aurand generously shared his research on this intriguing and elusive architect. I am also grateful to Samuel Albert, Ph.D., who shared his extensive knowledge of de Bobula.

[9] According to Samuel Albert, de Bobula arrived in New York City on May 29, 1896. T. W. A. Bobula is listed as working at McKim, Mead & White between October 1896 and November 7, 1896 in "Appendix II: Office Roll of McKim, Mead & White," 333; in Charles Moore, *The Life and Times of Charles Follen McKim* (Boston: Houghton Mifflin, 1929). I am grateful to Tom Josephi for providing this reference.

[10] Information from Martin Aurand.

[11] *Der Architekt* 6 (1900), plate 48.

[12] Tannler, "Austro-Germanic Secessionism and the Shaping of Early Modern Architecture in Pittsburgh." *PHLF News* 179 (December 2013), 18–20.

[13] In the 1908 city directory, de Bobula is listed as a member of the firm of De Bobula & Hazeltine with architect Louis R. Hazeltine.

[14] Martin Aurand, *The Progressive Architecture of Frederick G. Scheibler, Jr.* (Pittsburgh: University of Pittsburgh Press, 1994), 8.

[15] The demolished churches were Holy Ghost Greek Catholic Church in Allegheny City (1903) and St. Nicholas Greek Catholic Church in Duquesne (1904). I am grateful for information about these churches from Fr. David Lesko.

[16] St. Emory Hungarian Roman Catholic Church in Connellsville, PA. The building has been altered and is now Faith Bible Church, 425 Arch Street, Connellsville.

[17] *Ohio Architect & Builder* (December 1903), 74–75. The convent is gone but the parish house and the much-altered school building remain at 1135 Braddock Avenue. The architectural rendering of the school is illustrated in Aurand, *Progressive Architecture*, 8. The building, c. 1997, is illustrated in Walter C. Kidney, *Pittsburgh's Landmark Architecture: The Historic Buildings of Pittsburgh and Allegheny County* (Pittsburgh: Pittsburgh History & Landmarks Foundation, 1997), 471.

[18] *Construction* (December 2, 1905), 509; (December 9, 1905), 533; (December 16, 1905), 558. Illustrated in Aurand, *Progressive Architecture*, 55. De Bobula's designs for concrete row houses were discussed in "A Row of Concrete Houses," *Cement Age* 4:1 (January 1907), 62–63; also noted were his recent "patents for concrete doors and window frames which are made of the best grade of Portland cement, reinforced by a thick wire mesh." (63)

[19] Titus de Bobula, "American Style," *Inland Architect & Building News* (June 1905), 53, (July 1905), 64–65.

[20] *Catalogue of the Third Exhibition, Pittsburgh Architectural Club*, 1905, [no page] Fr. David Lesko discovered that St. Nicholas Greek Catholic Church in Duquesne was built as designed but was radically altered in 1911, and eventually demolished. Plans for the church were completed in May 1904. The cornerstone of the building at First Street and Viola Avenue was laid on July 3, 1904. St. Nicholas was dedicated on September 24, 1904. *Ohio Architect & Builder* (May 1904), 64; *The Duquesne Observer*, July 1, 1904, July 8, 1904, and September 22, 1905; [McKeesport, PA] *The Daily News*, August 11, 1905 and September 22, 1905 (both page 8). Driving home from the ceremony, de Bobula's car struck and killed a pedestrian; the architect was indicted for manslaughter, but acquitted in December. The following March, however, he ran down and injured another pedestrian, who sued him for $10,000. I am indebted to Fr. David Lesko for information about the church and the automobile tragedy, the first vehicular homicide in Allegheny County.

[21] *Catalogue of the Third Exhibition, Pittsburgh Architectural Club*, 1905, [no page]

[22] John T. Comes, "The Pittsburgh Architectural Club Exhibition, 1905," *House & Garden* (August 1905), 89.

[23] *Palmer's Pictorial Pittsburgh and Prominent Pittsburghers, Past and Present* (Pittsburgh, 1905), 107.

[24] *New York Times*, November 10, 1923, 2.

[25] "House at Spuyten Duyvil, New York City: Titus de Bobula, Architect," *The American Architect* (June 2, 1920), 667–673.

[26] "Schwab Answers Suit of de Bobula," *New York Times*, August 7, 1919, 15.

[27] Marc J. Seifer, *Wizard: The Life and Times of Nikola Tesla* (Secaucus, NJ: Carol Publishing, 1996), 431.

[28] *Washington Post*, February 1, 1961, B.4.

[29] "Greek Catholic Church Dedicated," *Homestead News-Messenger*, December 28, 1903, 1–2.

[30] *Ohio Architect & Builder* (October 1903), 16.

[31] Kidney, *Pittsburgh's Landmark Architecture*, 460.

[32] *Construction* (February 24, 1906), 173.

[33] *Ohio Architect & Builder* (November 1903), 74; (March 1904), 59.

[34] The first was Franklin Flats erected in 1903 in the Lower Hill (demolished). See Lubove, *Twentieth-Century Pittsburgh*, 32.

[35] *Construction* (May 19, 1906), 451.

[36] The definitive study is Aurand, *The Progressive Architecture of Frederick G. Scheibler, Jr.* See also James D. Van Trump, *The Architecture of Frederick G. Scheibler, Jr., 1872–1958*, Exhibition Catalogue, October 11–November 18, 1962, Department of Fine Arts, Carnegie Institute, and "Frederick G. Scheibler, Jr.: A Prophet of Modern Architecture in Pittsburgh," *Life and Architecture in Pittsburgh*, 283–290.

[37] Van Trump, "Frederick G. Scheibler, Jr.," 283.

[38] Aurand, *Progressive Architecture*, 6.

[39] Aurand, *Progressive Architecture*, 29.

[40] Aurand, *Progressive Architecture*, 30.

[41] Hans Berger, "Das Wohnhaus in Amerika," *Der Architekt* 14 (1908), 27; figure 5, page 30.

[42] The Mackintosh and Behren's designs were illustrated in *Dekorative Kunst* [Art], (July 1905); Scheibler owned a copy. For Rudy Brothers see Joan Gaul, "J. Horace Rudy and the Rudy Brothers' Company Stained and Leaded Glass," *Stained Glass Quarterly* 91:4 (Winter 1996), 277–282.

[43] Van Trump, "Frederick G. Scheibler, Jr.," 289–290.

[44] Kiehnel is listed in *The Lakeside Annual Directory of the City of Chicago*, Reuben H. Donnelley, compiler (Chicago: Chicago Directory Company, 1894 through 1898; 1900 through 1902).

[45] Biographical information from "Richard Kiehnel: Architect, Designer Well Known in Miami and Pittsburgh," *New York Times*, November 4, 1944. Kiehnel is listed in *Cleveland Directory for the Year Ending August 1904* (Cleveland, OH: Cleveland Directory Company, 1903), 693. For Cleveland architect J. Milton Dyer see Mary-Peale Schofield, *Landmark Architecture of Cleveland* (Pittsburgh, PA: Ober Park Associates, 1976), and Cleveland Chapter, AIA, *Guide to Cleveland Architecture* (Cleveland, OH: Carpenter Reserve Printing, 1991).

[46] *A Monograph of the Florida Work of Kiehnel & Elliott Architects*. Foreword by George H. Spohn and Henry P. Whitworth (Miami, FL: Miami Post Publishing Company, 1938), 1.

[47] He also designed traditional buildings, including two Gothic churches, and houses in a variety of styles.

[48] Kiehnel's renovation of the German Club is documented by a single photograph, "Screen in German Club, Pittsburgh," displayed at the 1911 Pittsburgh Architectural Club exhibit.

[49] Beth Dunlop, *Miami: Trends and Traditions* (New York: Monacelli Press, 1996), 40. For *El Jardin* see 40–49; another of Kiehnel's Mediterranean-style houses, *La Brisa* (1926–28), is discussed and illustrated, 30–33. See also Beth Dunlap, "Inventing

Antiquity: The Art and Craft of Mediterranean Revival Architecture," *The Journal of Decorative and Propaganda Arts 1875–1945: Florida Theme Issue* 23 (1998), 191–207.

[50] Barbara Capitman, et al, *Rediscovering Art Deco U.S.A.: A Nationwide Tour of Architectural Delights* (New York: Viking Studio Books, 1994), 22. See Francis S. Onderdonk, *The Ferro-Concrete Style* (New York: Architectural Book Publishing Company, 1928), 169–170; and Beth Dunlap, *Miami: Trends and Traditions* (New York: Monacelli Press, 1996), 92–103, for photographs of the building.

[51] The decorated piers on Brushton School are derived from Greco-Roman models, although the ornament is no longer classical. The form is often found in the work of Otto Wagner. There are also American examples: Paul Kruty, *Frank Lloyd Wright and Midway Gardens,* 175, 200, has an illuminating discussion of an architectural form of repeated piers often found in Chicago School buildings and called (with a nod to Hitchcock) a "Sullivan pilastrade" after their appearance on Sullivan's Wainwright Building (1890). The piers may be plain or decorated with floral and/or geometric capitals as they are on the Wainwright Building. Prairie School examples from 1902–16 include Hugh Garden's Schoenhofen Brewing Company, Richard Schmidt's Chapin and Gore Building, Dwight Perkins' Rogers School, and numerous buildings by Purcell & Elmslie, most notably Woodbury County Courthouse, Sioux City, Iowa.

[52] "Taylor & Dean, Pittsburgh, received the [ornamental iron work] contract for bank, store and apartment building, Pitcairn, Pa. Owner, First National Bank, Pitcairn, Pa." *Construction Record* [New Series] 45:2 (August 20, 1910), 13.

[53] Martin Aurand, "The Prairie School in Pittsburgh," *Pittsburgh History* 78:1 (Spring 1995), 13.

[54] Photographs of the bank appear in the 1913 Pittsburgh Architectural Club exhibition catalog.

[55] "Turn Verein Club House," *The Oaklander* 1:11 (June 29, 1911), 3.

[56] "Work Started on Turner Hall," *The Oaklander* 1:31 (November 16, 1911), 1.

[57] "Will Dedicate Home," *The Oaklander* 2:27 (October 17, 1912), 1.

[58] "Turnverein Opens New Club House," *Pittsburgh Chronicle Telegraph*, October 21, 1912, 11.

[59] Franz Fammler, "Die moderne Ladenfront," *Der Architekt: Wiener Monatshefte für Bauwesen und Dekorative Kunst* (Vienna: Kunstverlag Anton Schroll & Co., 1906), 1–3, plate 11.

[60] Ernst Wasmuth, ed., *Die Architekture des XX jahr hunderts* (1906), 81, plate 232; reprinted in *Architecture of the Early 20th Century*, 157, 97.

[61] In his discussion of the Turnverein in *Pittsburgh: A New Portrait* (2009), Franklin Toker states: "Cubist-style cement decoration … seems to pick up Frank Lloyd Wright's ornamental work at Chicago Midway Gardens." The Pittsburgh building opened October 20, 1912; the Chicago building opened June 27, 1914—twenty-one months after the Turnverein. No drawings or photographs of Midway

Gardens were exhibited before 1914. In this case, the German-trained architect who oversaw the 1907 PAC exhibition and the American architect who saw Austro-Germanic Secessionist design in St. Louis in 1904 and *in situ* in 1910 were independently influenced by the same European ornamental design movement. This influence on Wright is thoroughly documented by Paul Kruty, *Frank Lloyd Wright and Midway Gardens*.

[62]Like the German Club, the Central Turnverein became an organizational casualty of World War I. In 1920—eight years after it opened—the University of Pittsburgh purchased the facility and transformed it into a dental clinic. The building now serves as the University's Gardner Steel Conference Center. Only a few interior elements—the two transom windows, metal newel posts, and dramatic molding between the windows in what is now the computer center (possibly the "dancing hall")—remain.

[63]Four photographs—an exterior and three interiors—were printed in the *Pittsburgh Architectural Club: Tenth Exhibition 1915* (Pittsburgh, 1916), [no page] The exterior and a view of the living room are reproduced in Aurand, *Progressive Architecture*, 83.

[64]Frank Lloyd Wright, "In the Cause of Architecture," 59.

[65]Montgomery Schuyler, "The Buildings of Pittsburgh: Part Five—The Homes of Pittsburgh," *Architectural Record* (September 1911), 282.

[66]Blueprints, dated 1914, in the possession of the home owner.

[67]*Pittsburgh Architectural Club Annual 1916: School Houses* (1917) published a perspective, a plot plan, elevations, and floor plans ([no page]). See Aurand, "Prairie School," 15.

[68]*Moderne Bauformen: Monatschefte für Architectur* 6:6 (1907), 220–256, plates 39–44. Hermann Billing (1867–1946) practiced in Karlsruhe. U. M. Schumann, wrote: "Billing played a mediating role in the transmission of American forms (specifically those of H. H. Richardson) through his early residential architecture." See *Saur Allgemeines Künstler-Lexikon* (München/Leipzig: K. G. Saur, 1995), 2:47. Kathryn Bloom Hiesinger, *Art Nouveau in Munich* (Prestel, 1988) illustrates a room Billing exhibited in St. Louis in 1904—one of twenty-one interiors purchased by John Wanamaker for his Philadelphia department store, 22.

[69]Albert M. Tannler, "Historic Thornburg: Variations on a Theme," *PHLF News* 125 (September 1992), 4–5; "A Player of Architectural Themes and Variations," *Pittsburgh Tribune-Review, Focus* 22:12 (January 25, 1998), 8–9; "An Architect's House in Thornburg," *Pittsburgh Tribune-Review, Focus* 26:61 (January 6, 2001), 8–11; "Revisiting Thornburg," *PHLF News* 160 (April 2001), 12–15; and "Samuel T. McClarren—Before and After Thornburg," *PHLF News* 167 (September 2004), 14.

[70]The earliest publication, including photos of model houses, is "Thornburg," *Allegheny* 1:23 (October 21, 1899), [no page]

[71]See *Pittsburgh Gazette,* June 19, 1904, Section 4, page 3 for a positive contemporary view.

[72] *Construction* 1:13 (April 1, 1905), 3.

[73] S. T. McClarren published two books of his designs. The first is lost, but the *Second Annual Souvenir of Designs, S. T. McClarren, Architect, 64 Fifth Ave., Pittsburgh, Pa.* (c. 1891), contains elevations, plans, and photographs of some forty-five residential, commercial, industrial, and ecclesiastical buildings, as well as decorative elements. Many designs in his pattern book show the influence of Richardsonian Romanesque, evident in buildings by McClarren's first employer, James Bailey (in particular, the Butler County Courthouse, 1886, erected when McClarren was in the office from 1883–87) and by other prominent local architects, most notably Longfellow, Alden & Harlow, Richardson's successor firm in Pittsburgh.

[74] Florence Thornburg quoted in Alice C. Christner, *Here's to Thornburg* (Thornburg Community Club, 1966), 36.

[75] H. M. Phelps, "Hillside House," *House Beautiful* 29:5 (April 1911), 150.

[76] The Pfohl House blueprints are the only ones known to exist for pre-1908 Thornburg houses.

[77] *Myron Hunt, 1868–1952: The Search for a Regional Architecture* (Santa Monica, CA: Hennessey & Ingalls, 1984). By the Fall of 1905, architects Neal & Rowland, C. E. Willoughby, and W. H. Charles were designing residences in Thornburg.

[78] Randell L. Makinson, Thomas A. Heinz, and Brad Pitt, *Greene & Greene: The Blacker House* (Layton, UT: Gibbs Smith, 2000), 45.

[79] Its predecessor, erected in 1901, burned in November 1905.

[80] Louis Sullivan, "Artistic Brick," *Louis Sullivan: The Public Papers*, ed. by Robert Twombly (Chicago: University of Chicago Press, 1988), 203.

[81] Robert Winter, "Arthur S. and Alfred Heineman," *Toward a Simpler Way of Life: The Arts & Crafts Architects of California*, ed. by Robert Winter (Berkeley: University of California Press, 1997), 139–140.

[82] Winter, "The First Generation," *Toward a Simpler Way of Life*, 9.

[83] James D. Van Trump, "Art Deco," *Life and Architecture in Pittsburgh*, 73, 80.

[84] Information provided by Martin Aurand.

[85] Kidney, *Pittsburgh's Landmark Architecture*, 242.

[86] These Palm Beach buildings are illustrated and described in Barbara D. Hoffstot, *Landmark Architecture of Palm Beach* (Pittsburgh: Pittsburgh History & Landmarks Foundation, 1991), 58–59, 214–218. The Paramount Theatre building still stands but the auditorium was destroyed in 1980; see Michael D. Kinerk and Dennis W. Wilhelm, "Dream Palaces: The Motion Picture Playhouse in the Sunshine State," *Journal of Decorative and Propaganda Arts: Florida Theme Issue* 23 (Miami: Wolfsonian Foundation, 1998), 230–232.

[87] Carter/Cole 1992 were unaware of the William Penn designs (a section of the Urban Room ceiling painting is illustrated on p. 237 but misattributed). Two of the Kaufmann's Department Store project drawings are illustrated on p. 188.

Original, full-color renderings of the Urban Room ceiling and wall paintings have now been properly identified in the Urban Collection at Columbia University, where they are preserved together with the unexecuted 1926 Kaufmann's Department Store and 1928 William Penn Hotel project drawings. Loring (2010) illustrates the unexecuted designs for Kaufmann's Department Store, pp. 174–175, and for the ballroom, pp. 158–159, and men's lounge, p. 167, in the William Penn Hotel, but not the executed Urban Room designs. Both Carter/Cole 1992 and Loring 2010 illustrate a mural design, similar to but not identical with the Urban Room murals, and identify it as a design Urban used in the St. Regis Hotel; that design is dated August 1929—five months *after* the murals in the Urban room were in place at the end of April 1929; thus one has reason to assume that the Pittsburgh version was the prototype.

[88] Otto Teegen, "Joseph Urban's Philosophy of Color," 261.

[89] R. G. Frame to James D. Van Trump, September 20, 1972; James D. Van Trump Library, Pittsburgh History & Landmarks Foundation.

[90] "The Greater Wm. Penn Hotel," *Greater Pittsburgh* 9:51 (May 18, 1929), 29. See also *William Penn Points*. 12:1 (May 1929). Pittsburgh, PA: Eppley Hotels Company, 1929.

[91] The carpet used motifs found in the Urban Collection at Columbia University and recreated the original colors used in the murals. It was replaced in 2011.

[92] King's obituary in *The Builders' Bulletin* 37:21 (February 7, 1953), 1, 16, states that he served in the U.S. Air Corps during World War I.

[93] "Architects' Building Bulletin," *The Charette* (January 1929), 607; (March 1929), 633.

[94] Sydney Karpowich and Liesl Ostergaard, "Mt. Lebanon Municipal Building," Historic Resource Survey Form, 2010, 11.

[95] Kidney, *Pittsburgh's Landmark Architecture*, 504.

[96] Jason Togyer, *For the Love of Murphy's: The Behind-the-Counter Story of a Great American Retailer* (University Park: Pennsylvania State University Press, 2008), 34.

[97] Togyer, *For the Love of Murphy's*, 143. It is illustrated on page 145.

[98] Dissolution of the firm reported in *The Builders' Bulletin* 16:5 (October 3, 1931), 1.

[99] The life and career of Edward Weber is summarized by Patricia Lowry in "An Architect Out of Time," *Pittsburgh Post-Gazette, Sunday Magazine* (February 9, 1997), G1, G10–11. For a discussion of his buildings in Allegheny County, see Kidney, *Pittsburgh's Landmark Architecture*; the bibliography lists some of Weber's writings.

[100] Marion Markle Steen was burdened with an unwieldy name; after trying Marion M. Steen and M. Markle Steen he eventually settled on M. M. Steen.

[101] Information from Martin Aurand. My thanks to Tracy Myers, curator, Heinz Architectural Center, Carnegie Museum of Art, for providing the color scheme.

[102] An undated presentation drawing of Prospect School, in the collection of the Heinz Architectural Center, shows a recognizable but grander version of the building with gymnasium and auditorium wings at either end; the drawing is signed James T. Steen & Sons which suggests that the 1931 design as built was altered and simplified and that the 1936 additions were, in effect, the realization of an earlier scheme.

[103] Vernon Gay and Marilyn Evert, *Discovering Pittsburgh's Sculpture* (Pittsburgh: University of Pittsburgh Press, 1984), 150.

[104] "'Homes all to be Modern' in the Startling but Financially Sound Restriction in a Pittsburgh Subdivision," *Architectural Forum* 67:5 (November 1937), 442–443.

[105] "Only House of Its Kind in the World: Unique, Modern Home Built by Becks in Rosslyn Farms As Seen in Completed Form and During Construction," *Pittsburgh Post-Gazette*, June 8, 1934, 9. The house, purchased by Maynard Riemann in 1937, is located in Rosslyn Farms at 221 Puritan Road. Mr. Riemann remodeled the house in 1957 and eradicated all "modern" elements.

[106] Harry Pople misrepresented his role and the Becks' role in the 1937 *Architectural Forum* article. See Albert M. Tannler, "Swan Acres, 'the nation's first Modern subdivision,' Revisited and Reassessed." *PHLF News* 177 (April 2011), 19–21.

[107] "Swan Acres, A Planned Community in the Country, Opening Today," *Pittsburgh Press*, August 23, 1936, 15.

[108] Five simple brick houses on Circle Drive, designed and built 1939–40, may have been designed by Harry Clepper, who left the firm in 1940.

[109] The B.P.B. name continued until 1938 when it was replaced by the Swan Realty & Development Company Architecture Division.

[110] Tannler, "Swan Acres," 21.

[111] Homes of New American Design Will Feature Development Plan at Swan Acres," *Pittsburgh Press*, October 25, 1936, 42–43.

[112] "Swan Acres," *Pittsburgh Press*, 15.

[113] "Homes all to be Modern," *Architectural Forum*, 443.

[114] Tannler, "The Architect," *Allegheny County Courthouse and Jail Walking Tour* (Pittsburgh: Pittsburgh History & Landmarks Foundation, 2007), 1–2.

[115] Ralph Adams Cram, "Foreword," *The Art of Stained Glass: a note on the work of Henry Wynd Young, worker in glass, mosaic, church-decoration, 314 East 34th Street, New York*, by Walter E. Wheeler. (Printed privately for Henry Wynd Young, 1921).

[116] Peter Cormack, "Foreword," Albert M. Tannler, *Charles J. Connick: His Education and His Windows in and near Pittsburgh* (Pittsburgh: Pittsburgh History & Landmarks Foundation, 2008), vii.

[117] John T. Comes, "Calvary Church, Pittsburg, Pa," *Architectural Review* 15:1 (January 1908), 1–3.

[118] Jonathan L. Fairbanks, "Foreword," *The Stained Glass Work of Christopher Whall 1849–1924,* by Peter Cormack (Boston: Boston Public Library, 1999), 7.

[119] Douglass Shand-Tucci, *Ralph Adams Cram: An Architect's Four Quests—Medieval, Modernist, American, Ecumenical* (Amherst, MA: University of Massachusetts Press, 2005), 259.

[120] Ralph Adams Cram, *My Life* (Boston: Little, Brown & Co., 1936), 253.

[121] Shand-Tucci, *Ralph Adams Cram,* 496.

[122] "Architectural Criticism," *Architecture* 26:4 (October 15, 1912), 186.

[123] For First Baptist see Tannler, *Charles J. Connick,* 38–54. For Bertram Goodhue see Romy Wyllie, *Bertram Goodhue: His Life and Residential Architecture* (New York: W. W. Norton, 2007), and Richard Oliver, *Bertram Grosvenor Goodhue* (Cambridge, MA: MIT Press, 1983).

[124] Obituaries. "William P. Hutchins." *Pittsburgh Post-Gazette,* September 12, 1941, 9; *The Pittsburgh Catholic,* September 18, 1941, 13.

[125] Some of the windows are illustrated in Albert M. Tannler, "Harry Wright Goodhue: Stained Glass of Unsurpassed Distinction and Rare Beauty," *Stained Glass Quarterly* (Summer 2004), 134–147.

[126] James D. Van Trump and Arthur P. Ziegler, *Landmark Architecture of Allegheny County Pennsylvania* (Pittsburgh: Pittsburgh History & Landmarks Foundation, 1967), 107–108.

[127] Kidney, *Pittsburgh's Landmark Architecture,* 355.

[128] Curl, "Expressionism," *Oxford Dictionary of Architecture,* 271.

[129] Wim de Wit, ed., *The Amsterdam School: Dutch Expressionist Architecture, 1915–1930.* (Cambridge, MA: MIT Press, 1983), 32.

[130] These examples are selected from buildings listed by Curl, 271.

[131] [William H. Harrold] "The Jazz Period of Architecture," *The Charette* 4:12 (November 1924), 2–3.

[132] Kidney, *Henry Hornbostel,* 13.

[133] Kidney, *Henry Hornbostel,* 189.

[134] *American Architect* 134:2555 (October 20, 1928), 547.

[135] Leah Dickerman, "Bauhaus Fundaments," *Bauhaus 1919–1933: Workshops for Modernity,* ed. by Barry Bergdoll and Leah Dickerman (New York: Museum of Modern Art, 2009), 15.

[136] In 1941, Gropius and Breuer designed a housing project, Aluminum City Terrace, twenty-one miles northeast of Pittsburgh in New Kensington, Westmoreland County. Marcel Breuer designed a stone house near Ligonier, Westmoreland County, about fifty miles east of Pittsburgh, 1946–50, for Mrs. A. W. Thompson.

[137] Letter to M. A. Clegg, quoted in Isabelle Hyman, *Marcel Breuer, Architect: The Career and the Buildings* (New York: Harry N. Abrams, 2001), 332.

[138] Barry Bergdoll, "New Ways in the New World," *Häuser* (1/2009): English Text, vii–viii; German text, 84–93.

[139] Barry Bergdoll, www.thefrankhouse.org. On September 11, 2013, Alan Frank talked about his house with Louise Sturgess (editor) and me.

[140] Many of Cornelia's writings during the 1930s are included in Randolph C. Henning, ed., *At Taliesin: Newspaper Columns by Frank Lloyd Wright and the Taliesin Fellowship 1934–1937* (Carbondale, IL: Southern Illinois University Press, 1992), 58, 82, 85–87, 92, 94–95, 103, 110–112, 125–127, 129, 130, 139, 144, 151–155, 159–160, 170, 310.

[141] Cornelia Brierly, *Tales of Taliesin: A Memoir of Fellowship* (Tempe, AZ: Arizona State University, 1999).

[142] The Peter Berndtson collection at Carnegie Mellon University Architecture Archives contains references dated 1947 to the Bear additions and an "Agreement with the Contractor," dated June 3, 1953, regarding the additions for Mr. and Mrs. Mock.

[143] Cornelia Brierly, "Notz House: A Shelter of Warmth and Rest," *Pittsburgh Tribune-Review, Focus* 24:32 (June 13, 1999), 9. The current owner of the Notz House has blueprints dated 1950 and 1953.

[144] Introduction by James D. Van Trump. Peter Berndtson, "The Houses of Peter Berendtsen [sic]: A Tour for Members of Pittsburgh History & Landmarks Foundation," September 1971, 1.

[145] James D. Van Trump, "Architecture and the Pittsburgh Land: The Buildings of Peter Berndtson," *Life and Architecture in Pittsburgh* (Pittsburgh History & Landmarks Foundation, 1983), 65.

[146] Berndtson, "The Houses of Peter Berendtsen [sic]," 1.

[147] Donald Miller and Aaron Sheon, *Organic Vision: The Architecture of Peter Berndtson* (Pittsburgh, PA: Hexagon Press, 1980), 49.

[148] Quoted in Miller and Sheon, 1980, 23.

[149] Berndtson, "The Houses of Peter Berendtsen [sic]," 2.

[150] Miller and Sheon, 1980, 55.

[151] Brian D. Coleman, "Shelter: A House Designed by Pittsburgh Architects Peter Berndtson and Cornelia Brierly, Who Studied with Wright, Is Carefully Preserved" *Old–House Interiors* 17:6 (December 2011), 36.

[152] Miller and Sheon, 1980, 49.

[153] Miller and Sheon, 1980, 74–77.

[154] Wiseman, *Shaping a Nation*, 174.

[155] William R. Cooper, "Duquesne: Dramatic Change in Campus Scale," *Architectural Forum* (July/August 1967), 79, notes: "Mies agreed, provided Schweikher's firm would serve as supervising architects." Mies's letter is quoted in a final version of "Preliminary Statement of the Sciences at Duquesne University and an Appraisal

of our Current and Future Needs" (c. May 1962), Duquesne University Facilities Management Archives. Many thanks to Gregory R. Fuhrman, P.E., Project Manager, Design & Construction, for providing this document, and to Jeff Slack of Pfaffmann + Associates for calling the quote to our attention.

[156] Franz Schulze, ed., *An Illustrated Catalogue of the Mies van der Rohe Drawings in the Museum of Modern Art, Part 2: 1938–1967, The American Work* (Garland: 1992), 2.

[157] Franz Schulze and Edward Windhorst, *Mies van der Rohe: A Critical Biography, New and Revised Edition* (Chicago: University of Chicago Press, 2012), 373.

[158] Cooper, *Duquesne*, 79.

[159] Franz Schulze, "Speyer's Life and Career," *A. James Speyer: Architect, Curator, Exhibition Designer*, edited by John Vinci (Chicago: University of Chicago Press, 1997), 32. This source dates the Apt House to 1951–53, 118.

[160] Schulze, *A. James Speyer*, 32.

[161] On May 30, 2013, Joan Apt met in her home with Louise Sturgess, Luis Espinoza-Delgado (PHLF intern), and me. She talked about the design and construction of her house, and we toured the house and garden.

[162] All quotations in this paragraph are from Schulze, *A. James Speyer*, 39.

[163] The Arts Club and Speyer House staircases are white; the Arts Club has a double railing and the Speyer House has a single railing. The Mellon Hall staircase is black and has a triple railing.

[164] Curl, *Oxford Dictionary of Architecture*, 71.

[165] Henry-Russell Hitchcock, "Introduction," *Architecture of Skidmore, Owings & Merrill, 1950–1962* (New York: Frederick A. Praeger, 1962), 10.

[166] Franz Schulze and Edward Windhorst, *Mies van der Rohe*, 403.

[167] www.som.com/Myron Goldsmith

[168] Nathaniel A. Owings, *The Spaces in Between: An Architect's Journey* (Houghton Mifflin, 1973), 264–265. See also Judith Paine, "Natalie de Blois," *Women in American Architecture: A Historic and Contemporary Perspective*, ed. by Susan Torre (Whitney Library of Design, 1977), 112–114; and Patricia Lowry, "A Look at Local Woman Architects," *Pittsburgh Press*, Section F, April 3, 1988.

[169] Nory Miller, "Mies' Office Today: FCL, an Evolving Firm," *Inland Architect* (May 1977), 25–27.

[170] Marcus Whiffen, "Brutalism," *American Architecture Since 1780: A Guide to the Styles* (Cambridge, MA: MIT Press, 1996), 279.

[171] Anthony Alofsin, *The Struggle for Modernism: Architecture, Landscape Architecture, and City Planning at Harvard* (New York: W. W. Norton, 2002): Fig. 5.39, 169. See also *A Guide to the John Ormsbee Simonds Collection*, University of Florida Smathers Libraries, Box 178.

[172] *A Guide to the John Ormsbee Simonds Collection*, 1–2.

[173] A notarized partnership agreement between Mitchell and Ritchey dated May 17, 1956 states: "Mr. James Mitchell, during the life of the firm, has had the principal responsibilities for planning and design, equal participation in production of working drawings, detailing, and in business policy, and participated in all other phases of the work. Mr. Dahlen Ritchey has had the principal responsibilities for business administration, supervision of work under construction, checking of shop drawings, equal participation in production of working drawings, and participated in all other phases of the work." The firm dissolved acrimoniously on August 30, 1957. Mitchell relocated to Stamford, Connecticut, and Ritchey remained in Pittsburgh. Ritchey continued to practice as D. K. Ritchey Associates (1957–59); the firm then became Deeter & Ritchey (1959–65) and later Deeter Ritchey Sippel Associates (1965–79).

[174] [John Mauro] Pittsburgh Chamber of Commerce. "Magnificent Square in the Triangle," *Greater Pittsburgh* (October 1955). The article was reprinted in *The Charette* 35:12 (December 1955), 13–16.

[175] John O. Simonds, "Mellon Square: An Oasis in an Asphalt Desert," *Landscape Architecture* 48 (July 1958), 211–212.

[176] Whiffen, *American Architecture Since 1780*, 283. The Katselas House is illustrated on page 279.

[177] Bill Strickland, *Make the Impossible Possible: One Man's Crusade to Inspire Others to Dream Bigger and Achieve the Extraordinary* (New York: Doubleday, 2007), 89.

[178] Stickland, *Make the Impossible Possible*, 95. My thanks to Eric K. Rueter, Manchester-Bidwell Corporation, who provided much useful information and gave me a tour of the center.

[179] Victoria Newhouse, *Wallace K. Harrison, Architect* (New York: Rizzoli, 1989), 145–149; Janet Parks and John Harwood, *The Troubled Search: The Work of Max Abramovitz* (New York: Columbia University, 2004), 45–56; 58–63; 94–96; 98–100.

[180] John Harwood, "Architect of the Complex," *Troubled Search*, 45.

[181] Harwood, 46.

[182] Harwood, 51.

[183] Newhouse, 147.

[184] Harwood, 55–56.

[185] Newhouse, 147. The building is discussed in detail in "Alteration To Skyline $28,500,500," *The Charette* 30:11 (November 1950), 14–15, 33, 36.

[186] Harwood, 52.

[187] "Pittsburgh Office Building Has External Service Tower," *Architectural Record* 128 (September 1960), 214–216.

[188] "Pittsburgh Renaissance Historic District," Section 7, page 5.

[189] John O. Simonds, "Equitable Plaza, Pittsburgh," *Landscape Architecture* 53:1 (October 1962), 19.

[190] Karen Kingsley, "Curtis and Davis Architects," www.knowla.org.

[191] Arthur Q. Davis, *It Happened by Design: The Life and Work of Arthur Q. Davis* (New Orleans: University Press of Mississippi, 2009), 116.

[192] "New IBM Building to Rise in Pittsburgh," *The Charette* 42:1 (January 1962), 21.

[193] Kingsley, "Curtis and Davis Architects," www.knowla.org. It is estimated that the wall trusses required 250 tons less steel than conventional post-and-beam construction.

[194] Carl Condit, *American Building: Materials and Techniques from the Beginning of the Colonial Settlements to the Present* (Chicago: University of Chicago Press, 1968), 198, Fig. 72.

[195] Condit, *American Building*, 58.

[196] Gerald Beasley, "Foreword," *The Troubled Search*, 7.

[197] Harwood, 61.

[198] Harwood, 62.

[199] Mr. Flucker and Mr. Hossli discussed their work on the United States Steel Innovations Committee with Louise Sturgess and me on May 21, 2013.

[200] *The Steel Triangle: United States Steel Builds a Corporate Center* (Pittsburgh: United States Steel Corporation, 1969; reprinted 1971), 6.

[201] "Statement in Steel," talk given to U.S. Steel Building Design and Construction Workshop, Penn-Sheraton Hotel, Pittsburgh (March 15, 1967), Harwood, 59; 70n85.

[202] Paul O'Neill quoted in "Open for Business," *@Issue: The Journal of Business and Design* 5:2 (1999), 26.

[203] www.rusli.com/alcoainc.html

[204] www.alcoa.com/Alcoa Corporate Center—Pittsburgh

[205] Paul Heyer, "Edward L. Barnes," *Architects on Architecture: New Directions in America* (New York: Walker & Company, 1966), 327, 329.

[206] Curl, *Oxford Dictionary of Architecture*, 63.

[207] Curl, 195.

[208] Lu Donnelly, et al, *The Buildings of Pennsylvania: Pittsburgh and Western Pennsylvania* [Buildings of the United States] (Charlottesville: University of Virginia Press in association with the Society of Architectural Historians, 2010), 70.

[209] *Richard Meier Houses 1962/1997* (New York: Rizzoli, 1996), 130.

[210] *Richard Meier Houses*, 245.

[211] *Richard Meier Houses*, 12.

[212] *Richard Meier Houses*, 130.

[213] The exhibition was held at the Heinz Architectural Center, Carnegie Museum of Art, November 8, 2002 through February 2, 2003.

[214] Richard Pain, "Lost Property," *Blueprint* (June 2004), 50–53, 55.

[215] Pain, 53.

[216] Pain, 55.

[217] Pain, 54–55.

[218] Quoted in Jack Miller, "Abrams House Pledged to Landmarks," *PHLF News* 172 (April 2007), 7. Photographs of the Abrams House were published as "House in Pittsburgh," in "Venturi, Scott Brown and Associates, Inc.," *Dream Homes: Greater Philadelphia—Showcasing Greater Philadelphia's Finest Architects* (Dallas, TX: Panache Partners, LLC, distributed by Gibbs Smith, 2006), 92–95.

[219] Philip Johnson, "Foreword to the 1995 edition," *The International Style*, 15.

[220] Philip Johnson, *The Architect in His Own Words* (New York: Rizzoli, 1994), 132–136.

[221] Albert M. Tannler, *A List of Pittsburgh and Allegheny County Buildings and Architects 1950–2005* (Pittsburgh: Pittsburgh History & Landmarks Foundation, 2005), 12.

[222] Sonia R. Cháo and Trevor D. Abramson, *Kohn Pedersen Fox: Buildings and Projects 1976–1986* (New York: Rizzoli, 1987), 152. Models of the two-tower design are illustrated.

[223] Sam Spatter, "AI Office Tower Opening Pushed Back to '87," *Pittsburgh Press*, October 3, 1984.

[224] *Architecture … Energy: Arthur Lubetz Associates*, Exhibition Catalog (Pittsburgh: University Art Gallery, University of Pittsburgh, 1989).

[225] *Architecture … Energy*, 1989.

[226] Cynthia Davidson, "Michael Graves: O'Reilly Theater, Pittsburgh: The Reigning Prince of Post-Modernism Leaves His Unmistakable Signature on a Pittsburgh Theater," *Architecture* 90:5 (May 2001), 128.

[227] Davidson, 128.

[228] *Michael Graves Buildings and Projects 1995–2003* (New York: Rizzoli, 2003), 72–79.

[229] Information from Fr. David Lesko. A photograph appears in Walter C. Kidney, *Pittsburgh's Landmark Architecture*, 109.

[230] *Pittsburgh Press*, April 15, 1955, 7.

[231] "First Floor Redecorated: Famous Black Glass Columns Lightened." *Storagram* (September 27, 1955), 1. I am grateful to Richard Cleary for providing this reference. Thanks to Carole Mazzotta, Kaufmann's Media Center Manager,

for locating copies of *Storagram.* See Albert M. Tannler, "Two Interiors Destroyed: The May Company Déjà Vu," *PHLF News* 155 (August 1999), 16.

[232]Christopher Wilk, *Frank Lloyd Wright: The Kaufmann Office* (London: Victoria and Albert Museum, 1993), 68. For Wright's work for Edgar J. Kaufmann, Sr., see Richard Cleary, *Merchant Prince and Master Builder: Edgar J. Kaufmann and Frank Lloyd Wright* (Seattle: University of Washington Press, 1999).

[233]Carol H. Krinsky, *Gordon Bunshaft of Skidmore, Owings & Merrill* (Cambridge, MA: MIT Press, 1988), 18. See also *Architecture of Skidmore, Owings & Merrill, 1950–1962* (New York, Praeger, 1963), 35.

[234]Mitchell & Ritchey, "Lower Hill," *Pittsburgh in Progress Presented by Kaufmann's* (Pittsburgh: Kaufmann's, 1947).

[235]Lubove, 131.

[236]Bernice Strawn and Elizabeth Matthews, "House for Family Living," *Woman's Home Companion* 83:9 (September 1956), 101–103, 106–108, 110, 112, 114, 117, 119–122.

[237]For Pei's employment by Webb & Knapp (1948–60) and his relationship with William Zeckendorf see Michael Cannell, *I. M. Pei: Mandarin of Modernism* (Carol Southern, 1995), 89–152. For Washington Plaza Apartments see "Tete-a-tete," *The Charette* 37:7 (July 1957), 19; "Washington Plaza Apartments, Pittsburgh, Pa," *Architectural Record* (January 1963), 161; Arthur P. Ziegler, Jr. "Apartment Roundup," *The Charette* 43:11 (November 1963), 10; James D. Van Trump, "The Infinite Flat-House: Some new Pittsburgh and Philadelphia Apartment Buildings," *The Charette* 45:3 (March 1965), 15–19.

[238]Urs Büttiker, *Louis I. Kahn: Light and Space* (New York: Whitney Library of Design, 1994), 126–127. See also www.americanwindsymphonyorchestra.org/aboutus.html.

[239]Lescaze's quotation is from a letter to Arthur P. Ziegler, Jr., June 14, 1968, James D. Van Trump Library, Pittsburgh History & Landmarks Foundation. The mural is now in The Butler Institute of American Art, Trumbull branch, Howland Township, Ohio. See Tannler, *A List of Pittsburgh and Allegheny County Buildings and Architects*, 9. *Pittsburgh Art in Public Places: Downtown Walking Tour* (City of Pittsburgh Office of Public Art, 2006), No. 35, p. 62. Patricia Lowry, "Pierre Soulages Mural Finds New Home in Ohio," *Pittsburgh Post-Gazette*, February 22, 2010.

Bibliography (Chronological)

General

Chewning, J. A. "The Teaching of Architectural History during the Advent of Modernism, 1920s–1950s," *The Architectural Historian in America*. Washington, D.C.: National Gallery of Art, 1990: 101–110.

Wiseman, Carter. *Shaping a Nation: Twentieth-Century American Architecture and Its Makers*. New York: W. W. Norton, 1998.

Alofsin, Anthony. *The Struggle for Modernism: Architecture, Landscape Architecture, and City Planning at Harvard*. New York: W. W. Norton, 2002.

General—Pittsburgh and Western Pennsylvania Architecture

Catalogue of the Architectural Exhibition of Pittsburg, Pa. Held at Carnegie Art Rooms, Allegheny, From Thursday, September 16 to Saturday, September 25, inclusive. 1897. Supplement to *The Builder*. Pittsburgh: *The Builder*, 1897.

Pittsburgh Chapter, AIA. *Catalogue of the First Annual Architectural Exhibition by the Pittsburgh Chapter American Institute of Architects Held at the Carnegie Art Gallery, Pittsburgh, Pa., May 2nd to 31st*. Pittsburgh: Murdoch-Kerr Press [1898].

Orth, George S. "The Pittsburgh Chapter of the American Institute of Architects and Its Predecessors." *Interstate Architect and Builder* 1:37 (November 4, 1899): 6–7.

Pittsburgh Architectural Club. Exhibition Catalogues 1900, 1903, 1905, 1907, 1910–16.

Stamm, K. Salome. "Architectural Books in the Carnegie Library: The Bernd Collection." *The Charette* 5:5 (May 1925): 1–3.

Kropff, Henry M. "Recollections of Some of the Old Timers." *The Charette* 12:3 (March 1932): 1–2.

Beginning as "Carnegie Library News: the Architectural Book Collection—Additions for February" and listed under various titles. *The Charette* 5–29 (April 1925–October 1949).

Equitable Life Assurance Society of the United States. *Equitable Builds a Gateway*. Pittsburgh: Ben Rosen Associates, March 1964.

"Pittsburgh: Smoke, Architecture, and Architects." *The Charette* 49:4 (July–August 1969): 10.

Monkhouse, Christopher. "A Century of Architectural Exhibitions at The Carnegie: 1893–1993." *Carnegie Magazine* 61:12 (November/December 1993): 28–32, 37–43.

Lubove, Roy. *Twentieth-Century Pittsburgh: Volume 1, Government, Business, and Environmental Change*. 1969. Reprint. *Volume 2, The Post-Steel Era*. Pittsburgh: University of Pittsburgh Press, 1996.

Monkhouse, Christopher. "The ABC's of an Architectural Library in Pittsburgh: Anderson, Bernd and Carnegie." *Carnegie Magazine* 63:2 (March/April 1996): 20–26.

Greenwald, Maurine W. and Marge Anderson, eds., *Pittsburgh Surveyed: Social Science and Social Reform in the Early Twentieth Century*. Pittsburgh: University of Pittsburgh Press, 1996.

Kidney, Walter C. *Pittsburgh's Landmark Architecture: The Historic Buildings of Pittsburgh and Allegheny County*. Pittsburgh: Pittsburgh History & Landmarks Foundation, 1997.

Tannler, Albert M. "Two Beginnings: First Architectural Exhibitions Held in Pittsburgh 1898 and 1900." *Pittsburgh Tribune-Review, Focus* 26:51 (October 28, 2001): 8–10.

Tannler, Albert M. *A List of Pittsburgh and Allegheny County Buildings and Architects 1950–2005*. 3rd rev. ed. Pittsburgh: Pittsburgh History & Landmarks Foundation, 2005.

Bauman, John F., and Edward K. Muller. *Before Renaissance: Planning in Pittsburgh, 1889–1943*. Pittsburgh: University of Pittsburgh Press, 2006.

Aurand, Martin. *The Spectator and the Topographical City*. Pittsburgh: University of Pittsburgh Press, 2006.

Tannler, Albert M. "The 'First' Architectural Exhibition in Pittsburgh." *PHLF News* 176 (February 2010):18.

Donnelly, Lu, et al. *The Buildings of Pennsylvania: Pittsburgh and Western Pennsylvania*. Charlotte, VA: University of Virginia Press for the Society of Architectural Historians, 2010.

Architects and Their Buildings in Metropolitan Pittsburgh

Edward Larrabee Barnes

Paul Heyer, "Edward L. Barnes," *Architects on Architecture: New Directions in America*. New York: Walker & Company, 1966: 325–329.

"Museum, Architect Sign Pact: Edward Barnes to Work on Plans for the Addition." *Pittsburgh Post-Gazette*, May 30, 1970.

"The Sarah Mellon Scaife Gallery." *Carnegie Magazine* 46:1 (January 1972): 5–14.

"Barnes gratia artis." *Progressive Architecture* 56 (March 1975): 26–27.

Edward Larrabee Barnes Architect. Introduction by Peter Black. New York: Rizzoli, 1994.

Quentin S. Beck

"Only House of Its Kind in the World: Unique, Modern Home Built by Becks in Rosslyn Farms As Seen in Completed Form and During Construction." *Pittsburgh Post-Gazette*, June 8, 1934: 9.

"Swan Acres, A Planned Community in the Country, Opening Today." *Pittsburgh Press*, August 23, 1936: 15.

"Homes of New American Design Will Feature Development Plan at Swan Acres." *Pittsburgh Press*, October 25, 1936: 42–43.

"Four Houses Done." *Pittsburgh Post-Gazette*, April 4, 1937: 25.

"Four Dwellings of Modern Construction Completed in Swan Acres, North Hills." *Pittsburgh Press*, May 2, 1937.

"'Homes All to Be Modern' in the Startling but Financially Sound Restriction in a Pittsburgh Subdivision." *Architectural Forum* 67:5 (November 1937): 442–443.

"Opening Date Is Announced: Plan Public Inspection of Swan Acres Homes." *Pittsburgh Post-Gazette*, July 29, 1939: 9.

"Quentin S. Beck." *American Architects Directory 1962*. Ed. by George S. Koyl. New York: R. R. Bowker Company, 1962: 42.

Tannler, Albert M. "Swan Acres: First Modern Subdivision." *Pittsburgh Tribune-Review, Focus* 21:30 (June 1, 1997): 8–9

———"A Man Ahead of His Time." *Pittsburgh Tribune-Review, Focus* 21:48 (October 5, 1997): 6–7.

———"Swan Acres, 'the nation's first Modern subdivision,' Revisited and Reassessed." *PHLF News* 177 (April 2011): 19–21.

Peter Berndtson and Cornelia Brierly

"Squirrel Hill House on a Slope." [Landis House] *The Charette* 29:9 (September 1949): 32–33.

"House in the Round: A Residence for Dr. and Mrs. Abraam Steinberg, Peter Berndtson, Architect." *The Charette* 31:3 (March 1951): 18–19.

Ungar, Anne Jean. "Three Contemporary Houses." [Steinberg, Weinberger, and Fineman houses] *The Charette* 33:5 (May 1953): 9–17.

"Recipe for a House." [Lipkind House] *The Charette* 37:3 (March 1957): 20–21.

Sheon, Aaron. *The Architecture of Peter Berndtson*. Exhibition Catalogue. [An Exhibition of Contemporary Architectural Drawings, Photographs and Color Slides, The University Art Gallery, March 28th through April 18th, 1971.] Pittsburgh: University of Pittsburgh, 1971.

Berndtson, Peter. "The Houses of Peter Berendtsen [*sic*]: A Tour for the Members of Pittsburgh History & Landmarks Foundation." September 1971.

Miller, Donald, and Aaron Sheon. *Organic Vision: The Architecture of Peter Berndtson*. Pittsburgh: The Hexagon Press, 1980.

Van Trump, James D. "Peter Berndtson, Pittsburgh Architect." *Carnegie Magazine* 55:9 (November 1981): 27–29.

Van Trump, James D. "Architecture and the Pittsburgh Land: The Buildings of Peter Berndtson." *Life and Architecture in Pittsburgh*. Pittsburgh: Pittsburgh History & Landmarks Foundation, 1983: 64–68.

Henning, Randolph C., ed. *At Taliesin: Newspaper Columns by Frank Lloyd Wright and the Taliesin Fellowship 1934–1937*. Carbondale, IL: Southern Illinois University Press, 1992.

Besinger, Curtis. *Working with Mr. Wright*. Cambridge: Cambridge University Press, 1995.

Guggenheimer, Tobias S. *A Taliesin Legacy: The Architecture of Frank Lloyd Wright's Apprentices*. New York: Van Nostrand Reinhold, 1995.

Brierly, Cornelia. *Tales of Taliesin: A Memoir of Fellowship*. Tempe, AZ: Arizona State University in association with the Frank Lloyd Wright Foundation, 1999.

Rosenblum, Charles L. "Precedent and Principle: The Pennsylvania Architecture of Peter Berndtson and Cornelia Brierly." *Frank Lloyd Wright Quarterly* (Spring 1999): 12–15.

Tannler, Albert M. "Drafting a Plan for Protégés: Frank Lloyd Wright's Taliesin Fellowship Trains a New Generation of Architects." *Pittsburgh Tribune-Review, Focus* 24:32 (June 13, 1999): 8–10.

Brierly, Cornelia. "Notz House: A Shelter of Warmth and Rest." *Pittsburgh Tribune-Review, Focus* 24:32 (June 13, 1999): 9.

Coleman, Brian D. "Shelter: A House Designed by Pittsburgh Architects Peter Berndtson and Cornelia Brierly, Who Studied with Wright, Is Carefully Preserved." *Old–House Interiors* 17:6 (December 2011): 36–41.

Titus de Bobula

"Geschäfts-, Bureau und Wohnhaus." *Der Architekt* 6 (1900): plate 48.

Ohio Architect and Builder (October 1903): 16; (November 1903): 74; (December 1903): 74; (March 1904): 59; (May 1904): 64; (March 1905): 79.

"Greek Catholic Church Dedicated." *Homestead News Messenger*, December 28, 1903: 1–2.

De Bobula, Titus. "American Style." *Inland Architect and Building News* 45:5 (June 1905): 51–53; 45:6 (July 1905): 64–65.

Palmer's Pictorial Pittsburgh and Prominent Pittsburghers, Past and Present. Pittsburgh: R. M. Palmer, 1905: 107.

Pittsburgh Architectural Club. *Catalogue of the Third Exhibition*. Pittsburgh, 1905 [no page].

"Greek Catholic Church to Be Dedicated." *The Duquesne Times*, September 22, 1905: 1.

Municipal Record of Allegheny County/Construction, March 11, 1905: 8; April 29, 1905: 13; June 10, 1905: 5; June 17, 1905: 14; December 2, 1905: 509; December 9, 1905: 533; December 15, 1905: 558; January 13, 1906: 30; January 27, 1906: 85; February 24, 1906: 173; May 19, 1906: 451.

"A Row of Concrete Houses." *Cement Age* 4:1 (January 1907): 62–63.

Obituary. "Titus De Bobula Dead; Consulting Architect." *Washington Post*, February 1, 1961: B.4.

Seifer, Marc J. *Wizard: The Life and Times of Nikola Tesla; Biography of a Genius*. Secaucus, NJ: Carol Publishing, 1996: 427, 431–434, 457, 527, 528.

Tannler, Albert M. "Architecture with a Dash of Paprika: Titus de Bobula in Pittsburgh." *Pittsburgh Tribune-Review, Focus* 28:11 (January 19, 2003): 8–11.

———"Architect Titus de Bobula's Work in Pittsburgh." *The New Rusyn Times* 13:5 (September/October 2006): 6–10.

———"Austro-Germanic Secessionism and the Shaping of Early Modern Architecture in Pittsburgh." *PHLF News* 179 (November 2013): 18–20.

Harold E. Crosby

Koyl, George S., complier. *American Architects' Directory*. New York: R. R. Bowker, 1956: 117.

"Harold E. Crosby." *The Builders' Bulletin* 42:14 (January 15, 1958): 1, 16.

Tannler, Albert M. "Two Art Deco Commercial Buildings in the Heart of the Triangle." *PHLF News* 157 (April 2000): 10–11.

Beres, Joanna. "An Alternative Method for Redeveloping Downtown Pittsburgh: The Three Faces of Murphy's—Past, Present, and Future; An Historic Structures Report & Feasibility Study." M. Arch. thesis. Washington, D.C.: Catholic University of America, 2008.

Togyer, Jason. *For the Love of Murphy's: The Behind-the-Counter Story of a Great American Retailer*. University Park: Pennsylvania State University Press, 2008: 34, 90, 93, 141–142, 143, 144.

Curtis & Davis

"New IBM Building to Rise in Pittsburgh." *The Charette* 42:1 (January 1962): 21.

Messurier, William J. "The Return of the Bearing Wall." *Architectural Record* (July 1962): 168–171.

"IBM's exterior-truss walls: the new IBM building for Pittsburgh." *Progressive Architecture* 43 (September 1962): 162–167.

"New Pittsburgh Test: Steel Shows off a Wide Range of Strengths in the Multicolor Structure of the IBM Building." *Architectural Forum* 117 (December 1962): 15.

IBM Building, Pittsburgh, Pennsylvania: USS Structural Report [AIA File No. 13-A-1] 1963.

IBM Building, Pittsburgh, Pennsylvania [AIA File No. 17A] 1963.

"Welded Truss Walls of Tailored Steels—Big Building Breakthrough." *Welding Design and Fabrication* 36:3 (March 1963): 43–46.

Modern Architecture U.S.A.: Presented by the Museum of Modern Art and the Graham Foundation for Advanced Studies in the Fine Arts. New York: The Museum of Modern Art, 1965. [no page] (#66).

Dixon, John Morris. "I.B.M. Thinks Twice." *Architectural Forum* 124:2 (March 1966): 32–39.

"Curtis & Davis: Design Firm Case Study." *Contract Interiors* 126:7 (February 1967): 100–147.

Condit, Carl W. *American Building: Materials and Techniques from the Beginning of the Colonial Settlements to the Present.* Chicago: University of Chicago Press, 1968: 198; Fig. 72.

Davis, Arthur Q. *It Happened by Design: The Life and Work of Arthur Q. Davis.* Jackson, MS: University Press of Mississippi, 2009: 116.

The Design Alliance

www.tda-architects.com

Graham, Anderson, Probst & White

Graham, Ernest. *The Architectural Work of Graham, Anderson, Probst and White.* Vol. 2. London: Batsford, 1933: 259–260, 317–321.

Chappell, Sally. *Architecture and Planning of Graham, Anderson, Probst and White, 1912–1936: Transforming Tradition.* Chicago: University of Chicago Press, 1992: 208–209.

Tannler, Albert M. "Three Distinguished Offspring of a Not-So-Famous Family." *Pittsburgh Tribune-Review, Focus* 20:26 (March 5, 1995): 6, 11.

Michael Graves

Davidson, C. C. "Michael Graves: O'Reilly Theater, Pittsburgh." *Architecture* 90:5 (May 2001): 126–131.

"O'Reilly Theater, Pittsburgh, Pennsylvania, 1996," *Michael Graves Buildings and Projects 1995–2003*, ed. by Karen Nichols. New York: Rizzoli, 2003: 72–79.

Walter Gropius and Marcel Breuer

"House in Pittsburgh, Pa.: Walter Gropius and Marcel Breuer, Architects." *Architectural Forum* 74 (March 1941): 160–170.

Wolfe, Lawrence C., Jr. "Breuer Comes to Town: Internationally Famous Architect Sets Forth to Teach Students the Creed of Contemporary Architecture." *The Charette* 28:6 (June 1948): 12–13.

Berdini, Paolo. *Walter Gropius: Works and Projects*. Barcelona: Editorial Gustavo Gili, S.A., 1994: 176–177.

Driller, Joachim. *Breuer Houses*. London: Phaidon, 2000: 132–137.

Frampton, Kenneth, and David Larkin. *American Masterworks: Houses of the 20th and 21st Centuries*. Revised edition. New York: Rizzoli International, 2008: 98–105.

Bergdoll, Barry. "New Ways in the New World." *Häuser* (1/2009): English text, vii–viii; German text, 84–93.

Harrison & Abramovitz

[525 William Penn Place] "Alternation to Skyline $28,500,500." *The Charette* 30:11 (November 1950): 14–15, 33, 36.

"Skyscraper Sheathed in Aluminum." *Engineering News-Record*, 148:14 (April 3, 1952): 67–71.

"Alcoa Builds a Lightweight Building." *The Charette* 32:5 (May 1952): cover, 11–19.

"Faceted Metal Wall for Alcoa in Pittsburgh Sets New Style in Tall Buildings." *Architectural Forum* 97 (July 1952): 134–135.

"Alcoa Building: Innovations in Aluminum." *Architectural Record* 112 (August 1952): 120–127.

Holmes, B. H. "Alcoa Building: Lightweight Construction." *Progressive Architecture* 33 (August 1952): 87–91.

"Aluminum—234,000 sq. ft. of Stamping—Production Feat." *Light Metal Age* 11: 3–4 (April 1953): 12–15.

"Alcoa Complete: Pittsburgh's 30-Story Aluminum Waffle is America's most Daring Experiment in Modern Office Building." *Architectural Forum* 99 (November 1953): 124–131.

Aluminum on the Skyline. Pittsburgh: Aluminum Company of America, n.d.

[Four Gateway Center] "Contract." *The Charette* 38:9 (September 1958): 20.

"Pittsburgh Office Building Has External Service Tower: Four Gateway Center Building, Pittsburgh, Pa." *Architectural Record* 128 (September 1960): 214–216.

United States Steel Corporation. *The Steel Triangle: United States Steel Builds a Corporate Center*. Pittsburgh: United States Steel Corporation, 1969.

"U.S. Steel Headquarters Building." *Civil Engineering* 40:4 (April 1970): 58–63.

"Three Story Buildings Stacked in Triangular Frame." *Engineering News-Record* 185:4 (July 23, 1970): 22, 27.

"The Steel Triangle in Pittsburgh's Golden Triangle." *Contract Interiors* 131:5 (December 1971): 96–109.

"Big Steel Spike. …" *Architectural Forum* 135:5 (December 1971): 24–29.

"Tripleheader: U.S. Steel's New Headquarters Presents Three Faces to the Pittsburgh Skyline. …" *Industrial Design* 18:10 (December 1971): 62–65.

Newhouse, Victoria. *Wallace K. Harrison*, Architect. New York: Rizzoli, 1989: 145–149.

Parks, Janet, and John Harwood. *The Troubled Search: The Work of Max Abramovitz*. New York: Columbia University, 2004: 52–57; 58–63; 94–96; 98–100.

Henry Hornbostel

Kidney, Walter C. *Henry Hornbostel: An Architect's Master Touch*. Pittsburgh: Pittsburgh History & Landmarks Foundation, 2002.

Philip Johnson

Philip Johnson: The Architect in His Own Words. New York: Rizzoli, 1994: 104, 132–136.

Tasso Katselas

Tasso Katselas, Architect Planner. Pittsburgh: 1970.

Inoue, Bukichi. "Pittsburgh Architect Tasso G. Katselas." *SD: Space Design* 130 (June 1975), 27–59.

Tasso Katselas Architect/Planner: A Continuum 1970–1980. Pittsburgh: c. 1981.

Tasso Katselas Associates: Architects + Planners; An Architectural Anthology 1955 to 1995. Pittsburgh [1996].

Strickland, Bill, with Vince Rause. *Make the Impossible Possible*. New York: Broadway Books, 2007: 88–95.

Richard Kiehnel

Pittsburgh Architectural Club Exhibition Catalogues. 1905, 1907, 1910, 1911, 1912, 1913, 1914, 1915, 1916–17.

"To Show the City Beautiful: Forthcoming Exhibition of the Pittsburg Architectural Club in the Carnegie Galleries Will Typify the Improvement of American Cities." *Ohio Architect & Builder* 10:3 (September 1907): 46–48.

The Builder [Brushton School; City Hospital, Marshalsea photos] 28:11 (March 1911); [Central Turnverein photo] 30:7 (November 1912); [Bank of Pitcairn photo] 30:11 (March 1913); [TB hospital for the City of Pittsburgh photo] 31:9 (January 1914).

The Oaklander "Turn Verein Club House." 1:11 (June 29, 1911): 3; "Work Started on Turner Hall"; 1:31 (November 16, 1911): 1; "Will Dedicate Home." 2:27 (October 17, 1912): 1.

"Tenth Annual Exhibition, Pittsburgh Architectural Club." *American Architect* 109: 2093, Pt. 1. (February 2, 1916): 66–68.

Tannler, Albert M. "Richard Kiehnel: Architect of International Modernism and Topical Splendor." *Pittsburgh Tribune-Review, Focus* 21:30 (June 9, 1996): 6–7.

——"German, American Influences Accent School Design." *Pittsburgh Tribune-Review, Focus* 24:14 (February 7, 1999): 10–12.

——"Turtle Creek Treasure." *Pittsburgh Tribune-Review, Focus* 26:19 (March 18, 2001): 8–9.

——"Hospital Architecture: Despite Changes, Original Elements Remain in Two Early 20th-Century Medical Facilities." *Pittsburgh Tribune-Review, Focus* 26:25 (April 29, 2001): 8–9, 11.

——"Geometrically German-American: Two Buildings Exhibit Design in Turn of the Century Oakland." *Pittsburgh Tribune-Review, Focus* 26:38 (July 29, 2001): 8–10.

——"A Tale of Houses: Glass and Geometrics Reside in Proximity." *Pittsburgh Tribune-Review, Focus* 26:42 (August 26, 2001): 8–10.

William H. King, Jr.

"Student Goes to Many Cities." *Pittsburgh Press*, August 16, 1907.

"Competition for the Scholarship of the Pittsburg Chapter of the American Institute of Architects 1906: *Drawing for a Small House*. Perspective and Floor Plans." *The Builder* 26:11 (February 1909): Unnumbered plate.

"*A private swimming pool* (plan and perspective)." Carnegie Technical Schools. William H. King, Jr. No. 112. *Pittsburgh Architectural Club Annual 1910*. [no page]

Paris Prize Drawings—No. 133: *A Municipal Interborough Trolley Station and Assembly Hall*, Elevation; No. 134: Section; Nos. 135–136: Plans. Carnegie Technical Schools. William H. King, Jr. *Pittsburgh Architectural Club Annual 1911*. [no page]

"Competition for the Scholarship of the Pittsburg Chapter of the American Institute of Architects 1906: *Drawing for a Small House*. Perspective and Floor Plans." *The Builder* 30:9 (January 1913): 2 plates.

"*House of W. G. Chambers, Pittsburgh; House at Edgewood Park, Pa.*" [illustrated] William H. King, Jr. *Pittsburgh Architectural Club Annual 1915*. [no page]

[Mt. Lebanon Municipal Building] "Architects' Building Bulletin." *The Charette* (January 1929): 607; (March 1929): 633.

"William Henry King." *The Builders' Bulletin* 37:21 (February 7, 1953): 1, 16.

Tannler, Albert M. "Classy Classical Moderne: Mt. Lebanon Municipal Building Was Architect's Shining Moment." *Pittsburgh Tribune-Review, Focus* 29:50 (October 17, 2004): 8–9; 11.

Kohn Pedersen Fox

The Architecture of Kohn Pedersen Fox: An Exhibition of the Royal Institute of British Architects, June 10–July 9, 1985. New York, 1985: 15.

Cháo, Sonia R., and Trevor D. Abramson. *Kohn Pedersen Fox: Buildings and Projects 1976–1986*. New York: Rizzoli, 1987: 152–157.

McQuade, Walter. "The High Rise of Kohn Pedersen Fox." *Architecture* 78:5 (May 1989): 120–127.

Ichinowatari, Katsuhiko, et al. *Process Architecture: Kohn Pedersen Fox Associates* 86 (November 1989): cover, 40–41.

Arthur Lubetz

Architecture ... Energy: Arthur Lubetz Associates. Pittsburgh: University of Pittsburgh, Frick Fine Arts Gallery, 1989.

Kidney, Walter C. "Standouts: Arthur Lubetz's Bold New Geometry." *In Pittsburgh* (December 13, 1989): 11.

Kidney, Walter C. "Where Fiction Meets Function." *In Pittsburgh* (April 11, 1990): 16.

Richard Meier

"Giovannitti House, Pittsburgh, Pennsylvania, 1981–83." *GA [Global Architecture] Houses* 17 (February 1985): 32–47.

"Giovannitti House," *Richard Meier Houses 1962/1997*, with an introduction by Paul Goldberger and an essay by Sir Richard Rogers. New York: Rizzoli, 1996: 130–149.

Ludwig Mies van der Rohe

Cooper, William R. "Duquesne: Dramatic Change in Campus Scale," *Architectural Forum* (July/August 1967): 79.

Speyer, A. James. *Mies van der Rohe*. Chicago: Art Institute of Chicago, 1968.

"The Duquesne University Science Center." *The Charette* 49:6 (December 1969): 4–5.

Schulze, Franz, ed. *An Illustrated Catalogue of the Mies van der Rohe Drawings in the Museum of Modern Art, Part 2: 1938–1967, The American Work*. New York: Garland Publishing Company, 1992: 2.

Schulze, Franz, and Edward Windhorst. *Mies van der Rohe: A Critical Biography, New and Revised Edition*. Chicago: University of Chicago Press, 2012: 372–373.

Mitchell & Ritchey

James A. Mitchell and Dahlen K. Ritchey, "Impressions and Reflections: Part 1." *The Charette* 17:7 (July 1937): 1–2.

——"Impressions and Reflections: Part 2." *The Charette* 17:8 (August 1937): 1–2.

James A. Mitchell and Dahlen K. Ritchey, et al. "The Carnegie International." *The Charette* 18:11 (November 1937): 3.

Pittsburgh in Progress. Pittsburgh: Kauffmann's Department Store, 1947.

"Pittsburgh in Progress: Towards a Master Plan." *Progressive Architecture* 28:6 (June 1947): 14, 67–72.

"Mellons Give City $4 Million Gift for Triangle Park." *Pittsburgh Post-Gazette*, April 24, 1949: 1, 3.

"Pittsburgh's Redevelopment Progresses: Mitchell & Ritchey, Executive Architects." *The Charette* 33:3 (March 1953): 15–17.

"P/A Annual Design Survey for 1954 and First Design Awards Program." *Progressive Architecture* 35 (January 1954): 111. [Award citation. Civic Auditorium, Lower Hill Cultural Center]

"P-A Cites Pennsylvania Architects." *The Charette* 34:1 (January 1954): 13.

Mauro, John. "Magnificent Square in the Triangle." *The Charette* 35:12 (December 1955): 13–16.

Van Trump, James D. "Pittsburgh's Pleasure Dome: The New Civic Auditorium." *The Charette* 41:10 (October 1961): 8–22.

Kornwolf, James D., ed. *Modernism in America 1937–1941: A Catalog and Exhibition of Four Architectural Competitions*. Williamsburg, VA: College of William and Mary, 1985: 186, 188, 252, 256, 259, Figures 188–189.

Rosenblum, Charles. "Renaissance Man: Evaluating the work of the late Dahlen Ritchey." *Pittsburgh City Paper* (February 6–13, 2002): 17.

Office of Mies van der Rohe

Miller, Nory. "Mies' Office Today: FCL, An Evolving Firm." *Inland Architect* 21:5 (May 1977): 25–28.

Agus Rusli

www.rusli.com/

Frederick G. Scheibler, Jr.

Jordon, John W., compiler. "Frederick Gustavus Scheibler, Jr." *A Century and a Half of Pittsburg and Her People*. Vol. 4. [New York]: Lewis Publishing Company, 1908: 16.

Shear, John Knox, and Robert W. Schmertz. "A Pittsburgh Original." *The Charette* 28:9 (September 1948): 4–5.

Shear, John Knox. "Pittsburgh Rediscovers an Architect Pioneer, Frederick Scheibler." *Architectural Record* 106 (July 1949): 98–100.

Van Trump, James D. *The Architecture of Frederick G. Scheibler, Jr., 1872-1958.* Exhibition Catalogue. [An exhibition organized by James D. Van Trump and James H. Cook, October 11–November 18, 1962, Department of Fine Arts, Carnegie Institute]. Pittsburgh: Carnegie Institute, 1962.

Wilkins, David G., et al. *Art Nouveau: Works by Tiffany, Mucha, Toulouse-Lautrec, Gallé, Beardsley, Scheibler, and Others.* Exhibition Catalogue. [University Art Gallery, January 13–February 12, 1978]. Pittsburgh: University of Pittsburgh, 1978: 15–16.

Aurand, Martin. *The Progressive Architecture of Frederick G. Scheibler, Jr.* Pittsburgh: University of Pittsburgh Press, 1994.

Simonds & Simonds

"An Open Place at the Heart of a City." *Architectural Record* 121 (February 1957): 195–198.

Simonds, John O. "Mellon Square: An Oasis in an Asphalt Desert." *Landscape Architecture* 48 (July 1958): 208–212.

"Mellon Square Park." *Carnegie Magazine* 33 (June 1959): 185–189.

Simonds, John O. "Equitable Plaza, Pittsburgh." *Landscape Architecture* 53:1 (October 1962): 18–19.

Van Trump, James D. "Figures in a Landscape: Simonds and Simonds of Pittsburgh." *Landscape Architecture* 54:2 (January 1964): 127–130.

Vondas, Jerry. "John Simonds, Kilbuck: Architect Was Influenced by Travels in Asia [Obituary.]" *Pittsburgh Tribune-Review,* May 27, 2005: C4.

Lowry, Patricia. "John O. Simonds: Prominent, Influential Landscape Architect [Obituary.]" *Pittsburgh Post-Gazette,* May 28, 2005: B3.

Skidmore, Owings & Merrill—Natalie de Blois and Myron Goldsmith

Owings, Nathaniel Alexander. *The Spaces in Between: An Architect's Journey.* Boston: Houghton Mifflin Company, 1973: 264–265.

"Bank to Start Main Office Construction." *Pittsburgh Post-Gazette,* January 25, 1974.

"First Movement into Equibank This Weekend." *Pittsburgh Press,* September 14, 1975.

Paine, Judith. "Natalie de Blois," *Women in American Architecture: A Historic and Contemporary Perspective,* ed. by Susana Torre. New York: Whitney Library of Design, 1977: 112–114.

Lowry, Patricia. "A Look at Local Women Architects." *Pittsburgh Press* (Section F), April 3, 1988.

[Myron Goldsmith] "Appendix A: Protégés," *Mies van der Rohe: A Critical Biography, New and Revised Edition,* by Franz Schulze and Edward Windhorst. Chicago: University of Chicago Press, 2012: 403–405.

Dunlap, David W. "An Architect Whose Work Stood Out, Even if She Did Not." *New York Times*, July 31, 2013.

A. James Speyer

Vinci, John, et al. *A. James Speyer: Architect, Curator, Exhibition Designer*. Chicago: University of Chicago Press for the Richard Nickel Committee, 1997.

Myers, Tracy. "Less Was More for A. James Speyer." *Carnegie Magazine* 59:1 (January/February 1998): 14–16.

M. M. Steen

Harper, Frank C. "M. Markle Steen." *Pittsburgh of Today: Its Resources and People*. Vol. 3. New York: American Historical Society, 1931: 69.

Tannler, Albert M. "Moderne Masterpieces: Pittsburgh's Landmark Public Schools 1931–1941." Parts 1 and 2. *Pittsburgh Tribune-Review, Focus* 22:48 (October 4, 1998): 6–7; 22:49 (October 11, 1998): 6–7.

Joseph Urban

"Metropolitan Pittsburgh + Greater William Penn Hotel Edition." *William Penn Points* 12:1 (May 1929). Pittsburgh: Eppley Hotels Company, 1929.

"The Greater Wm. Penn Hotel." *Greater Pittsburgh* 9:51 (May 18, 1929): 29.

Teegen, Otto, "Joseph Urban" (251–256); and Otto Teegen, "Joseph Urban's Philosophy of Color" (257–271); Ralph Walker, "Joseph Urban, the Man" (271–274); Deems Taylor, "The Scenic Art of Joseph Urban" (275–290), *Architecture* 69:5 (May 1934): 250–290.

Van Trump, James D. "A Palace Up to Date." *Pittsburgher Magazine* 3:12 (May 1980): 25–27.

Tannler, Albert M. "The Joseph Urban Room." *PHLF News* 146 (June 1997): 8–9.

Robert Venturi

Pain, Richard. "Lost Property." *Blueprint* (June 2004): 50–53, 55.

Carabet, Brian G. and John A. Shand. "House in Pittsburgh" in "Venturi, Scott Brown and Associates, Inc.," *Dream Homes: Greater Philadelphia—Showcasing Greater Philadelphia's Finest Architects*. Dallas, TX: Panache Partners, LLC, distributed by Gibbs Smith, 2006: 92–95.

Edward J. Weber

Lowry, Patricia. "An Architect Out of Time." *Pittsburgh Post-Gazette, Sunday Magazine* (February 9, 1997): G1, G10–11.

Tannler, Albert M. "Common Brick, Uncommon Buildings." *Pittsburgh Tribune-Review, Focus* 30:4 (November 28, 2004): 8–10.

Archival Collections:
Carnegie Mellon University Architecture Archives

Check website listed below for information on these collections and other relevant holdings.

Peter Berndtson Collection
Henry Hornbostel Collection
Tasso Katselas Collection
Arthur Lubetz Collection
Mitchell & Ritchey Collection
Rubin & VeShancey Collection
Frederick G. Scheibler, Jr. Collection

Websites:

AIA Historical Directory of American Architects [1857–1978]
http://www.aia.org/about/history/aiab082017

American Architects and Buildings Database
Baltimore Buildings Project
www.baltimorebuildings.org

Philadelphia Architects and Buildings Database
www.philadelphiabuildings.org

Carnegie Library of Pittsburgh
Construction Record [1910–16]: http://hdl.handle.net/10493/719

Carnegie Mellon University Architecture Archives
http://www.andrew.cmu.edu/user/ma1f/ArchArch/index.html

http:/dli.library.cmu.edu/charette/

Postwar Pittsburgh Architecture Bibliography 1945–75:
http://www.andrew.cmu.edu/user/ma1f/ArchArch/postwarPGHarchbibliography.html

Alan I W Frank House
http://www.thefrankhouse.org

Historic Pittsburgh
http://www.digital.library.pitt.edu/pittsburgh/

Pittsburgh History & Landmarks Foundation
www.phlf.org
Home/*PHLF News* publication 1966–present
Education/Architectural History

Society of Architectural Historians
Research Resources: Brief Biographies of American Architects [d. 1897–1947]
www.sah.org

Index

The page numbers for sites in the Guide are given in bold face. The page numbers for illustrations of particular importance to the discussion of a place, that are not within the site description, are given in italics. Map locations are usually only given for the current name of the site.

48th Street Row, Lawrenceville, 216
56 South 16th Street, South Side, 215
139 South 22nd Street, South Side, 215
200 East Elizabeth Street: Apartment Building, Hazelwood, 54, **65**
201 Stanwix Street Place (former Bell Telephone Building), downtown Pittsburgh, 38, 41, *44–45*, 50, 234n62
221 38th Street, Lawrenceville, 216
425 Sixth Avenue, downtown Pittsburgh (former Alcoa Building), 50, **162–163**
500 Second Street (former First National Bank of Pitcairn), Pitcairn, PA, 54, **73–74**, 239n52, 239n53, 239n54
525 William Penn Place, downtown Pittsburgh, 50, *156*, 161, 163, 170
625 Liberty Avenue, downtown Pittsburgh (EQT Plaza), 50, **185–187**
625 Stanwix Tower Apartments, downtown Pittsburgh, 37, 41, 50
4209 Butler Street, Lawrenceville, 216

Abbe, Charles H., 168
Abramovitz, Max (Harrison & Abramovitz), 161–165, 168–170
Abrams, Betty and Irving: House, 31, 54, **180–183**, 249n213, 249n218

Akoun, Bernard Sauveur, 28
Alan I W Frank House, 54, **126–131** (*see also:* Frank, Cecelia and Robert: House)
Alcoa Building (former), 50, *156*, 161, **162–163**
Alcoa Corporate Center, 50, *160*, 163, **171–173**
Alden & Harlow/Longfellow, Alden & Harlow, *14*, 66, 175–177, 241n73
Allegheny Conference on Community Development, 15, 29, 33, 38, 41
Allegheny County Courthouse and Jail, 12, *13*, 183
Allegheny International Tower (former), **185–187**, 249n222
Allegheny Ludlum Steel Corporation, 186
Allegheny Towers Penthouse Apartments (now 625 Stanwix Tower), 37, 234n62
American Gothic, **112–121**
Anderson, Edwin H., 16
Apt, Joan and Jerome: House, 30, 54, 146, **147–150**, 151, 246n161
Architectural Exhibitions in Pittsburgh, 14–23, 230n10, 230n11, 231n22, 232n24, 232n28, 232n29, 232n30, 232n31, 232n32
Architectural League of America, 1, 61

265

Aretz, Franz, 117, 118
Arimoto, Tadao, 158
Armour Institute of Technology, Chicago, 6, 145, 146, 152
Art Moderne, 3–4, 71, 95, 100, 103, 111, 117
Art Nouveau, xvii, 2, 6, 47, 59, 60, 61, 62, 71
Arthur Lubetz Associates (now Front Studio Architects, LLC), 187–188, 214, 217
Arts and Crafts movement, 2, 16, 18, 19, 22, 85, 113
Ashbee, Charles R., xv, 17, 18, 19, 227n1, 230n12, 230n14
Attia, Eli, 184
Aurand, Martin, 22, 66, 67, 68, 74
Austrian Museum of Art and Industry, 22, 232n28

Baillie Scott, M. H., 66, 67
Balfour, R. S., 17
Barnes, Edward Larrabee, 175–177
Barr, Alfred H., Jr., 5
Barragán, Luis, 182
Bauhaus, 127, 130, 145, 207
Bear, Mr. & Mrs. Fay: House, 135, 136
Bearden, Romare, 213
Beck, Quentin S., 108–111
Beck, Pople & Beck, 108–111, 243n106
Behrens, Peter, 66, 68, 127
Bell Telephone Building (former), 38, 41, *44–45*, 234n62
Benedictus, Edouvard, 94
Bergdoll, Barry, 129–130
Berlage, H. P., 21
Bernd [Julius] Collection, Carnegie Library of Pittsburgh, 16
Berndtson, Peter, 31, *132*, 134–143

Bidwell Training Center, 158
Billing, Hermann, 81, 240n68
Bindley, John, 70
Blois, Natalie de, 152
Bobula, Titus de, 19, 23, *24*, 60–65, 76, 193, 236n8, 237n18, 237n20
Boudreau, Robert, 202
Bourgeois, Louise, 190
Bowman, John G., 120
Brenenborg Brown Group Architects, 92
Breuer, Marcel, xvi, 30, 126–131, 147, 175, 178, 244n136
Brierly, Cornelia, 31, *132*, 134–141, 245n140
Brinkman, William J., 70
Bruckman, Fred, 66
Buckland, Herbert, 17
Builder, The [Pittsburgh] 1897, 1901, 1903–19, 17
Builders' Bulletin [Pittsburgh] 1916 to present, 16
Bunshaft, Gordon, 34, 152, 197
Burgee, John, 183
Burne-Jones, Edward, 113
Burnham, D. H. & Company, 93
Burnham & Root, 70, 93
Butler Institute of American Art, The, 203
Butz, E. M., 92

Callery, Mary, 162
Calvary Episcopal Church, 54, **114**
Carnegie Art Gallery (Carnegie Library, Allegheny City), 17
Carnegie Institute and Library of Pittsburgh, 14–16, 18–23, 199
—Branch libraries, 217
—Carnegie Museum of Art, Sarah Mellon Scaife Galleries, 54, **174–177**, 181

Index

Carnegie Mellon University (Carnegie Institute of Technology; Carnegie Technical Schools), 15, 16, 18, 28, 38, 91, 92, 98, 102, 118, 124, 134, 136, 145, 146, 155, 156, 157, 171, 187
—Gates Hillman building (Gates Center for Computer Science and Hillman Center for Future-Generation Technologies), 211–212
—Immigrant faculty, 28, 233n44

Carnegie Mellon University Architecture Archives, 22, 200

Center for Sustainable Landscapes (Phipps), 217, *218–219*

Central Turnverein, 74–76, 79, 239n58, 239n61, 240n62

Century of Progress International Exposition, Chicago, 1933–34, 91, 95, 108

Chandler, Theophilus P., 120

Charette, The 1920–74, xvi–xvii, 15, 16, 21–22, 166

Children's Museum of Pittsburgh, *204–205*, 210–211

Church of the Redeemer, The Episcopal, 54, **120**

City of Pittsburgh Hospital at Marshalsea, 70, **193–194**

Civic Arena (Mellon Arena), *39, 192,* **197–200**, *201*

Clarke & Rapuano, 37

Clavan, Irwin, 37

Cleary, Richard, 28, 30, 233n34, 233n39

CNG Tower (former), **185–187**

Comes, John T., 62, 114, 116–117

Companion House for Family Living No. 1, 200

Comstock, William T., 1

Condit, Carl, 167

Connick, Charles J., 113, 114, 116, 120

Construction [Pittsburgh] 1905–06, 84, 237n18

Construction Record [Pittsburgh] 1910–16, 16

Conterato, Bruno P. (Office of Mies van der Rohe), 153

Cooper, C. J. Harold, 17

Cope & Stewardson, 120

Corbusier, Le (Charles-Édouard Jeanneret), xvi, 4, 5, 38, 155, 157, 175, 235n66

Cormack, Peter, 114

Craftsman [American; California], **82–89**

Cram, Ralph Adams, 113–116, 120

Crane, Lionel Francis, 17

Crane, Walter, 17, 18

Crosby, Harold E., 100–101

Curtis & Davis, 166–167, 170

David L. Lawrence Convention Center, *206,* 207–209, 210

Davidson, Cynthia, 189–190

Davison, Allen Lape, 29

Davison, Thomas, 17

Design Alliance Architects, The, 171–173

Destiny International Ministries, 54, **104–105**, *224*

Dominion Tower (former), **185–187**

Douglas, Dr. and Mrs. Harlan: House, 52, **142–143**

Douglas, John, 19

Dowler, Pressley, 89, 99, 234n62

Duquesne University, 145

Dyer, J. Milton, 70

East Liberty Presbyterian Church, 54, **115–116**

Ecole des Beaux-Arts, 99, 102, 124

Eden, F. C., 17

267

EDGE Studio, 212, 217
Egan & Prindeville, 70
Eggers & Higgins, 37
Eleven Stanwix Street, 38, 50
Emerald Art Glass, 214
Emmanuel Episcopal Church, 12, 149
EQT Plaza, 50, **185–187**, 249n222
Equibank Building (former), **152**, 153
Equitable Life Assurance Society of the United States, 35–36, 164
Evans, John, 114
Evert, Marilyn, 106
Exposition Internationale des Arts Décoratifs et Industriels Modernes (International Exposition of Modern Decorative and Industrial Art), Paris, 1925, 3–4, 22, 24, 71
Eyre de Lanux, Elizabeth, 94

Fallingwater, 28, *29*, 133, 134, 135, 195, 214
Filler, Martin, 178–179
First Baptist Church, 54, **116**, 120
First Hungarian Reformed Church, 54, **64**
First National Bank of Pitcairn (former), **73–74**
Fisher, Eric (FISHER ARCHitecture), 214
Flucker, Ronald L., 170, 248n199
Fort Couch Tower, 56, **187–188**
Four Allegheny Center, 52, **153**
Four Gateway Center (including The Plaza at Gateway Center; Equitable Plaza), 7, 38, 42, *43*, 50, **164–165**
Frame, R. G., 97
Frank, Cecelia and Robert: House, 30, 54, **126–131**, 147, 151, 181, 245n139
Frank, Josef, 28, 30, 233n46
Freyssinet, Eugene, 34
Front Studio Architects, LLC, 214

G. C. Murphy Company Store 12 (former), **100–101**, *226*
Gábor, László, 28
Garden, Hugh, 21, 231–232n22, 239n51
Gardner Steel Conference Center, University of Pittsburgh, 54, **74–76**
Gates Hillman building (Gates Center for Computer Science and Hillman Center for Future-Generation Technologies, Carnegie Mellon University), 211–212
Gateway Center, 35–42, 234n62
—One, Two, and Three Gateway Center, 36–42, 50
—Four Gateway Center, 7, 38, 42, *43*, 50, **164–165**
—Five Gateway Center [former IBM Building]: United Steelworkers, 38, 50, **166–167**
—Six Gateway Center (now Eleven Stanwix Street), 38, 50
Gateway Towers, 37, *39*, 41, *42*, 50, 234n62
Gateway T Station, 212–214
Gensler, 217
George, Ernest, 17
German Museum for Art in Trade and Commerce, 22, 232n28
Geyling, Remigius, 21
Giovannitti, Frank: House, 54, **178–179**
Glass Lofts, 214
Goldberger, Paul, 179
Goldsmith, Myron, 152
Goodhue, Bertram Grosvenor, 113, 114, 116, 120
Goodhue, Harry Eldredge, 114, 117
Goodhue, Wright, 115, 117, 118, *119*
Graduate School of Design, Harvard University, 6, 127, 155, 156, 166, 175, 183, 189
Graham, Anderson, Probst & White, 93–94
Graves, Michael, 182, 189–191

Greene & Greene, 85, 86, 88
Griffin, Marion Mahony, 21, 231n22
Griffin, Walter Burley, 21, 59, 231n22
Griswold, Ralph E., 33, 34
Gropius, Walter, xvi, 5, 6, 7, 22, 30, 126–131, 147, 166, 175, 244n136
Grueby, William, 114

Hanwell, Thomas Leopold, 77
Harrison [Wallace K.] & Abramovitz [Max], 161–165, 168–170
Harwood, John, 161, 162–163
Hazen, Joseph, 38, 40
Hearn, M. F., 188
Heineman & Heineman, 88
Heinz Architectural Center, Carnegie Museum of Art, 92, 177, 181
Heinz, Henry J. II (Jack), 40, 151, 191
Heinz Memorial Chapel, *113*, **120**, *121*
Heinz Vinegar Plant, **196–197**
Highland Towers, *xiii*, 54, *58*, **68**, 76, *220*
Hilton Hotel (now Wyndham Grand Pittsburgh Downtown), 37, *39*, 40, *42*, *43*, 234n62
Hitchcock, Henry-Russell, xvii, 4–5, 6, 152, 155, 239n51
Hochenleitner, Xavier, 118
Hoffman & Crumpton, 99
Hoffmann, Julius, 21
Holy Ghost Greek Catholic Church, 60, **193**
Holy Rosary Roman Catholic Church, *v*, 54, **115**
Hoover, Herbert, 3
Hoover, Joseph W., 108
Hornbostel, Henry, 18, 102, 123–125
Horst, Frederick: House, 52, **110–111**
Hossli, Robert, 170, 248n199
Howard Heinz Endowment, 151
Hunt, Myron, 86

Hunt & Egar, 84
Hunt Stained Glass Studios, 118
Hutchins, William P., 116, 118, 184

IBM Branch Office Building (former), **153**
IBM Building, 38, 164, **166–167**, 170
Illinois Institute of Technology (IIT), 6, 145, 146
Ingham, Boyd & Pratt, 157
International Style, The: Architecture Since 1922, 5
Irving & Casson, 116

Jacobs, Jane, 40
Janssen & Abbott, 96
Janssen, Benno, 24–25, 28, 96
Janssen & Cocken, 24, 96, 99, 194
Jensen, Jens, 21, 231n22
Johnson, Philip, xi, 5, 182, 183–185
Jugendstil, 59, 71, 72, 76, 235n2

Kahn, Louis I., 181, 202
Kahn, Ned, *204–205*, 210
Kaiser, Neal & Reid, 117
Kato, Kantero, 68
Katselas, Tasso, 157–159
Katz [Agnes R.] Plaza, 50, **189–191**
Kaufmann, Edgar J., Sr., 24–30, 151, 197 (*see also* Fallingwater)
— Kaufmann's Department Store, 24–28, **194**, 201, 249n231
— Kaufmann, Edgar J., Sr., Office, 28, **195**
Kaufmann, Edgar, jr., 28, 195
Kidney, Walter C., xii, xiv, xvi, 10–12, 64, 94, 100, 120, 125

Kiehnel, Elliott & Chalfant, 71, 72
Kiehnel, Richard (Kiehnel & Elliott), *xvii*, 21, 23, *24*, 70–81, 193–194, 232n23, 238n45, 238n46
Kiley, Daniel Urban, 190
King, Jr., William Henry, 98–100
Kingsley, Karen, 166, 167
Kirchmayer, John, 114
Klauder, Charles Z., 120, *121*
Klimt, Gustav, 60
Kohn Pedersen Fox, 185–187
Koning Eizenberg, *204–205*, 210–211
Koppers Building, 50, **93–94**
Krinsky, Carol, 197
Kruty, Paul, 235n5, 239n51, 239–240n61
Kupka, Frantisek, 21

Landis, Mr. & Mrs. Jack: House, 54, **137–138**, 139
Larkin Building, Buffalo, New York, 6, 68
Lawrence, David L., 33, 35 (*see also* David L. Lawrence Convention Center)
Lawrie, Lee, 116
Lemington Engine Company No. 15 (former No. 38), 54, **71**, 72
Lescaze, William, 5, 202–203, 250n239
Lethaby, William R., 2
Letter Carriers' Local 84 Union Hall, 52, **92**
Lieftuchter, Felix B., 117
Lindeberg, H. T., 108
Link, Albert F., 116
Link, Weber & Bowers, 102–104
Lipkind, Saul and Edith: House, 30, 54, *132*, 139, **140–141**
Lissitzky, El, 187
Live/Work Studio, 215
Locke & Preston, 84, 86

Lofts of Mount Washington, The, 56, **105–107**, 243n102, *275*
Lorántffy, Princess Zsuzsanna, 64
Lower Hill Cultural Center, 151, **197–200**, *201*
Loysen + Kreuthmeier Architects, 217
Lualdi, Angelo, 118
Lubetz, Arthur, 187–188, 214, 217
Lubove, Roy, 31, 32, 40, 197–198

MacClure & Spahr, 98, 102
Mack Scogin Merrill Elam Architects, 211
Mackintosh, Charles Rennie, 19, 66, 67, 68, 73
Mackintosh, Margaret Macdonald, 19
Maher, George W., 21, 76, 231n22
Manchester Bidwell Corporation Headquarters, 52, *154*, **158–159**
Manchester Craftsmen's Guild, 158
Market Square Place, 50, **100–101**, *226*
Martin, Edward, 33
McClarren, Samuel Thornburg, 84, 86–89, 241n73
McKim, Mead & White, 6, 60
McMullen, Leo A., 116
Meier, Richard, 178–179
Mellon Arena (Civic Arena), *39*, *192*, **197–200**, *201*
Mellon, Richard King, 33, 156–157
Mellon [Richard King] Hall of Science, 50, **144–146**, 151, 153, 245n155
Mellon Square, 50, **156–157**, 161, 165
Mellon-U.S. Steel Building, *156*, 161, 163, 170
Mendelsohn, Eric, 123
Metzner, Franz, 60
Mies van der Rohe, Ludwig, xi, 5, 6, 7, 144–153, 183
Miller, Donald, 138, 141

Mitchell, Arnold, 17
Mitchell, James A. (Mitchell & Ritchey), 155–157, 198, 200
Mitchell & Ritchey, 30, 155–157, 197–198, 200, 247n173
Modern Architecture—International Exhibition, 5, 22–23, 229n26
Modernista, 228n12
Möhring, Bruno, 21, 231n18
Moore, Temple, 19
Moose Building, 187
Morris, William, 18, 113, 114
Möser, Henry, 66
Moss Architects, 216
Mt. Lebanon Municipal Building, *46*, 56, **99–100**, *222*
Muriel Street: house, 215

National Carpatho-Rusyn Cultural Center, 54, **63–64**
National Historic Preservation Act, 6, 8
National Trust for Historic Preservation, 101, 210
Neutra, Richard, 5, 30, 229n26
New Brighton Theatre (former), **92**
Newton, Ernest, 17
Notz, Hulda and Louise: House, 54, 134, **135–136**, 142

Olbrich, Joseph M., 59, 60, 66, 67
Old Heidelberg, 19, 54, **66–67**, *69*, 76
Oldenburg, Claes, 187
Olmsted, Frederick Law, Jr., 31
Omni William Penn Hotel, Urban Room, xv, 50, *90*, 95, **96–98**, 241n87
O'Neill, Paul, 171, 173
O'Reilly Theater, 50, **189–191**
Osterling, Frederick J., 70
Oud, J. J. P., 5

Pain, Richard, 181–183
Parigot, Y., 94
Parkstone Dwellings, *viii–ix*, 54, **69**
Paul Rodriguez Architect, 105
Peabody & Stearns, 102
Pei, I. M., 201, 250n237
Pennsylvania Society of Architects, 15, 22
Pennsylvania Station, New York City, 6
Perkins, Dwight H., 21, 231–232n22, 239n51
Perry, William R., 116
Pewabic Pottery, 116
Pfaffmann + Associates, 212, 217
Phipps (Center for Sustainable Landscapes), 217, *218–219*
Pitassi, A. Leo, 117
Pite, Beresford, 17
Pittsburgh Architectural Club, 15, 17–23, 70, 74, 91, 98, 123, 230n9
Pittsburgh Board of Public Education, 102
Pittsburgh Chapter, American Institute of Architects, 15, 17–22
Pittsburgh Cultural District, 40, **189–191**
Pittsburgh Cultural Trust, 40, 191
Pittsburgh History & Landmarks Foundation, xi, xii, xvi, 6, 10, 22, 40, 41, 42, 48, 49, 102, 105, 137, 199, 200
Pittsburgh Parks Conservancy, The, 157
Pittsburgh Planning Commission, 31
PPG [Pittsburgh Plate Glass] Place, xi, *9*, 50, **183–185**
Pittsburgh Public Schools (PPS) (*original names*)
—Brushton, *xvii*, **72**, 80, 239n51
—Greenfield, 54, 76, **80–81**
—Lemington (former), 102, **104–105**, *224*
—Mifflin, 54, 102, **103–104**, 105
—Prospect (former), 102, **105–107**, 243n102, *275*

271

—Schiller, 52, 102, **125**
—Stevens, Thaddeus (former), 49, 56, 102, **107**
Pittsburgh Renaissance, 15, 31–42
Pittsburgh Renaissance Historic District, 42
Pittsburgh Student Achievement Center (formerly, Brushton School), *xvii*, 54, **72**, 239n51
Pittsburgh Survey, 31
Plaza at Gateway Center, The (Equitable Plaza), 38, 42, 50, **164–165**
Plečnik, Jože, 75, 76, 81
Point Counterpoint II, **202**
Point State Park, 33–35, *39*, 41–43
—Fort Pitt Block House (1764), 34, 227n1
—Fort Pitt Museum (1969), 34
—Portal Bridge, 34, *35*, 50, 234n59, *276*
Pond & Pond, 74, 231n19, 231–232n22
Pople, Harry: House, 52, 108, **111**
PPG Place, xi, *9*, 50, **183–185**
Prairie School, 16, 21, 60, 133
Pressley Associates, 41
Price, C. Matlack, 2–3, 59
Prior, Edward S., 19
Purcell & Elmslie, 239n51

Rafael Viñoly Architects, 206–209
Regional Enterprise Tower (former), **162–163**
Reynolds, W. Bainbridge, 19
Richard King Mellon Hall of Science, 50, **144–146**, 151, 153, 245n155
Richardson, George S., 34
Richardson, H. H., 12, *13*, 17, 31, 66, 113, 149, 183
Riesmeyer, Lydia A.: House, 54, **78–79**
River Vue Apartments (former State Office Building), 38, *39*, *42*, 50

Robb, E. Donald, 120
Robertson, Leslie E., 170
Robinson, Boardman, 24, *25*, 28, 233n37
Rodriguez Associates, A. M., 106–107
Roehrig, F. L., 85
Rookwood Pottery, 68
Rosen, Jan de, 118
Rothschild Doyno Collaborative, 99, 100
Roush, Stanley, 21
Rubin & VeShancey, 91–92
Rudolph, Paul, 38, 200
Rudolsky, Bernard, 28
Rudy Brothers, 68, 238n42
Ruskin, John, 18, 113
Rusli, Agus [Rusli Associates], 171–173
Russian Constructivism, 187, 214

Saarinen, Eero, 181, 208
Saarinen, Eliel, 21, 195
Saarinen, Loja, 195
Sacred Heart Roman Catholic Church, 54, **117–118**
St. Agnes Roman Catholic Church (St. Agnes Center of Carlow University), 54, *112*, 117
St. James Roman Catholic Church, 54, **118–119**
St. John the Baptist Greek Catholic Church and Rectory, 60, **63–64**, 76
St. Louis World's Fair 1904 (Louisiana Purchase Exposition), 21, 59, 61, 63, 66, 94, 231n19
St. Mary of Mercy Roman Catholic Church, *45*, 184
St. Peter & St. Paul Ukrainian Orthodox Church (originally St. Peter's & St. Paul's Russian Greek Catholic Church), 56, **65**
Sarah Mellon Scaife Galleries, Carnegie Museum of Art, 54, **174–177**

Scheibler, Jr., Frederick G., 19, 23, *24*, 66–69, 76, 238n42

Schell & Deeter, 164

Schiller Building, Chicago, 6

Schindler, Rudolph, 229n26

Schmertz, Robert, 23

Schmidt, Richard, 21, 231–232n22, 239n51

Schulze, Franz, 145–146, 147–149

Schumacher, Fritz, 21, 22, 231n21

Schuyler, Montgomery, 78

Schwab, Charles M., 62–63

Schweikher, Paul, 38, 145, 245n155

Scott Brown, Denise, 181, 182

Scully, Vincent, 6–7

Secessionism/Secessionist, xvii, 2–3, 6, 16, 48, 59–81, 235n3, 235n4

Seifer, Marc, 63

Serra, Richard, 187

Sheon, Aaron, 138, 141

Simonds, John O., 155–157, 164–165

Simonds & Simonds, 38, 152, 155–157, 164–165

Skidmore, Owings & Merrill, 151
—New York Office, 34, 152, 178, 197
—Chicago Office, 152

Sobotka, Walter, 28, 30, 233n43

Society of Arts and Crafts, Boston, 114

Sommerfeld house, Berlin, 129

Sotter, George and Alice, 117, 118

Soulages, Pierre, **203**, 250n239

South Park Golf Club House, 56, *122*, **124–125**

Speyer, A. James, 30, 146–151

Speyer, Tillie S.: House, 30, 54, **151**

Sports & Exhibition Authority of Pittsburgh and Allegheny County, 198–199

Stamatakis, Nick, 41

State Office Building (now River Vue Apartments), 38, *39*, 41, *42*

Steen, M. M. (James T. Steen & Sons; M. M. Steen), 102, 105–107

Steinberg, Dr. and Mrs. Abraam: House, 30–31, 54, **138–139**

Stengel, George H.: House, *3*, 54, **76–77**, 79

Stern, Robert A.M., 182, 183

Stickley, Gustav, 86

Stotz, Charles Morse, xi, 34

Strada Architecture, LLC, 100–101, 103

Strickland, Bill, 158

Strong, Carlton, 116, 117–118

Studio d'ARC, 215–216

Sturgis, Russell, 2

Sullivan, Louis H., 1, 6, 21, 59, 60, 86, 228n7, 231–232n22

Swan Acres, 108–111

Taliesin Fellowship, 28, 31, 133–134, 135

Taylor, F. Steward, 17

Teegen, Otto, 96

Tesla, Nikola, 63

Thaddeus Stevens School (*see* Pittsburgh Public Schools)

Thalman, V. Wyse, 66

Theater Square, **189–191**

Thomas, Francis Inigo, 17

Thomas, Leo (Georg Boos Studios, Munich), 117

Thornburg, 56, **82–89**
—1109 Cornell Road, **86**
—1124 Cornell Road, *82*, 85
—1137 Cornell Road, **86**
—501 Hamilton Road, **84**
—529 Hamilton Road, **86**
—545 Hamilton Road, **88–89**
—560 Hamilton Road, **88**
—1132 Lehigh Road, *84*, **87–88**
—1060 Stanford Road, **85**

Thoughtful Balance, Inc., 217

Tower at PNC, 217

Townsend, Charles Harrison, 17, 18
Train & Williams, 85
Two PNC Plaza, 50, **152**

United States Steel Innovations Committee, 168–170, 248n199
United Steelworkers, 38, 50, **166–167**
University of Pittsburgh Cathedral of Learning Campus (Cathedral of Learning, Heinz Memorial Chapel, Stephen Foster Memorial), 54, **120–121**, 183
University of Pittsburgh Medical Center (UPMC), 169
Urban, Joseph, xv, 24, 94–98, 233n35, 241n86
Urban [Joseph] Room, Omni William Penn Hotel, xv, 50, *90*, 95, **96–98**, 241n87
Urban Redevelopment Authority of Pittsburgh (URA), 35, 38
U.S. Steel Tower (United States Steel Building; USX Tower), *vi*, *39*, 50, 165, **168–170**

Van Trump, James D., xii, xvi–xvii, 22, 24, 66, 69, 91, 120, 136, 232n27
Venturi, Robert, 8, 31, 181–183
Venturi & Rauch, 181–183
Vetter, Hans, 28
Vibert, Max, 94
Vokral, Joseph: House, 52, **109–110**

Wagner, Otto, 21, 59, 60, 229n26, 239n51
Warhol, Andy, 187
Warren, Charles Bradley, 106–107

Warren, Edward, 17
Washington Plaza Apartments, *39*, *199*, **201**
Wasmuth, Ernst, 21, 75
Watson, Vernon, 21, 231–232n22
Weber, Edward J., 102–105, 116, 125, 242n99
West, James, 109
Western Architect, The, 16, 21
Westinghouse Building (former), 38, 161, 234n62
Whiffen, Marcus, 48, 155, 157
Wilbert, Howard Gilman, 120
William Penn Hotel (*see* Urban Room)
Williams, J. L., 17
Wiseman, Carter, 7–8
Wittmann, Konrad, 125
Wlach, Oskar, 28, 30
Wood, Edgar, 17, 18, 21
Wright, Frank Lloyd, xi, xv–xvi, 2, 3, 5, 6, 21, 28–30, 47, 59–60, 66, 68, 77, 86, 123, 133–135, 195, 228n10, 229n26, 231–232n22, 235n5, 236n6, 236n7
Wyndham Grand Pittsburgh Downtown (former Hilton Hotel), 37, *39*, 40, *42*, *43*, 50, 234n62

Yeates, Alfred Bowman, 17
Young, A. N., 109

Ziegler, Arthur P., Jr., xii

Eagle and shield entrance detail, The Lofts of Mount Washington (formerly, Prospect School)

The Portal Bridge, illuminated at night, in Point State Park